ANIMAL THEOLOGY

Andrew Linzey

University of Illinois Press
Urbana and Chicago

First Illinois paperback, 1995

© 1994 by Andrew Linzey
Manufactured in the United States of America
⊚ This book is printed on acid-free paper.

Library of Congress Cataloging-in-Publication Data

Linzey, Andrew.
    Animal theology / Andrew Linzey.
        p.   cm.
    Includes bibliographical references and index.
    ISBN 0-252-02170-3 (alk. paper). —
  ISBN 0-252-06467-4 (pbk. : alk. paper)
        1. Animals—Religious aspects—Christianity. 2. Animal
    rights—Religious aspects—Christianity. I. Title.
    BT746.L56   1995
    241'.693—dc20   94-35580
                                                            CIP

First published in 1994 by SCM Press, Ltd., London

P 5 4

UNIVERSITY OF ILLINOIS PRESS
1325 SOUTH OAK STREET
CHAMPAIGN, ILLINOIS 61820-6903
WWW.PRESS.UILLINOIS.EDU

Contents

For my children:
Adam, Clair, Rebecca and Jacob

Introduction

This book is based on a series of lectures on 'The Theology of Animal Rights' given in the Faculty of Theology at Oxford during Trinity Term 1993. It would not, I think, be an exaggeration to say that they were the first lectures on this subject in the history of the Faculty, if not of the University itself. I am enormously grateful to the students who attended and engaged me in lively and critical debate – so much so that even the one and half hours allotted to each session proved insufficient for the controversy which each topic engendered.

These lectures are in turn the result of a reworking of my major papers in the field of animals, theology and ethics over the last eight years. They represent even in their present form a continued wrestling with issues which are still sadly neglected by the theological world. Despite the fact that some of these chapters are speculative, combative and controversial, I have done my best at each stage seriously to consider objections and to give good space to critics. My overall intention is to question the all too comfortable assumption that if theology is to speak on this question, it must do so only on the side of the oppressors of animals. Whatever the limitations of this present collection, it at least raises the issue in a way that, sadly, few other theologians seem prepared to countenance.

The title of this book – and the endeavour it represents – will inevitably be subject to two sets of criticisms. The first, from the theological community, will be that animal theology coming as it does on the heels of feminist theology, black theology, gay theology, and liberation theology generally, represents nothing short of a contemporary dissipation of theology itself. A flight from 'real' theology into the arms of secular moral fashion.

I hope that some of those who argue in this way will at least *read* some of the subsequent pages in this book. For while they will find exemplified here a passionate concern for moral justice for animals, they will also at one and the same time find an equal concern to explore and appropriate some of the central themes of Christian doctrine. My argument throughout is not only that justice requires a thoroughgoing revision of our treatment of animals but also, quite specifically, that historical theology creatively expounded also requires this. Indeed, in some ways the theological kernel of this book derives from what to some will appear an overly conservative, unabashed trinitarian formulation of Christian orthodoxy. I hold that Christian theology provides some of the key categories of thought which enable a fully satisfying ethical conception of the place of non-human creatures in our world.

Indeed, I question the timidity of those who hold fast to trinitarian faith and at the same time seemingly oppose, as a matter of principle, any exploration of its relevance beyond familiar boundaries. I propose that it has to be a matter of regret, even repentance, that the community of faith which holds to the objective truth of the self-revelation of God in Christ should have advanced its world-affirming doctrine without much more than a passing thought for the billions of non-human inhabitants within creation itself. What are we to say of a theology which has so proceeded on the basis of a moral neglect of God's creatures?

I cannot pretend to unravel this conundrum here. All I seek to do is to suggest ways in which the doctrine of the incarnation – among others – can help ethically motivated Christians to perceive meaning in the suffering of the animals all around them. Whatever may be the final judgment on the Christian tradition in respect of its moral legacy in the contemporary world, at least in this area the time is over-ripe for a theological change-of-heart leading to ethical re-evaluation. This volume can only begin to repay the moral debt and redress the balance.

The second line of criticism will come from animal activists who are understandably, if erroneously, wary of more theoretical discussion of the rights and wrongs of our treatment of animals. For those passionately concerned for animal rights, the moral case has already been made and is already, even philosophically, unassailable. I wish I could accept this view. Despite the impressive nature of much recent philosophical discussion of animals, its failure to enter seriously and sympathetically into a specifically theological understanding of animals has meant that the case has *not* been made for the many millions of human beings who continue to adhere, even in a weak form, to Christian doctrine. Moreover, even as stout a defender of animal rights as myself can see that rights language does not by itself resolve each and every moral problem that our contemporary abuse of animals confronts us with. While rights language has value as a provider of checks and markers on our way to eliminating animal exploitation, it fails by itself to provide a sufficiently holistic and positive interpretation of the place of animals in God's world. Negative moral prescription, however essential from time to time, is no substitute for a vision of moral goodness.

In short: moralism is not enough. The Western intellectual tradition which animal rightists properly criticize for failing to take animals seriously has also unplumbed theological resources – in language, rhetoric, argumentation – and not least of all in spirituality – which can provide a broader, more compelling theoretical backcloth to animal rights imperatives than has hitherto been imagined. Theology provides a way in which animal rights theory can be released from its current philosophical straightjacket.

Perhaps it is not going too far to say that the contemporary animal rights movement *needs* theology to help save itself from its own degeneration into moralism and self-righteousness, the second of which in particular strikes me as very serious indeed. I have frankly written of those who 'enjoy a moral condemnation the way others enjoy a good dinner' (p. 112). Moral prescriptivism divorced from a thoroughgoing sense of the utter sinfulness of humankind leads inevitably to the cul-de-sac of moral triumphalism.

As regards the structure of the book: part one contains my more specifically theological arguments regarding animals, and part two is focussed, chapter by chapter, on specific areas of animal abuse: experimentation, killing for food, genetic engineering, patenting, and sport hunting. All the pieces have been revised and reworked to avoid wherever possible repetition or overlap. In one instance, however, I have not avoided repetition and that is in the case of my central argument concerning christology. I hold that human dominion over animals needs to take as its model the Christ-given paradigm of lordship manifest in service. This is so pivotal to my expanding argument, especially in the area of ethics, that I have not hesitated to draw upon it throughout. To have circumvented references to it would have weakened the theological thrust of the book.

Various people have read one or more chapters of the book in earlier forms and given me the benefit of their advice. In this regard, I am especially grateful to Peter Wexler, Stephen R. L. Clark, Paul Clarke, Richard Jurd, Elaine Kaye, Charles Brock, John B. Wilson, Frank Schulman and John Muddiman. Margaret Lydamore of SCM Press prepared the manuscript for publication and provided me with invaluable editorial assistance. My thanks are also due to Toni Tattersall who typed the manuscript with much skill and patience.

I owe two special debts. The first is to the International Fund for Animal Welfare (and especially its Executive Director, Richard Moore) for ambitiously funding the world's first fellowship in theology and animal welfare which I am privileged to hold. IFAW is unparalleled not only in its pioneering work for animals but also in its appreciation of the significance of the contemporary intellectual discussion of the status of animals. My second debt is to Mansfield College itself which has graciously received me into its fellowship and provided an environment which is second to none in its intellectual openness and personal conviviality. During the writing of this book, I became aware that Albert Schweitzer visited Mansfield to give the Dale Lectures in 1922. In these lectures Schweitzer first formulated and publicly presented his doctrine of reverence for life which was subsequently published in his outstanding books *The Decay and Restoration of Civilization* and *Civilization and Ethics* in 1923. I would like to think that this is a book of which Schweitzer as well as the Non-Conformist founders of Mansfield would have approved.

Andrew Linzey

Mansfield College, Oxford
Trinity, 1993

Part One

Establishing Theological Principles

1

Reverence, Responsibility and Rights

This chapter is principally concerned with what we owe animals morally – as God's creatures. I discuss three questions: (1) Should we show respect, or reverence, to animals? (2) Do we have responsibility to animals? and (3) Do animals have rights? I propose that all three questions should be answered in the affirmative. While holding tenaciously to a doctrine of the moral rights of animals, it will be seen that I do not think that rights terminology should obliterate other notions such as 'respect' or 'responsibility'. I have treated the issue of animal rights at length in my books *Animal Rights: A Christian Assessment* and *Christianity and the Rights of Animals*[1] and I do not want to simply rehearse the arguments again here. The concept of rights, I suggest, is fully compatible with moral theology and should be properly extended to include animals. At the same time, I resist the idea that rights language is exhaustive of everything that should be said from a theological perspective about animals. In my view, there are good theological grounds for respecting the worth of animals, accepting responsibility *and* recognizing their God-given rights.[2]

Reverence for Life

The idea that the specifically animal creation should be the subject of honour and respect because it is created by God, however elementary that idea may now appear to us, is not one that has been given endorsement throughout centuries of Christian thought. Whilst it can be claimed to have some grounding in scripture in, for example, the psalmist's sense of wonder and beauty at God's creation and in the regard that Jesus claimed even for sparrows,[3] these intimations have never been developed into systematic theological thought, still less full-blown doctrine. Again whilst it is true that many saints, sages, divines and poets within the tradition have shown or articulated respect for animals,[4] the idea remains largely vague and unfocussed.

In order to sharpen this issue, I intend to examine the opposing views of two significant, but very different, thinkers: Albert Schweitzer and Karl Barth.

Schweitzer's Concept

It is Schweitzer, of course, who is most well-known for his development of this concept. In his *Civilization and Ethics*, he surveys successive Western world-views and finds them wanting. 'Our philosophizing has become more and more involved in the discussion of secondary issues,' argues Schweitzer. 'It has lost touch with the elemental questions regarding life and the world which it is man's task to pose and solve, and has found satisfaction more and more in discussing problems of a purely academic nature and in a mere virtuosity of philosophical technique.'[5] The answer to the 'spiritual crisis' of our civilization, maintains Schweitzer, is the development of ethical thought which must seek to conceive life-affirmation as 'a manifestation of an inward, spiritual relation to the world' and which does not 'lapse into abstract thinking' but remains – as Schweitzer calls it – 'elemental', that is, 'understanding self-devotion to the world to be self-devotion of human life to every form of living being with which it can come into relation'.[6] From this, Schweitzer deduces a classic definition:

> Ethics consists, therefore, in my experiencing the compulsion to show to all will-to-live the same reverence as I do to my own. There we have given us that basic principle of the moral which is a necessity of thought. It is good to maintain and encourage life; it is bad to destroy life or to obstruct it.[7]

Three characteristics of this basic principle of reverence should be noted. First, the principle is comprehensive. Schweitzer does not posit reverence as one principle among many, even as the most satisfying or coherent principle, but as the *sole* principle of the moral. Love and compassion, for example, whilst important notions for Schweitzer, are entirely subsumed under the concept of reverence. Compassion which suggests only 'interest in the suffering will-to-live' is regarded as 'too narrow to rank as the total essence of the ethical'. Whereas the ethics of reverence 'include also feeling as one's own all the circumstances and all the aspirations of the will-to-live, its pleasures, too, and its longing to live itself out to the full, as well as its urge to self-perfecting'.[8]

Second, the principle is universal. Schweitzer sees reverence as applying to *all* life forms, human or animal, insect or vegetable. The ethical person 'does not ask how far this or that life deserves one's sympathy as being valuable, nor, beyond that, whether and to what degree it is capable of feeling'. 'Life as such is sacred to him,' maintains Schweitzer. In order to grasp the ramifications of reverence-in-practice, it is worth enumerating some of the examples given. 'The ethical man', writes Schweitzer,

> tears no leaf from a tree, plucks no flower, and takes care to crush no insect. If in summer he is working by lamplight, he prefers to keep the window shut and breathe a stuffy atmosphere rather than see one insect after another fall with singed wings upon his table.
>
> If he walks on the road after a shower and sees an earthworm which has strayed on to it he bethinks himself that it must get dried up in the sun, if it does not return soon enough to the ground into which it can burrow, so he lifts it from the deadly stone surface, and puts it on the grass. If he comes across an insect which has fallen into a puddle, he stops a moment in order to hold out a leaf or a stalk on which it can save itself.

As if to anticipate the mirth, even incredulity, of his readers, Schweitzer continues: 'He is not afraid of being laughed at as sentimental.' 'It is the fate of every truth', he reminds us, 'to be a subject for laughter until it is generally recognized.'[9]

Third, the principle is limitless. Schweitzer is no exponent of casuistry. Apart from one possible exception, namely animal experimentation,[10] he enters into no discussion about the relative rights and wrongs of this or that action when confronted with this or that dilemma. 'Ethics', he insists with stark, perhaps unreasonable, simplicity, 'are responsibility *without limit* to all that lives.'[11]

In order to understand Schweitzer at this point, however, we must clear our minds of two common, but deeply erroneous, perceptions of his position. The first is that he is advocating an absolutist stance, and second, that he was himself an absolutist in practice, or an absolutist in principle and inconsistent in practice. For, in the first place, as much as Schweitzer speaks of the limitless demand of reverence, he prefaces this claim with the significant statement that there will come a time when 'people will be astonished that mankind needed so long a time to learn to regard *thoughtless* injury to life as incompatible with ethics'.[12] In other words, Schweitzer did not regard all forms of life as inviolable under all circumstances. The very word 'reverence' (*ehrfurcht*) indicates to us that

Schweitzer is not depicting obedience to law but the promotion of the good which in turn requires a holistic response of the individual including attitude, disposition, motive as well as action. Some individuals have simply read Schweitzer's examples and been taken with the sheer practical impossibility of their implementation. But such a reading is to mistake Schweitzer's intention. What he gives us are examples of what reverence requires without the pressure of necessity. 'Whenever I injure life of any sort, I must be quite clear whether it is *necessary*,' argues Schweitzer. 'Beyond the *unavoidable*, I must never go, not even with what seems insignificant.'[13]

In his personal life, Schweitzer was no absolutist in practice as he was not in principle. He was no thorough-going vegetarian, vegan, or anti-vivisectionist, for example. At least on one occasion, his biographer reminds us, he was involved in a pre-emptive strike against poisonous spiders.[14]

Nevertheless, Schweitzer does open himself up to the charge of absolutism by his apparent claim that reverence for life knows 'nothing of a relative ethic'. 'Only the most universal and absolute purposiveness in the maintenance and furtherance of life, which is the objective aimed at by reverence for life, is ethical. All other necessity or expediency is not ethical, but only a more or less necessary necessity, or a more or less expedient expediency.'[15] This does not mean, however, that we do not sometimes have to make the choice between more or less necessary necessity or more or less expedient expediency. The vital point to grasp is that when we have to do so, as we all surely do, we are not acting ethically as Schweitzer understands this term. In other words, even if we do our best most of the time, we are guilty, and guilty most of the time – a point that Schweitzer never tires of reminding us. 'The good conscience', he warns, 'is an invention of the devil.'[16]

What is required in order to place into perspective Schweitzer's thought is a recognition that reverence for life – far from being a new moral law – is more like a religious experience. He says almost as much. 'The surmisings and the longings of all deep religiousness is contained in the ethic of reverence for life.'[17] Philosophers, like Peter Singer, immersed in utilitarian calculations, simply miss this point entirely when they debate Schweitzer's apparent inconsistencies as do, to be fair, some religious commentators as well.[18] It was Paul Tillich in his penetrating study on *Morality and Beyond*, who held that 'a moral act is not an act in obedience to an external law, human or divine'; rather it is 'the inner law of our true being, of our essential and created nature, which demands that we actualize what follows from it'. Moreover: 'the religious dimension of the moral imperative is its unconditional character'.[19] Now if this is true, we may say that it is especially true of Schweitzer's thought. For what gives Schweitzer's concept its unconditional character is precisely its religious dimension. 'True philosophy', maintains Schweitzer, 'must start from the most immediate and comprehensive fact of consciousness, which says "I am life which wills to live, in the midst of life which wills to live."' This for Schweitzer is not – as he calls it – 'an ingenious dogmatic formula'. He speaks personally as one who has encountered revelation:

> Day by day, hour by hour, I live and move in it. At every moment of reflection it stands fresh before me. There bursts forth from it again and again, as roots that can never dry up, a living world- and life-view – which can deal with all the facts of Being. A mysticism of ethical union with Being grows out of it.[20]

It is this experiential, mystical identification of individual life with life, and through life with Being itself, which lies at the heart of Schweitzer's philosophy. It is not so much a new law, code or maxim but essentially an unconditional religious experience of great power. The insight that lies at its heart is actually quite simple, namely an apprehension of the value of other life-forms as given by God. Life, in other words, is sacred or holy.

Karl Barth's Reply

Although Schweitzer's concept has received commentary of various kinds, only one theologian, namely Karl Barth, has – to my knowledge – given it detailed and critical attention. Before we address ourselves to his criticisms, anticipating that these two great Germanic thinkers could hardly agree on any theology, it is worth noting that Barth's discussion of Schweitzer is initially at least, and to some degree throughout, sympathetic, even eirenical. Barth begins by accepting that theological and naturalistic ethics have suffered from a certain narrowness of ethical concern. He quotes with some approval Schweitzer's well-known comparison of the place of animals in European philosophy with that of a kitchen floor scrubbed clean by a housewife who is 'careful to see that the door is shut lest the dog should come in and ruin the finished job with its footprints'.[21] Barth then recounts some of Schweitzer's examples concerning the compassion to be shown to worms and insects and even to the wayside flower. Barth's response does not fail to show the essential seriousness which Schweitzer's thought elicits. 'Those who can only smile at this point', he writes, 'are themselves subjects for tears.'[22] Such thought, Barth concludes, is certainly not 'sentimental'. Nor, according to Barth, can we justify ourselves in the face of it by taking 'the easy course of questioning the practicability of the instructions given'. In short: 'whatever the solutions proposed, the problem itself is important'.[23]

Barth develops three kinds of criticisms. First, Barth is clearly unhappy about the lumping together of vegetables and animals as though what was owed to vegetables was of the same order as that owed to the higher mammals. The destruction of a plant and the destruction of an animal are not comparable. An animal is 'a single being, a unique creature existing in an individuality which we cannot fathom but also cannot deny', whereas the using of vegetable life does not constitute its destruction but rather involves 'sensible use of its superfluity'.[24] Barth comes to this conclusion because respect for life only arises in 'a primary sense' in the relationship between human beings. The concept of reverence may apply 'analogically' to animals who are distinct individuals but dissolves entirely when it comes to vegetables.

Secondly, and relatedly, reverence and responsibility – for he uses these two words almost interchangeably – properly belong to the world of human-to-human relationships. Barth accepts that the care of animals may constitute 'a serious secondary responsibility' but he is clearly troubled by the universality and unconditional nature of Schweitzer's ethic. Although Schweitzer is right to protest at our 'astonishing indifference and thoughtlessness', what he proposes cannot be understood as 'doctrine, principle and precept'.[25] And if we ask why Barth is so adamant on this issue, despite the clearly humanitarian sympathies displayed, there is only one answer, which constitutes his third – and by far the most important – theological criticism.

This third criticism runs as follows: Schweitzer does not appreciate the moral distinction between animals and humans because he fails to grasp the meaning of the doctrine of the incarnation. According to this doctrine, as Barth expounds it,

> [man] is the animal creature (*sic*) to whom God reveals, entrusts and binds Himself within the rest of creation, with whom He makes common cause in the course of a particular history which is neither that of an animal nor of a plant, and in whose life-activity He expects

a conscious and deliberate recognition of His honour, mercy and power.

What follows from this is the 'higher necessity' of human life and hence the right to 'lordship and control'.[26] Students of Barth will not of course be surprised by this argument. The one pivotal assumption throughout the twelve chapter-volumes of his magisterial *Church Dogmatics* is precisely this: 'that God's eternal Son and Logos did not will to be an angel or animal but man'.[27] For Barth, humans are a cherished creature.

Reverence: Schweitzer v. Barth

How then are we to begin an assessment of Schweitzer's reverence and Barth's criticism of it? At least one of Barth's criticisms is well made. There are morally relevant distinctions between one kind of creature and another; it may not be sufficient but it is at least relevant to ask whether a being on which one is to bestow reverence can at least have some consciousness of what reverence, or lack of it, might mean. Barth may be right or wrong about whether plants are ethical individuals,[28] but he is not wrong in supposing that what is done to a beast is – in his own words – 'something which is at least very similar to homicide'.[29] There are good biblical as well as biological reasons for sensing a continuity in living agents but also for positing greater capacities in spiritual self-awareness in humans and mammals.[30]

That accepted, what is difficult in Barth is not just that he proposes a fundamental theological distinction between humans and animals, but rather what he wants to deduce from such a distinction. What is so problematic is the way in which God's 'yes' to humankind in the incarnation becomes a 'no' to creation as a whole. There are three christological relationships which seem strangely absent, not just from Barth's own discussion of Schweitzer, but also throughout his four volumes on creation doctrine as a whole.[31] First, according to orthodox doctrine, the same Christ incarnate is also the *Logos* through whom all things come to be. The *Logos* is the source and destiny of all that is. 'For God who made and brought into existence all things by his infinite power contains, gathers, and limits them and in his Providence binds both intelligible and sensible beings to himself and to one another,' maintains St Maximus. 'All beings which are by nature distinct from one another, he makes them converge in each other by the singular force of their relationship to him as origin.'[32] If this is true, we should abandon our sharp, sometimes arrogant, separation of humankind from nature, often buttressed by non-theological considerations. With Eric Mascall we shall reject the misconception that 'Jesus Christ is of immense significance for human beings, but of no importance whatever to the rest of creation'.[33]

Second, we need to bring to light the ancient patristic principle that what is not assumed in the incarnation is not healed in the redemption. The Barthian view that there is a specifically human nature, absolutely differentiated from all other natures or nature itself, is untenable if Christ is also the *Logos*, the co-creator through whom all things come to be. 'When the Word visited the holy Virgin Mary, the Spirit came to her with him, and the Word in the Spirit moulded the body and conformed it to himself,' writes St Athanasius, 'desiring to join and present *all* creation to the Father, through himself, and in it to reconcile *all* things, having made peace, whether things in heaven or things upon the earth.'[34] Athanasius is not a lone voice. 'In uniting himself with man,' writes St John of the Cross, God 'united Himself with the nature' of all creatures. In other words, the 'yes' of God the creator extends to all living beings: the *ousia* assumed in the incarnation is not only specifically human, it is also creaturely. 'The sheer profundity of St John's thought is expressed in this line: "To behold [all creatures] and find them very good was to make them very good in the Word, His Son."'[35]

Third, the same Christ who is the co-creator, the *Logos*, the one who becomes incarnate in the very heart of being, is also the reconciler of all things. Indeed the work of creation, incarnation and reconciliation are three sides of the one mysterious divine activity accomplished in Christ. Far too many interpreters have held that the cosmic strands in the New Testament belong to a past age and represent transient cosmological wrapping. For us in our time their significance could not be greater. God's purpose 'which he set forth', is as Ephesians puts it, 'a plan in the fullness of time to unite all things in him, things in heaven and things in earth'.[36] In Romans the non-human creation groans and travails awaiting the redemption promised by the one who subjected it in hope.[37] Athanasius speaks of Christ as the 'Saviour of the Universe' (*tou pantos*).[38] Once again, Athanasius is not alone in his interpretation of the New Testament. In the well-known passage from *Against Heresies*, St Irenaeus insists that:

This is our Lord, who in the last times was made man, existing in this world, and who in an invisible manner contains all things created, and is inherent in the entire creation, since the Word governs and arranges all things; and therefore He came to his own, in a visible manner, and was made flesh, and hung upon the tree, that He might sum up all things in Himself.[39]

Enough has been said to question the adequacy of Barth's christological argument. It may appear presumptuous to claim that the one christological theologian this century *par excellence* has a deficient christology, and yet it has to be said that the cogency of Barth's view rests upon a drastically over-simplified conception of orthodox christological relationships. In short: Barth's theology too easily severs the connection between the Revealing Word and the cosmos in which that Word is revealed.

An appeal to christology, to the specialness of humankind in the light of the incarnation, such as made by Barth, simply does not rule out a conception of reverence for all life as advanced by Schweitzer. Indeed, the reverse is the case. Whatever the limits of what Barth calls the 'mystico-cosmic ethics' which Schweitzer expounds, they cannot be so easily opposed to Christian doctrine. For if the *Logos* inheres in creation, and if the act of uniting human nature involves the whole of created nature, then we may reasonably suppose some value to the created order, quite independent of human utilitarian calculations. It is understandable, given his presuppositions, that Barth should faintly recoil at what he takes to be Schweitzer's undeveloped theology and supposedly commonsensical approach. No theologian could be more disturbed than Karl Barth by the notion that anything is self-evident in creation. But all this should not blind us to the real possibility that Schweitzer has uncovered a practical moral imperative that is deducible from, if not integral to, christological doctrine.

Barth is properly fearful of any attempt to build a theological perspective upon specific creaturely insights or feelings no matter how heartfelt they may be. But what he overlooks is the possibility that Schweitzer may have implicitly grasped an essential implication of Christ-centred theology. The common origin of all creatures is a doctrine that carries with it implications and consequences which so far only a few in the Christian tradition have fully appreciated. 'Surely we ought to show kindness and gentleness to animals for many reasons,' writes St Chrysostom, 'and chiefly because they are of the *same origin* as ourselves.'[40] A view similar to that of St Bonaventure who says of St Francis that 'when he considered the primordial source of all things, he was filled with even more abundant piety calling creatures no matter how small by the name of brother and sister because he knew that they had the *same source* as himself'.[41] Thomas Traherne likewise speaks of how God 'enjoyeth' the whole world so that 'all that is therein' are God's own 'peculiar treasures', and that since we are made in God's image, 'to live in His similitude, as they are His, they must be our treasures [too]'.[42]

In short: Doubtless Barth is right that Schweitzer's concept of reverence cannot constitute 'doctrine' as such, but it can be easily defended with the most impeccable Christian doctrines, if not actually an integral moral imperative of the same. The value of Schweitzer's thought may lie precisely in this area: that he articulates a frequently-forgotten implication of doctrine which whenever heard – however strange, laughable or incredible it may sound – resonates with some sense of the Creator's will for individual creatures.

Responsibility to Animals

I want now to turn to the question of responsibility to animals. If the notion of reverence has not had a high profile within the Christian tradition, still less has the concept of responsibility. Although there are signs of an awakening sense of concern – most notably in papal pronouncements and in the work of some scholars[43] – it is still true as far as I can determine that Roman Catholic moral theology denies that humans have *direct* duties to animals. This, at least, is the position that continues to be repeated in one moral theology textbook after another.[44] In order to understand this position we have to examine the thought of that giant of the Catholic tradition, namely St Thomas Aquinas, whose theology still dominates much Catholic thinking – not least about animals.

The Scholastic Rejection

I propose to discuss two questions raised and answered by St Thomas in his *Summa Theologica*. The first concerns whether it is unlawful to kill any living thing.[45] St Thomas notes three kinds of objections that might be brought against killing. First, on the basis of divine providence, namely that God has 'ordained that all living things should be preserved'. Second, since depriving an individual of life is murder and since murder is a sin and life is also common to animals and plants, killing animals and plants is also a sin. Third, since in Mosaic law the killing of another man's ox or sheep is an offence punishable by death, it follows that killing an animal must be sinful.

Aquinas finds all three objections unconvincing. Following Augustine, he insists that 'when we hear it said, "Thou shalt not kill", we do not take it as referring to trees, for they have no sense, nor to irrational animals, because they have no fellowship with us'.[46] If we inquire concerning the philosophical basis of this view, we may not be surprised to find Aristotle cited as its source. 'There is no sin in using a thing for the purpose for which it is,' answers Aquinas. 'Now the order of things is such that the imperfect are for the perfect, even as in the process of generation nature proceeds from imperfection to perfection … Wherefore it is not unlawful if man uses plants for the good of animals, and animals for the good of man, as the Philosopher states.'[47] It is this appeal to the natural 'order of things' that predominates in Thomist thought about animals. Only subsequently, and almost secondarily, is this interpretation reinforced by an appeal to scripture. Aquinas cites Genesis 1.29 and 9.3 which concern the giving of food for humans to corroborate what he has already accepted, following Aristotle and Augustine, as the providential design of nature.

To the three objections noted earlier, Aquinas replies briefly as follows. To the first objection, namely that God preserves all life in existence, he maintains that 'the Divine Ordinance of animals and plants is preserved not for themselves but for man', and hence 'as Augustine says … both their life and their death are subject to our use'.[48] To the second objection, namely that life is a common possession of humans and animals, Aquinas answers in a line almost entirely taken over from Aristotle and worth citing in full:

> Dumb animals and plants are devoid of the life of reason whereby to set themselves in motion; they are moved, as it were by another, by a kind of natural impulse, a sign of which is that they are naturally enslaved and accommodated to the uses of others.[49]

To the third objection, namely that killing another's oxen is contrary to Mosaic law, Aquinas answers that it is only the life of an ox considered as human property that is disputed in the Old Testament. The act of killing another's ox is 'not a species of the sin of murder but of the sin of theft or robbery'.[50]

In summary, three elements distinguish Aquinas' view of the status of animal life: First, animals are irrational, possessing no mind or reason.

Second, they exist to serve human ends by virtue of their nature and by divine providence. Third, they therefore have no moral status in themselves save in so far as some human interest is involved, for example, as human property.

In case it is thought that this might be a caricature or misreading of Aquinas' position, it is worth noting that this view is consistently defended without substantial deviation throughout the whole of his work. Indeed, there are passages where he underlines the absence of moral status by claiming the legitimacy of *absolute* human prerogatives over animals. 'By divine providence', he argues in *Summa Contra Gentiles*, animals 'are intended for man's use in the natural order. Hence it is not wrong for man to make use of them, either by killing them or in any other way whatever.'[51]

It is sometimes argued that whilst Aquinas did not accept specific duties to animals, such as refraining from killing, he nevertheless espoused general care and love towards animals.[52] Close reading of Aquinas does not support this view, however. Question 65, article 3, in the *Summa Theologica* is precisely concerned with this question whether 'irrational creatures also ought to be loved out of charity'.[53] Here the line taken by Aquinas entirely supports his earlier view that we have no fellowship with animals. 'The love of charity extends to none but God and our neighbour', maintains Aquinas. But can animals be regarded as or at least analogous to human neighbours? No, claims Aquinas. 'The word neighbour cannot be extended to irrational creatures, since they have no fellowship with man in the rational life,' and therefore, 'charity does not extend to irrational creatures.'[54]

If we ask why Aquinas is so insistent upon this point, we find that the answer lies in the already defended axiom that animals are irrational. Charity is, according to Aquinas, a kind of friendship, which is 'impossible, even metaphorically speaking' to extend to animals. It may be objected that surely God loves all creatures, to which Aquinas replies 'yes', charity towards animals may be appropriate 'if we regard them as the good things we desire for others', that is, for 'God's honour and man's use'.[55] And it is only in this way, Aquinas suggests, that God loves the non-human, namely in so far as they are good and of use to human beings.

We see then that Aquinas' position is quite consistent in its own terms. It has been not incorrectly reproduced by one Catholic textbook after another. For example in 1962 by the *Dictionary of Moral Theology* which argues that animal welfare workers 'often lose sight of the end for which animals, irrational creatures, were created by God, viz., the service and use of man. In fact Catholic moral doctrine teaches that animals have no rights on the part of man.'[56] We may summarize Aquinas in this way: considered *in themselves* animals have no reason and no rights, and humans no responsibility to them.

The Challenge of Mercy

Aquinas' doctrine has become the dominant Western religious position on animals since the thirteenth century. Those in any doubt about this should consult Keith Thomas' excellent survey entitled *Man and the Natural World*.[57] Only in the eighteenth and nineteenth centuries do we find Aquinas seriously challenged. I want now to consider the best of these challenges made by a little-known eighteenth-century divine, Humphry Primatt. That so few should have even heard of Primatt may itself be suggestive of oblivion, but in a number of practical ways, his theology, if not his name, lives on.

Primatt's sole known work is his *Dissertation on the Duty of Mercy and the Sin of Cruelty to Brute Animals*, published in 1776. Without directly mentioning Aquinas, he takes on many of the key elements within the scholastic tradition. He appears to agree with Aquinas in rejecting the idea that creation has in some way 'fallen' from the original designs of the Creator, but unlike Aquinas (who then goes on to postulate the innocency of parasitical existence and man's part in it), Primatt sees in nature 'a transcript of the divine goodness'.[58] Beginning from this starting-point that creation is fundamentally good, the outward result of a Creator who is 'wise and just and good, and merciful', Primatt deduces the principle that 'every creature of God is good in its kind; that is, it is such as it ought to be'. It follows, according to Primatt, that whatever the 'perfections or defects may be, they cannot be owing to any merit or demerit in the creature itself, being not prior, but consequential to its creation'.[59] In this way Primatt agrees with Aquinas about the essential goodness of creation, but gives this doctrine a new twist in underlining the value of each kind of creature in itself.

Primatt also agrees with Aquinas that there is a natural 'order of things' and in particular that humans are mentally superior to other animals. 'At the top of the scale of terrestrial animals we suppose Man,' argues Primatt, 'and when we contemplate the perfections of body, and the endowments of mind, which, we presume, he possesses above all the other animals, we justly suppose him there constituted by his Maker.'[60]

So far then there is much in common between Primatt and Aquinas. But Primatt goes on to make two further distinctions. Whilst he accepts significant differences between humans and animals, he insists upon the common misery of pain:

> Pain is pain, whether it be inflicted on man or on beast; and the creature that suffers it, whether man or beast, being sensible of the misery of it whilst it lasts, suffers evil; and the sufferance of evil, unmeritedly, unprovokedly, where no offence has been given; and no good end can possibly be answered by it, but merely, to exhibit power or gratify malice, is Cruelty and Injustice in him that occasions it.[61]

The appeal here to justice is significant. For Aquinas – whether he thought animals could feel pain or no – certainly did not include animals, even analogically, within the sphere of human justice. Indeed because, strictly speaking, animals could, for Aquinas, have no friendship with humans, and therefore be subject to charitable constraints, animals could not actually be wronged. The new note in Primatt is the insistence that what happens within the sphere of animal-human relations is not just a question of locating some human interest, hidden or otherwise, nor a question of taste or skill, but of plain justice. His argument from consistency is developed in a way that has a familiar ring to modern ears:

> It has pleased God the Father of all men, to cover some men with white skins, and others with black skins; but as there is neither merit nor demerit in complexion, the *white* man, notwithstanding the barbarity of custom and prejudice, can have no right, by virtue of his *colour*, to enslave and tyrannize over a black man; nor has a *fair* man any right to despise, abuse and insult a *brown* man. Nor do I believe that a *tall* man, by virtue of his *stature*, has any legal right to trample a *dwarf* under his foot. For, whether a man is wise or foolish, white or black, fair or brown, tall or short, and I might add *rich* or *poor*, for it is no more a man's choice to be poor, than it is to be a fool, or a dwarf, or black, or tawny, – such he is by God's appointment; and, abstractly considered, is neither a subject for pride, nor an object of contempt.[62]

And in a crucial step, Primatt – contrary to the Thomist tradition – places animals within this widening circle of sympathy and justice.

> Now, if amongst men, the differences of their powers of the mind, of their complexion, stature, and accidents of fortune, do not give any

one man a right to abuse or insult any other man on account of these differences; for the same reason, a man can have no natural right to abuse and torment a beast, merely because a beast has not the *mental* powers of a man.[63]

This further point that mental superiority does not justify moral abuse is developed by Primatt throughout his whole work. In short: unlike Aquinas, who found all-embracing support for the notion that humans had a right to kill animals precisely because of their rationality, Primatt insists that 'superiority of rank or station may give ability to communicate happiness, and seems so intended; but it can give no right to inflict unnecessary or unmerited pain'.[64]

Some may think Primatt is here simply anticipating the later secular arguments for equality between animals and humans in the matter of moral treatment. But to understand Primatt properly, we have to appreciate the deeply theological, indeed christological, character of his endeavours. Living mercifully is, according to Primatt, a matter of revelation.[65] It is because God loves and cares for creation and because, moreover, that great creative generosity is shown us in Jesus Christ, that we have a sure moral imperative for our dealings with fellow creatures.

Again, contrary to Aquinas, the usefulness of animals is a sign of the very generosity of God which should inspire in humans a corresponding generosity towards them. For the purpose of animals is not to serve the human species but to glorify God. In other words, they have a justification for existence which humans themselves have yet to earn, and earn they may supremely through the exercise of mercy. Primatt does not pull his punches in this matter so central, as he sees it, to Christian faith:

> We may pretend to what religion we please, but cruelty is atheism. We may make our boast of Christianity; but cruelty is infidelity. We may trust to our orthodoxy, but cruelty is the worst of heresies.[66]

Responsibility: Aquinas v. Primatt

How then are we to assess the views of Aquinas and Primatt's protest against them? From a theological perspective, a major weakness in Aquinas stems from what appears to be most derived in his thought from Hellenistic sources. Two axioms from Aristotle are taken over almost without question. The first is that humans alone have a rational capacity. Animals are thought to 'have the power of locomotion' and yet in none but man, 'is there intellect'.[67] We find this idea taken over lock, stock and barrel by Aquinas. The second is that animals have no other purpose save that of serving human beings. Aristotle arrives at this conclusion from the rather weak argument that since all nature has a purpose, and animals must have a purpose too, 'it must be that nature has made all of them for the sake of man'.[68] Again this idea of a creation entirely pleasing and naturally ordered for the sake of humankind is assumed throughout the *Summa* by Aquinas. All that Aquinas does is to give these essentially Greek ideas a scriptural and/or theological over-writing. Rationality, for example, is justified in terms of the giving of the divine image which is described wholly in terms of an intellectual capacity which separates humans from beasts.[69] And as regards the utility of animals, the biblical notion of dominion is used to confirm human despotism over animals.[70] Unluckily for Aquinas one would have to look very hard nowadays to find one Old Testament scholar who thought 'dominion' simply meant despotism; if anything at all, the concept underlines human respons-ibility for God's creation.[71] Worst still, when, as we have seen, Aquinas wants to support scripturally Aristotle's dictum that animals were made for human use and that we are therefore justified in using them indiscriminately for food, the actual texts he utilizes – Genesis 1.29 and 9.3 do not unambiguously support his case. In Genesis 9.4, humankind is only allowed flesh on the condition that they do not appropriate the *nephesh*, the life symbolized by blood, and in Genesis 1.29, humans are actually commanded to be vegetarians. In other words, influenced by Aristotelian philosophy, Hebrew monarchy becomes created hierarchy. Genesis is interpreted in terms of the Aristotelian pattern which sees nature as a hierarchical system in which it is assumed – as with human society – that the male is superior to the female, the female to the slave, and the slave to the beast and so on in declining intellectual order. The animals are as 'naturally' subject to humans as slaves are to their masters. No wonder that Robin Attfield argues that 'the tradition which holds that in God's eyes the non-human creation has no value except in its instrumental value for mankind has Greek rather than Hebrew sources'.[72]

What is so problematic then about Aquinas is that this great Christian scholar was not quite Christian or scriptural enough in allowing for theological argument either drawn from the humanitarian tradition of the Old Testament which acknowledged that humans had at least some responsibilities to animals, on the one hand, or to theological argument centred on the exercise of costly merciful loving expressed for us in Jesus Christ, on the other. We may be tempted to go further. For the emphasis upon rationality in Aristotle, Augustine and Aquinas has left a bitter legacy in Christian theology. These people, not unfairly described by Alec Whitehouse as 'aristocrats of the mind' are 'frequently disposed to treat as fully actual, and to envisage as finally actual only what is incorporated into the activity of rational agents'.[73] Hence Christian theology – from this perspective – comes increasingly to consist in the cure of souls, the development of souls, and the salvation of souls. The affect of all this on the non-rational and therefore mortal souls of animals is not, to say the least, advantageous. God's providential care, attested by scripture, becomes telescoped into the continuing obsession with individual human soul-cultivation, at the expense of the rest of creation.

One historical footnote is desirable. Although, as regards the treatment of animals, Aquinas remains the dominant historical force throughout Western Christianity, the views of Primatt and others have gained increasing acceptance. We know, for example, that the person who was responsible for the revision of a second edition of Primatt's work was Arthur Broome, the man responsible for the foundation of the first national animal welfare society in the world, the SPCA, later the RSPCA, in 1824. The Society's first Prospectus spoke in Primatt-like terms about the extension of Christian compassion towards suffering creatures, and one of its subsequent meetings affirmed its foundation in Christian faith and specifically Christian principles.[74] Little do people appreciate how divided the Christian house is on the question of animals. Whilst the Primatt-like forces were increasing their strength behind the new Society, at the same time in the middle of the nineteenth century, Pope Pius IX forbade the opening of an animal protection office in Rome on the familiar Thomist principle that humans had duties to fellow humans but none to animals.[75]

The Rights of Animals

I want now to turn to our third question, whether animals have rights. The language of rights is sometimes viewed within contemporary Christian circles as being a secular import into theological ethics. In fact it is the Christian theological tradition that has been one of the main inspirations for the language of rights, and for many centuries right up until the present day, Christians, both Catholic and Protestant, have placed notions of rights within their theological systems. The question is, however, should the language of rights extend to animals? Again it is worth reminding ourselves that even this question is not as new as it may sound. The first person who used the term 'rights' in relation to animals was Thomas Tryon in the sixteenth century. In his lyrical 'Complaints of the birds and fowls of heaven to their Creator' published in 1688, Tryon gives voice to the creatures pleading for justice.

> But tell us, O men! We pray you to tell us what injuries have we committed to forfeit? What laws have we broken, or what cause given you, whereby you can pretend a right to invade and violate our part, and natural rights, and to assault and destroy us, as if we were the aggressors, and no better than thieves, robbers and murderers, fit to be extirpated out of creation ... From whence did thou [O man] derive thy authority for killing thy inferiors, merely because they are such, or for destroying their natural rights and privileges?[76]

We may notice here both an appeal to negative, as well as positive, rights such as is also found in the work of Primatt. Primatt argues, at least on one occasion for the 'undoubted right' of animals 'entrusted to our care' to minimal requirements such as, food, rest and tender usage'.[77] But he also speaks, more characteristically, of humans having no right to treat animals unmercifully.[78]

Rights and Sentiency

We have seen that the particular basis on which Primatt includes animals within this sphere of human justice is sentiency; it is because animals can feel pain like humans that we should regard their treatment as morally significant. But can sentiency by itself, understood as self-consciousness and the ability to experience pain, be regarded as the criterion for the possession of moral rights? Such was certainly the view of Justus George Lawler, who in 1965, argued:

> To the question of where one draws the line ... it must be replied that one would imagine the line to be drawn at the limits of flesh and blood. One draws the line then at the lowest extremity of creatures who share in spirit, and who are compounded of tissues, nerves and blood ... Any creature when it reaches the threshold of experiencing and anticipating pain possesses rights.[79]

Following Lawler, I adopted his position to a great extent and in my *Animal Rights: A Christian Assessment*, published in 1976, I tried to give an account of sentient rights within a theological context. In it, I queried what has become the classical view that either 'personhood' or 'rationality' were by themselves sufficient grounds for awarding moral rights. I pointed out that these criteria were 'necessarily exclusive' of the claims of animals; their inevitable result was to exclude the non-human from proper moral consideration. The unsatisfactoriness of these criteria should also be obvious, I argued, from the marginal cases, such as newly-born children or the mentally handicapped, who on these bases also possessed no or diminished moral rights. To be fair, I was not entirely oblivious of the difficulties associated with basing rights on the criterion of sentiency. 'I think the question we have to ask', I wrote, 'is whether we have erred on the right side. Has the criterion of sentiency met the problem of serious differences of potential and capacity for life and suffering which exist in the non-human world?'[80] The sentiency criterion, I maintained, was one way in which we could make sense of the value of created beings, the scriptural sense of human responsibility towards animals and the fact that animals could be harmed in ways that plants and stones could not.

Not surprisingly, my view, together with that of Peter Singer whose book *Animal Liberation*[81] followed closely on the heels of my own, aroused much discussion. Philosophers who particularly enjoy detecting inconsistency and unreason in theological argument especially found my youthful book an easy source of both.[82] In addition, the book attracted one detailed theological critique from a conservative evangelical standpoint, and it is to this critique that I now turn.

The Critique of Sentiency

The Human Use of Animals by Richard Griffiths makes many criticisms of my work, but three I think are of central importance. First, he queries whether there can be any purely natural basis for rights whether based on sentiency, intelligence or evolutionary kinship. Now I shall not concern myself at this time with Griffiths' detailed arguments against the sentiency criterion for rights, except to note that he does not rule out all rights talk completely. But he concludes that the 'search for an adequate secular basis for animal rights is bound to fail because of the overriding difficulty of establishing any rights at all (even human rights) on a purely two-dimensional plane, without including some notion of God'.[83] This interesting criticism is related to his second that from a theological perspective all nature, not just animals, have worth and

value. 'The value that God places on *all* nature is a biblical principle
which means that the Christian does not have to draw the line anywhere
in valuing the world.'[84] Third, Griffiths strongly argues that the language
of rights is divisive amongst Christians and obscures many of the
positive elements which can be found within a biblical view of animals.
Griffiths enumerates some of these positive elements: animals have
intrinsic value to God; God delights and rejoices in differentiated
creation; they are in God's gracious keeping; God feeds them; even the
sparrows and the Ninevite cattle are objects of concern; animals praise
their Creator and reflect God's glory.[85] Moreover, Griffiths queries the
view that animals 'were simply created for man alone'.

> In the creation story God makes the animals before man, and
> pronounces them good without man (Gen. 1.24–5): they are made by
> God and for God.[86]

In addition, although Griffiths accepts that humans may use animals in
various ways, he does not accept the common view of dominion as
despotism. Rather humans made in God's image are called 'to be
morally *like God*' and this enormous privilege in creation involves the
highest exercise of responsibility: 'it means that man must regard
creation, including the animals, as God does. It is in this light that his
dominion is to be understood'.[87]

It seems to me now that all three of Griffith's major criticisms can be
accepted in part at least, and I am grateful to him for his work has helped
provide stimulus for a substantial rethinking of the question on my part
and not least of all a new book on *Christianity and the Rights of Animals*.[88]
But the irony for Griffiths is that accepting at least some of his criticisms,
it is now possible to make not a weaker but a stronger case for animals,
and worst of all, from Griffith's standpoint, for the idea that animals
have moral rights as well.

Rights: Linzey v. Griffiths

For I agree with Griffiths that if there are such things as rights, it is only
God who can properly and absolutely claim them. God is, after all, the
Creator, and if Creator then sovereign in power, however we may
understand that sovereignty to be manifest. All creatures are God's
creatures. All things proceed from the Creator's hands. I like the line
from von Balthasar that 'the whole point of creation is for us to know that
we are not Creator'. If, as Karl Barth would have it, creation is 'grace',

the result of the sheer generosity of God, then we do well to pause, as he suggests, in wonder and awe and thanksgiving.[89] But if this is true, it seems to me perfectly possible, nay desirable, to talk of *God's own rights* in creation which we should respect by reverencing what is given. Alas, I cannot claim originality even for this idea, for it is expounded and defended with sutblety by Dietrich Bonhoeffer in a much neglected section of his *Ethics*:

> To idealistic thinkers it may seem out of place for a Christian ethic to speak first of rights and only later of duties. But our authority is not Kant; it is the Holy Scripture, and it is precisely for that reason that we must speak first of the rights of natural life, in other words of what is given to life, and only later of what is demanded of life. God gives before he demands. And indeed in the rights of natural life it is not to the creature that honour is given, but to the Creator. It is the abundance of his gifts that is acknowledged. There is no right before God, but the natural, purely as what is given, becomes the right in relation to man. The rights of natural life are in the midst of the fallen world the reflected splendour of the glory of God's creation. They are not primarily something that man can sue for in his own interest, but they are something which is guaranteed by God Himself.[90]

Second, I agree with Griffiths that from this perspective all life, indeed all nature, has some kind of value, precisely because it is given by God. And third, I also agree with Griffiths that the biblical picture of animals contains many elements that are much more favourable to animals than is commonly supposed. But our common ground in one sense is precisely the ground of our difference. While the biblical material does suggest that all nature has value to God the Creator, it also points us to an appreciation that different forms of life have increased capacities for responding self-awareness in the presence of God. It is true that we are not given in the Bible precise instructions as to the relative value of different beings, but it is also true that the commonness of the lot of humans and animals is frequently articulated. Humans and animals, for example, are made on the same day, recipients of a common blessing, subject both to the blessing and curse of the Lord, and are both to be redeemed.[91] I shall explore in detail some of the elements of this commonality in subsequent chapters.[92] All I would argue at this stage is that to hold the biblical principle that all life has value is not to hold that all being has the same value or to hold that there are not morally relevant distinctions between one kind of being and another.

Theocentric Orientation

I want to propose, therefore, that there is a Christian basis for what I shall term 'the theos-rights' of animals that is consistent with those same notions of reverence and responsibility which the tradition has, at its better moments, espoused. At the heart of this proposal is the conviction that we need a theocentric view of creation. There are four aspects to this which require some brief elaboration.

The Basis of Theos-Rights

The first is that creation exists *for* God. If the question be asked 'What is creation for?' or 'Why do animals exist?' there is only one satisfactory theological answer. Creation exists for its Creator. Years of anthropo-centrism have almost completely obscured this simple but fundamental point. What follows from this is that animals should not be seen simply as means to human ends. The key to grasping this theology is the abandoning of the common but deeply erroneous view that animals exist in a wholly instrumental relationship to human beings. Even if humans are uniquely important in creation, it does not follow that everything in creation is made for us, to be pleasing for us, or that our pleasure is God's chief concern. We need to be wary of making absolute claims about God's chief concerns. The point is made starkly by James Gustafson: 'If God is "for man", he may not be for man as the chief end of creation. The chief end of God may not be the salvation of man.'[93]

The second is that God is *for* creation. I mean by that that God, as defined by trinitarian belief, cannot be fundamentally indifferent, nega-tive or hostile to the creation which is made. Creation, as Barth suggests, is not only 'actualization' but also 'justification'.[94] Every creature is a blessed creature or it is no creature at all. The point is grasped by Oliver Wendell Holmes Sr who argued that 'if a created being has no rights which his Creator is bound to respect, there is an end to all moral relations between them'.[95] There is a sense in which this dictum is false and another in which it is true. It is false if it supposes some rights that exist independently of divine graciousness, almost external constraints which must tie the hands of the Almighty to obey them. But the dictum is true if it conveys the sense that God the Creator is tied to what divine nature has created in creation. Since God's nature is love, and since God loves creation, it follows that what is genuinely given and purposed by that love must acquire some right in relation to the Creator. I do not see how God can be the kind of God as defined by trinitarian doctrine who is morally indifferent to the creation which is sustained, reconciled and which will in the end be redeemed. To posit that the Creator can be indifferent to creatures, especially those who are indwelt by the Spirit, is ultimately to posit a God indifferent to his or her own nature and being.

The third point is that this – what I shall have to term – 'for-ness' of God towards creation is dynamic, inspirational, and costly. It is dynamic because God's affirmation of creation is not a once-and-for-all event but a continual affirmation otherwise it would simply cease to be. It is inspirational because God's Spirit moves within creation – especially within those creatures that have the gift of a developed capacity to be. It is costly because God's love does not come cheap. Jürgen Moltmann writes movingly of how Christian theology is 'found' not in 'the ascent of man to God but the relevation of God in his self-emptying in the crucified Christ which opens up God's sphere of life to the development of man in him'.[96] But if this same Christ is the *Logos* through whom all things come to be, how can we be justified in supposing that this 'self-emptying' is for the human sphere – as Moltmann here implies – alone? The contrary implication must be engaged that the self-emptying which the cross represents is the self-emptying for all creation. Once again we encounter the tendency so strong in systematic theology to restrict, and therefore to distort, the sacrificial work of Christ as though the non-human was worthless in God's sight. The cosmic dimension of the cross is a sadly unexplored aspect in modern theology.[97]

The fourth point or rather question is this: If creation exists for God, and if God is for creation, how can human beings be other than for creation? To the criticism that this theological perspective under-rates or minimizes the special, perhaps unique, gifts of human beings, we should reply that on the contrary, it may well be the special task of humans within creation to do what other creatures cannot do, at least in a consciously deliberate way, namely honour, respect and rejoice in the creation in which God rejoices. The notion of 'theos-rights' then for animals means that God rejoices in the lives of those differentiated beings in creation enlived by the Spirit. In short: If God is for them, we cannot be against them.

An Objection to Theos-Rights

To my proposal, I anticipate one important objection. It may be argued that whilst it may well be that the case for reverence and responsibility towards animals has been overlooked in the Christian tradition, the language of rights is unnecessary and undesirable. Why confuse the issue with the concept of rights which adds nothing and is practically divisive? This is a serious objection if it comes from people who are convinced for one or more reasons that *all* rights language is misplaced, inappropriate or misleading in a theological context. There are some people so powerfully convinced of the sheer generosity of God in creation that they would prefer not to speak the language of rights. This position surely deserves respect. But it is equally possible, following Bonhoeffer, to argue the reverse, namely that the sheer givenness of creation gives rights a secure theological basis. The position which I think is untenable, however, is the one that holds that human rights have a solid basis but then goes on to 'query the appropriateness of rights language when it comes to animals'.[98] Again, it should not be forgotten that the Christian tradition has historically inspired, if not pioneered, some kinds of rights language, and even now it is hardly possible to read a document from a collective gathering of churches from the Lambeth Conference, the United States Roman Catholic Synod of Bishops or the World Council of Churches that does not make ample, some might think effusive, reference to human rights.[99] Theologically speaking, the language of rights is no novelty.

Nevertheless, this does not mean that all appeals to rights of whatever kind are acceptable, nor that all understandings of rights are theologically defensible, and nor that some claims for rights language have not been exaggerated. My proposal is modest. It does not involve us positing that rights language is the only kind of acceptable moral discourse, nor that rights language is comprehensive so that nothing else needs to be added from a Christian context.

To those who argue that the appeal to rights makes no difference, I can only say that it is amazing that so much ink should have been spilt on an issue of supposed indifference. In fact rights language obviously makes a difference, and at least in two directions as I have elsewhere tried to show. In the first place it concretely reverses years of scholastic neglect, and rejects precisely the Thomist view of animals as morally without status. 'Language and history are against those who want the better treatment of animals and who also want to deny the legitimacy of the language of rights. For how can we reverse centuries of scholastic tradition if we still accept the cornerstone of that tradition, namely that all but humans are morally rightless?' Second, whatever the limitations of rights language and however it may be open to misunderstanding, the quite fundamental point is that 'to grant animal rights is to accept that they can be wronged' and in analogous terms to the wrong that may be inflicted upon human beings. 'According to theos-rights what we do to animals is not simply a matter of taste or convenience or philanthropy. When we speak of animal rights we conceptualize what is owed to animals as a matter of justice by virtue of their Creator's right. Animals can be wronged because their Creator can be wronged in his creation.'[100]

To reiterate: the language of theos-rights is not exclusive, comprehensive or essential, but it is plausible, consistent and desirable. It is for those who reject rights language to show how it is possible to give credence to the theological insights I have outlined 'without participating in the moral neglect of the non-human which still characterizes continuing elements within the Christian tradition'.[101]

If utilized carefully, the language of theos-rights helps bring out the fundamental point that what we are dealing with is God's own Spirit-filled life which does not belong to us and over which we certainly have no rights as of right. Such language – whatever its limitations or deficiencies – serves to convey to us that the claims of animals are God-based claims of justice. Far from usurping God's own prerogative in creation, the perspective of theos-rights champions it, brings it into sharpest contact with our own wants and desires, and determines that we recognize the generosity of God even in what often appears, to us, insignificant.

2

The Moral Priority of the Weak

Is what is owed animals as God's creatures satisfied by the language of respect, responsibility, and rights? In this chapter I argue, from a theological perspective, that we need to go even further: that a morally satisfying interpretation of our obligations to animals cannot simply rest with a claim for equal consideration as advanced by some animal liberationists. Drawing upon the notion of divine generosity exemplified in the person of Jesus, I suggest that the weak and the defenceless should be given not equal, but greater, consideration. The weak should have moral priority.

The Equality Paradigm

My starting point is an examination of one of the earliest arguments for animal liberation advanced by Peter Singer in 1974. His article, provocatively entitled 'All Animals are Equal', has been both widely discussed and widely reprinted.[1] Singer's argument is as simple as it is clever. He begins by observing that liberation movements require of us 'an expansion of our moral horizons and an extension or reinterpretation of the basic moral principle of equality'. Hence we have become familiar with a variety of minorities: blacks, gays, Spanish-Americans and other groups campaigning for equality and an end to discrimination. If we are not to be counted among the oppressors we need from time to time to examine ourselves, and in particular ask whether our own actions are not based on some arbitrary bias in favour of our own group or prejudice against some other. Singer argues that when surveyed in this light 'practices that were previously regarded as natural or inevitable come to be seen as the result of an unjustifiable prejudice':

> My aim is to advocate that we make this mental switch in respect of our attitudes and practices towards a very large group of beings: members of species other than our own – or, as we popularly though misleadingly call them, animals. In other words, I am

urging that we extend to other species the basic principle of equality that most of us recognize should be extended to all members of our own species.[2]

Singer offers one fundamental qualification to his thesis.

> The extension of the basic principle of equality from one group to another does not imply that we must treat both groups in exactly the same way, or grant exactly the same rights to both groups. Whether we should do so will depend on the nature of the members of the two groups. The basic principle of equality, I shall argue, is equality of consideration; and equal consideration for different beings may lead to different treatment and different rights.[3]

So Singer's notion of equality is prescriptive rather than factual; he goes on to elucidate the grounds for equal consideration. Following Bentham, he argues that sentience provides such a basis:

> If a being suffers, there can be no moral justification for refusing to take that suffering into consideration. No matter what the nature of the being, the principle of equality requires that its suffering be counted equally with like suffering – in so far as rough comparisons can be made – of any other being. If a being is not capable of suffering, or of experiencing enjoyment or happiness, there is nothing to be taken into account. This is why the limit of sentience (using the term as a convenient, if not strictly accurate, shorthand for the capacity to suffer or experience enjoyment or happiness) is the only defensible boundary of concern for the interests of others.[4]

What should be the appropriate theological response to Singer's argument for equal moral consideration between humans and animals? So far it would be fair to say that the theological response has been no response. The idea that animals are in any way morally equal with humans may be judged by many as a non-starter within the Christian tradition. Indeed Mary Midgley dismisses the idea; one chapter of her book, *Animals and Why They Matter* is headed: 'Equality and Outer Darkness'.[5] Many of these responses or non-responses rest on the unchallenged assumption of human superiority. But it is precisely this assumption, it seems to me, that can be best defended by critical examination. Singer, for his part, makes hay with this assumption:

Faced with a situation in which they see a need for some basis for the moral gulf that is commonly thought to separate humans and animals, but can find no concrete difference that will do the job without undermining the equality of humans, philosophers tend to waffle. They resort to high-sounding phrases like 'the intrinsic dignity of the human individual'; they talk of the 'intrinsic dignity of all men' as if men (humans?) had some worth that other beings did not, or they say that humans, and only humans, are 'ends in themselves', while 'everything other than a person can only have value for a person'.[6]

He continues with a calculated side-swipe at the Christian tradition:

This idea of a distinctive human dignity and worth has a long history; it can be traced back directly to the Renaissance humanists, for instance to Pico della Mirandola's *Oration on the Dignity of Man*. Pico and other humanists based their estimate of human dignity on the idea that man possessed the central, pivotal position in the 'Great Chain of Being' that led from the lowest forms of matter to God himself; this view of the universe, in turn, goes back to both classical and Judeo-Christian doctrines. Contemporary philosophers have cast off these metaphysical and religious shackles and freely invoke the dignity of mankind without needing to justify the idea at all ... [But] in elevating our own species we are at the same time lowering the relative status of all other species.[7]

This kind of counterblast must be taken seriously not least because of the way in which Christian tradition has culpably reinforced, if not generated, a whole range of negative responses to animal welfare. It will not do for Christians simply to respond (as many of them still do) by saying: 'The Christian view is that humans are worth more than animals.' Rather we have to ask: What is the theological insight that makes Christians claim humans as superior or as possessing special status? In what does this special value of humans consist?

The Generosity Paradigm

I want to begin by agreeing with Singer that no such appeal can properly be sustained by appealing to merely factual difference, e.g. that humans are more clever, more powerful, more rational and so on. Rather I want to stress that any decent theological insight must be grounded in God and in particular God's attitude towards creation. And that insight can properly be summed up in one word: *generosity*. The special value of humankind consists in the generosity of God: Creator, Reconciler and Redeemer. This idea is of course a perennial theme throughout the Old and New Testaments, is found consistently in the work of the Fathers, and in my view reaches its richest expression yet in the theology of Karl Barth. Barth writes eloquently of how the 'Yes' of God the Creator to the creature involves a historical 'No' to all the forces of non-being and disintegration that persistently threaten creation itself:

> In order that this No should be spoken by man in his weakness and frailty as it was spoken by the Creator from all eternity, God Himself willed to become man, to make His own the weakness and frailty of man, to suffer and die as man, and in this self-offering to secure the frontier between His creation and the ruin which threatens it from the abyss. God is gracious to man. He has appointed him to stand firm on this frontier to say No in covenant with him to what He has not willed but negated. But He knows man's incapacity to fulfil this destiny. And because he is unwilling to leave him unaided in the attempt to fulfil this destiny, He takes up his cause at this point and shares his creatureliness. He does this in order to rescue and preserve His creature. He does it because it is unable to rescue and preserve itself.[8]

The internal logic of this christological paradigm deserves some reflection. For here is a God supreme above all who in Christ humbles him/herself to identify with and suffer for the weakly and frail creature. As Barth puts it crisply: 'Without the condescension of God there would be no exaltation of man.'[9] At first sight all this might appear a wholly humanocentric, indeed anthropocentric, doctrine quite unhelpful to concerns about non-human creatures. And, there is no getting away from it, Barth's doctrine does suffer from some severe anthropocentric limitations. Yet even Barth is tantalizingly open to extending the meaning of the incarnation well beyond the human sphere. In discussing the gift of freedom as the basis of evangelical ethics, he declares that 'God is beyond doubt also before, above, after, and with all of His other creatures.' While accepting that we have no precise knowledge about the freedom of other creatures, he maintains:

> God was not and is not bound to choose and to decide Himself for man *alone* and to show his loving kindness to him *alone*. The thought of any insignificant being outside the human cosmos

being far more worthy of divine attention than man is deeply edifying and should not be lightly dismissed.[10]

I would not want to speculate here about God's possible incarnation as ants, aliens or ETs, though like Barth I would not want to rule anything out absolutely. What I want rather for us to focus our attention on is how the concept of generosity, of the higher sacrificing itself for the lower, is at the heart even of highly anthropocentric doctrine. That even Barth sees – albeit tentatively – that this doctrine may well have meaning beyond its human sphere is not insignificant.

I want, however, to go further than Barth and suggest that if it is true that this paradigm of generous, costly service is at the heart of the Christian proclamation then it must also be the paradigm for the exercise of human dominion over the animal world. We do well to remind ourselves of that ethical imperative arising from early Christian reflection upon the work and person of Jesus:

> Take to heart among yourselves what you find in Christ Jesus: He was in the form of God; yet he laid no claim to equality with God, but made himself nothing, assuming the form of a slave. Bearing the human likeness, sharing the human lot, he humbled himself, and was obedient even to the point of death, death on a cross (Phil. 2.5–9; REB).

If we 'take to heart' this paradigm of generosity we can perceive moral meaning to our relationship of power over the non-human creation. The pattern of obligation disclosed by Christ makes no appeal to equality. The obligation is always and everywhere on the 'higher' to sacrifice for the 'lower'; for the strong, powerful and rich to give to those who are vulnerable, poor or powerless. This is not some by-theme of the moral example of Jesus, it is rather central to the demands of the kingdom, indeed those who minister to the needs of the vulnerable and the weak minister to Christ himself:

> I was hungry and you gave me food, I was thirsty and you gave me drink, I was a stranger and you welcomed me, I was naked and you clothed me, I was sick and you visited me, I was in prison and you came to me (Matt. 25.35–37; RSV).

In this respect, it is the sheer vulnerability and powerlessness of animals, and correspondingly our absolute power over them which strengthens and compels the response of moral generosity. I suggest that we are to be present to creation as Christ is present to us. When we speak of human superiority we speak of such a thing properly only and in so far as we speak not only of Christlike lordship but also of Christlike service. There can be no lordship without service and no service without lordship. Our special value in creation consists in being of special value to others.

Drawing the Line

Before proceeding, I anticipate two objections both related to the problem of where one draws the line. The first objection maintains that historically the line has always been drawn at human beings. Humans, it is argued, are cherished creatures in a way that applies to none other. The limit of generosity must be drawn at the human/animal boundary. The second objection maintains that the line cannot be drawn at all. All God's creation is valuable to God and, as far as we can possibly know, in precisely the same way. When we say that God values one being more than another we are only expressing humanocentric prejudice.

I certainly do not want to suppose that drawing a line here is a straightforward matter. Are we to draw it at adult humans bearing in mind that children – for the most part of the Christian tradition – have *not* (in a straightforward way at least) been included within the moral circle? Are we to draw the line at humans excluding all other beings including animals? Are we to extend the circle to include humans, children and animals but not vegetables? Or should we include *all* life-forms even including vegetables but excluding inanimates?

I want to justify the middle choices – the extension of the circle to include adults, children and animals – against their two neighbours. In particular, it is sometimes supposed by modern Christians that concern for animal rights cannot and should not be distinguished from concern for creation as a whole. We now hear that the concern for animal rights lacks a holistic doctrine of creation and fails to recognize creaturely interdependence. In other words, God is supposed to take an undif-ferentiated view of all creation. Those who argue in this way have to contend against three major concepts – each located in the Bible and subsequently developed by later tradition: common creation or co-existence, dominion, and covenant. I shall briefly take them in turn.

First, common creation or co-existence. It is commonly supposed that Genesis 1 describes created hierarchy with the elements of creation made first, then vegetables, followed by the animals and eventually humankind as the summit of creation. I do not accept that hierarchical order was the prime intention of the author at this point, but I do not dissent from the view that Genesis 1 does posit circles of greater or lesser intimacy with God. But what is often overlooked is that animals belong to the innermost circle of intimacy. On the fifth day, birds and fishes are created while the land animals and humans are created together on the sixth. It is difficult to avoid the conclusion that Genesis 1 here envisages the special proximity of some (predominantly mammalian) animals to humankind. After having surveyed the variety of ways in which animals are specifically associated, if not identified, with humans themselves, Barth concludes: "'O Lord, thou preservest man and beast" (Ps. 36.6) is a thread running through the whole of the Bible; and it first emerges in a way which is quite unmistakable when the creation of man is classified in Gen. 1. 24f. with that of the land animals.'[11]

Secondly, the concept of dominion. Again it is commonly supposed that the power given to humankind over animals justifies their use or abuse by humans. Dominion has frequently been interpreted as despotism. But there is another and altogether more satisfying interpretation of this notion. Judged from its context, God shares his or her moral rule with humans so that they can look after and care for the creation which is made (cf. e.g. Gen. 2.15 where humans are specifically given the task of tilling and keeping the garden). It is important to note, however, that this divinely given commission to look after the earth eschews any right to kill for food. The dominion granted is such that *subsequent upon* its bestowal, God commands a vegetarian diet (Gen. 1.29f.). The giving of dominion over animals which was once thought to be the touchstone justifying any abuse is now becoming central to the view that what we owe animals is more than what we owe vegetables or arguably even ecosystems.

Thirdly, the concept of covenant. Even after the Fall and the Flood, God maintains a special relationship with the creatures. Once again, it is commonly supposed that humans alone are elected into this covenant relationship. Not so. The description of the covenant in Genesis 9 is worth recalling. The promise is that never again will God destroy 'all living things' (Gen. 9. 8–17). While it is true that on one occasion the covenant is extended to include earth itself (9.13), the principal subjects of the covenant are not just humans but 'every living creature that is with you' and specifically, 'the birds, the cattle, and every beast of the earth with you' – and this, as if to underline the point, is five times repeated (Gen. 9. 10, 12, 15, 16, 17).[12] Although many theologians seem to overlook the significance of these words, Barth – at least in one place – grasps the underlying vision of commonality. He writes of how

> Man's salvation and perdition, his joy and sorrow, will be reflected in the weal and woe of this animal environment and company … the animal will participate with man (the independent partner) in the covenant, sharing both the promise and the curse which shadows the promise.[13]

These sketches, brief though they are, are enough to indicate how some of the foundational material in scripture does indeed make distinctions not only between humans and animals but also between animals and vegetables. The characteristic thrust of scripture certainly distinguishes between animals and humans but it does so in such a way that the commonality of both is also stressed in relation to creation as a whole.

Even when it comes to the New Testament where it is often supposed that concern for animals can nowhere be found among its pages, there are signs that this understanding of commonality is continued and developed. John Austin Baker argues that in 'his parables Jesus encourages care and concern for animals (cf. Luke 13.15; 15.4; Matt. 12.11 = Luke 14.5), even if these are only illustrations incidental to his main point'.[14] Whatever we think of this, it does seem indisputable that Jesus is presented in the Gospels as upholding the 'basic attitude of the Old Testament that the created order is God's work and as such is good'. In particular Baker suggests that Jesus presents 'God's providential care' as extending 'even to the most insignificant animals, and the beauty of the wild flowers springing up in the fields of Galilee is greater than that of Solomon in all his glory (Matt. 6.26 = Luke 12.24; Matt. 10.29 = Luke 12.6; Matt. 6.28f.)'.[15] Although Jesus is presented as underlining the special value of humankind over that of sparrows, the main point does seem to be that God is generous so much so that what is taken by the world to be of little account, namely sparrows 'sold for two pennies', are in fact so valuable that 'not one of them is forgotten by God' (Luke 12.6–7). To be pedantic: the lilies are not to be compared with the glory of Solomon but it is the sparrows who are not forgotten by God. At the very least we should say that in this one case alone Jesus exhibits an *inclusive* understanding of divine generosity, one that is in contrast to past and present humanocentrism.

Now it would be difficult to contend that this inclusive paradigm of moral generosity has been widespread throughout Christian tradition as a whole, but it is worth noting that it has not been without some powerful

advocates within some of the sub-traditions of Christendom: St Bonaventure, St Gregory of Nyssa, St Catherine of Siena, St John Chrysostom, St John of the Cross, St Thomas More, John Wesley and, more
recently C. S. Lewis, are but a few examples.[16] The prayer of St Basil the
Great in the fourth century, for example, speaks of animals as 'our
brothers' and thus predates St Francis and the subsequent and substantial body of hagiography linking divine generosity with the value of all
living creatures.

It is not until the nineteenth century that we see the first flourishing of
these insights with the advent of the movements against animal cruelty.
We often forget that these movements drew their inspiration directly
from Christian notions of generosity and charity. We have already noted
that Arthur Broome wrote the first Prospectus of the SPCA in 1824 in
which he argued that divine benevolence was incompatible with animal
abuse.[17] But it is to the seventh Lord Shaftesbury that we should turn for
the fullest and most satisfying statement of the generosity paradigm:

> I was convinced that God had called me to devote whatever
> advantages He might have bestowed upon me to the cause of the
> weak, the helpless, both man and beast, and those who had none
> to help them ... Whatever I have done has been given to me; what I
> have done I was enabled to do; and all happy results (if any there
> be) must be credited, not to the servant, but to the great Master,
> who led and sustained him.[18]

Special Relationships: Children and Animals

Shaftesbury's words indicate his conviction that the weak and the
oppressed constitute a special moral category based on our special
relationship of power over them. Similarly, I propose that animals
constitute a special category of moral obligation, a category to which the
best, perhaps only, analogy is that of parental obligations to children. In
both cases, I hold that our special relationships involve special obligations. Generosity is the concept especially applicable to both.

At first sight the idea that we owe animals generous, that is, *more* than
equal consideration, might appear faintly ludicrous. To those who
respond in this way, I ask them to reflect upon the range of special
relationships in which we find ourselves and which require of us more,
much more, than the exercise of equal consideration. As the father of
four wonderful children, for example, I find the idea that my moral

obligations consist in equal consideration of interests laughable. If it was the case that Daddies possessed the same consideration as children, my life over the past ten years would surely have been different. I would have had *my* fair share of sleep, *my* fair share of tender loving care, even indeed an equal chance to watch the television programmes *I* like. Equality between adult human beings may well be a desirable norm, but between parents and children nothing less than the exercise of costly, generous loving is the daily moral obligation.

Nothing said so far as regards children would nowadays be regarded as contentious. Very few people would deny that we owe special obligations to children. That does not mean, of course, that children are not sometimes cruelly treated, abused, even murdered, but very few people regard these activities as anything less than morally shocking. But this has not always been so. As animals have been regarded as property without any rights or value in themselves so also have children. Indeed there is a formal similarity between the two, for not only have the same arguments justified abuse in both cases, so too have the arguments opposing cruelty to animals also opposed cruelty to children. Indeed the similarity is not only formal, it is historical. In Britain, it was members of the RSPCA who helped found the first anti-child cruelty society in the world. In the United States, it was the ASPCA founder, Henry Bergh, who also campaigned against child cruelty and who was instrumental in setting up the first anti-child cruelty society in the States.[19]

I anticipate that some may still be profoundly unhappy with the language of parenthood when applied to human relations with animals. As a one-time counsellor, I am more than aware that not every individual's experience of being subject to parenting has been a happy one. There are plenty of lousy fathers as well as hateful sons. I propose 'parenthood' only as an analogy and like all analogies there are points at which it breaks down. For some the responsibility of parenthood sometimes involves the right to coerce a child or physically chastise it. I propose that such 'rights' – if such they be – cannot and do not apply to animals. What I do accept, however, is that humans can and should use their power for the benefit of the animals themselves. As a result of our previous use or abuse of animals, such intervention has now become morally essential whether it be to reduce the ever-increasing unwanted pet population through neutering or spaying programmes, or through the preservation of animals which would otherwise perish. But I add this all-important caveat. When we act to take power on behalf of animals it must be just that: for *their* interests as individuals and not – as usually happens – for the advancement of ours.

Nevertheless, some animal rightists like myself are certainly nervous of the idea that humans have divinely appointed power over animals. And with good reason. In the past both Jews and Christians have thought of the exercise of power as itself sufficient justification for the abuse of power. In the words of the former Bishop of Exeter, foxhunting could be justified because it reinforced 'man's high place in the hierarchy of being'.[20] It is precisely that implication, christologically unenlightened as it is, that must be countered. I posit a counter-principle: whenever we find ourselves in a position of power over those who are relatively powerless our moral obligation of generosity increases in proportion. If our power over animals confers upon us any rights, there is only one: the right to serve.

In passing I also want to oppose the view, so comforting to those who wish to exploit children or animals, that children or animals do not really suffer like adult humans. It seems to me that the reverse is most likely to be the case. So many philosophers and theologians are guilty of 'adultism' in that they take the model of relations between adult humans – free, self-conscious, rational beings – as the sole model of ethical interaction. Animals – and also and especially children – are marginalized by this procedure. Logically enough, Peter Singer supports infanticide, that is, the killing of defective children.[21] For myself I do not deny that our power over both infants and animals does sometimes involve making burdensome choices on their behalf about the quality of their life and even in extreme cases whether they should live. But, unlike Singer, I dispute that these instances can simply be resolved by an appeal to some utilitarian rule of thumb. The relative weakness of both infants and animals should make us draw back from the immediate exercise of power until we are quite sure that *their* claims have been given greater consideration.[22] When it comes specifically to suffering, I suggest that animals and children who cannot fully vocalize or comprehend their misery, and who – in the case of animals at least – frequently suffer the deprivation of their natural instincts, are the victims of a greater cruelty.[23]

Ill-Gotten Gains

The question may be pressed, however, why precisely should we opt for the *Generosity* Paradigm rather than – what I call – the *Equality* Paradigm proposed by Singer?

In the first place, it must be questioned whether Singer himself is sufficiently consistent in his own interpretation of the Equality Paradigm. As we have seen, Singer indicated that the claim for equality 'does not imply that we must treat both groups in exactly the same way, or grant exactly the same rights to both groups'. 'Whether we should do will depend on the nature of the members of the two groups.' But this qualification, honest as it is, must make us question what kind of equality it is that is being proposed. Equal consideration is equal consideration. Singer it seems often wants to have it both ways. For example, when considering our obligation to promote racial equality, or equality of opportunity as he sees it, Singer defends 'reverse discrimination' or preferential options. 'Properly applied, it is in keeping with equal consideration of interests, in its aspirations at least.'[24] This, I suggest, is already to go substantially beyond any strict appeal to the Equality Paradigm. The Paradigm only holds up if sufficiently modified to allow for beneficent but essentially unequal treatment. This is no mere debating point. That Singer so qualifies his position is a sign that what is owed animals (or any other category) must go beyond any simple appeal to equality as such. In short: Singer offers animals equality of consideration. But it turns out that that phrase is to be interpreted *considerately* only in the case of (adult?) humans. Orwellian indeed.

Secondly and relatedly, the Equality Paradigm fails to offer positive vision of the animal/human relationship. Like so much pro-animal literature, it is only concerned with setting minimum limits to what we may do to them. Because of this, it simply does not go far enough in recognizing the full extent of our obligations to animals. According to the Generosity Paradigm, our obligations to animals are not exhausted by the attempt to minimize suffering or wanton destruction. What we owe animals is more than the demand for equality. What the Generosity Paradigm requires is generous, costly action to promote animal well-being. One example may illustrate this.

Singer expresses the view that many of our contemporary practices are the result of speciesism, one in particular: animal experimentation. 'The same form of discrimination may be observed in the widespread practice of experimenting on other species', he argues, 'in order to see if certain substances are safe for human beings, or to test some psychological theory ... or to try out various new compounds just in case something turns up ...'[25] But notice that however critical of the practice of experimentation Singer might be, he does not endorse its abolition or say that all such use of animals is wrong. Indeed in another context

Singer makes his position plain: '... if one, or even a dozen animals had to suffer experiments in order to save thousands (presumably Singer means here thousands *of the same species*), I would think it right *and* in accordance with equal consideration of interests that they should do so'.[26] The Equality Paradigm then does not and will not save animals from experimental suffering, indeed the reverse is the case. On Singer's argument there is a moral obligation to sacrifice one species to another, even a weaker species, if this is what 'equal consideration of interests' requires.

In contrast, the Generosity Paradigm I have outlined goes much further. It resists the idea that we have the right to promote human welfare and happiness at the expense of other creatures. The idea that animals are simply here for human use or benefit is as morally grotesque as supposing that children are morally the property of their parents or may be used for parental benefit. Far from asking what minimal harm or suffering we can inflict upon animals for human use, the Generosity Paradigm insists that humans must bear for themselves whatever ills may flow from not experimenting upon animals rather than sanction a system of institutionalized abuse.

Such a judgment may well appear a hard one. Yet, we may recall here the view of Lord Shaftesbury himself. Not only was he an abolitionist when it came to slavery and child labour, he was also one of the founding members of the first anti-vivisection society in the world. 'We are bound in duty', he wrote, 'to leap over all limitations and go in for the total abolition of this vile and cruel form of Idolatry; for idolatry it is, and like all idolatry, brutal, degrading and deceptive.'[27] Nowadays most of us would view as rather far-fetched the extension of that language to include scientific research concerned to advance the frontiers of knowledge beneficial to humankind. But it may be that this idea – that human life and well-being is of such enormous significance that it justifies the institutionalized use of millions of animals in experimental procedures which inflict great suffering – does have to be defined in idolatrous-like-terms. Do not animals now suffer in our laboratories to make our life easier, to help prolong our lives, to fulfil our therapeutic wants, even if the benefit concerned is as trivial as a new face cream, lipstick or nail-varnish? Are not animals now sacrificed for a species that increasingly takes to itself God-like powers and who regards its own interests as unquestioningly the goal and purpose of creation itself? Demythologized, we might say that our idolatrous tendency consists in thinking that our own estimation of our own worth and value can be the main or exclusive criterion by which we judge the worth and value of all other species. If we find this language disconcerting, it may be because we have come to accept, bit by bit, the utilitarian position even in its enlightened Singerian form, which accepts axiomatically that the interests of the weak can be traded against those of the strong.

The time has now come for me to crystalize my argument. I argue that whatever the merits of the Equality Paradigm, Singer's use of it is far from consistent and by itself is incapable of sparing animals from some existing abuses. The Generosity Paradigm I propose is based on the special relationship we have with animals as testified in scripture and continuing elements within the Christian tradition. This Generosity Paradigm takes as its model the moral priority of the weak as exemplified in the teaching and example of Jesus. It requires of us a massive reorientation in our attitudes towards animals as it has done (or begun to do in relatively recent times) in the case of our attitude towards children and the weaker members of the human community.

Two Objections

I anticipate two fundamental objections to my thesis. The first is that the language of generosity – preferable though it might be from a Christian standpoint – represents a departure from the historic language of justice and in particular the related ideas of equality and rights. It invites a return to the old notions of paternalism and philanthropy, whereas the modern movement for animal liberation is precisely concerned to cast off this framework of *noblesse oblige*.

I, for one, would not want to jettison the historic language of justice or in any way suggest that what we owe animals is simply a question of sentiment, emotion or even (understood in a disparaging sense) philanthropy. But to reiterate, what we owe animals requires *more* – not less – than adherence to concepts of equality and rights. I have already argued that the language of rights is indispensable as the provider of markers and pointers to the minimum obligations we should extend to animals, such as not harming, not causing suffering, not wantonly destroying. But at the same time we need to be aware of the limitations of this language and especially be cognizant that such rights, even if widely respected, will fall short of meeting the moral claim that animals make on us.

One example may help. It is quite possible for a parent to respect all the rights of a child and still be less than what a parent should be. He or she may not beat the child, provide as far as possible for its education, even care for it in times of sickness or need, and yet may still fall short of being the loving, forgiving parent that all children actually need for their growth into adult personhood. We should certainly speak of the rights of children[28] – as we should speak of the rights of animals – but what parents owe their children – as humans owe animals – goes beyond the respecting of their rights.

While I suggest that the Equality Paradigm is unsatisfactory, it does not follow that we should therefore jettison the concept of rights, and for one theological reason in particular. At the heart of the theological conception of rights – as I have defended it – is not a self-awarding system of obligation but a recognition that the Creator has rights to have creation treated with respect. Central to the theological debate about rights, unlike the concept of equality, is a debate about what we owe the Creator in view of the Creator's generosity in creation. Perhaps we can best encapsulate this point by combining both words and speaking of the 'right to generosity' or the 'right to generous treatment'.

The second objection is that the Generosity Paradigm would be impossible – practically and legally – to implement and, if attempted, would result in a substantially diminished quality of life for human beings.

At first sight this seems a strong objection. I readily accede that it is problematic to legislate for moral generosity (no less so for equality), and I am not one of those who think that all moral obligations can be transformed without difficulty into legal prescriptions. We need to be much more modest about what law can actually achieve in terms of securing a just and benevolent society. Nevertheless, as I see it, the strongest moral justification for government as well as law is that they should ensure the protection of the weak and the powerless. Because of this, it is inevitable that we turn to law at least to embody a framework that can prevent the worst, even if it cannot guarantee the best.

Can law provide a framework supportive of, even requiring of, the exercise of human generosity to animals? To answer this question I want to tackle a practical case, namely the protection of bats. At first sight a more hopeless case could not be envisaged. Bats have few devotees. They are not cuddly or friendly to human beings. Despite the fact that they are intelligent mammals with a highly sophisticated social life, bats are seldom thought well of. Indeed there is a large, even voluminous – and wholly libellous – literature associating bats with blood-sucking vampires, even the powers of darkness. Moreover, not only are bats in some cultures symbols of evil, they have also frequently been persecuted, even tortured. Poor public image, irrational persecution, and lack of FCF – 'friendly, cuddly factor' – must make us think that the Generosity Paradigm here faces its severest test.

Yet consider: in the United Kingdom, the Wildlife and Countryside Act of 1981 accords the bat special protection in law:

> It is illegal for anyone without a licence intentionally to kill a bat, injure or handle a bat of any species ... to possess a bat, whether alive or dead; or to disturb a bat when roosting. Ringing or marking or photographing them ... requires a licence from the Nature Conservancy Council. It is also an offence to sell or offer for sale any bat, whether alive or dead, without a licence. But the law does allow you to tend a disabled bat in order to release it when it recovers or to kill a seriously disabled bat which has no reasonable chance of recovery.[29]

Not only are bats accorded these rights, but also individual householders are unable under this legislation to disturb bats nesting in their roofs even when they are causing damage or even running the risk of disease. Hence it is illegal without a licence to disturb when roosting, block up their entrances, or even use any pesticides or wood preservatives which would harm them or disturb their dwelling place.[30]

What is interesting about this legislation is that not only are bat rights upheld by law, but also even in competing situations with human rights, the bat is to be given preferential treatment. In practice, even though a bat colony has invaded your house, may be causing damage to your home, incurring financial disadvantage, even unsightly mess and unwelcome noise, humans have no automatic right to self-defence. Licences to destroy bats can only be given after investigation and consultation with a third party who normally recommends non-violent preventative measures.

Now I do not want to pretend that all is now well with bats. Some individuals act illegally and kill them. Some licences doubtless are given after more scrupulosity than others. Some humans will go on persecuting and hating bats whatever the law prescribes. We need to be aware of the irreducible role of prejudice in any act of legal interpretation. Nevertheless what is astonishing about this legislation is the way in which human rights, in particular what may be legitimately construed as a right of self-defence against intruders, are not upheld without consultation and arbitration. The Equality Paradigm would surely permit the destruction of bats in these circumstances. After all bats are technically 'pests' in the sense that they are a species which interact with humans to the detriment of human habitats. The Generosity Paradigm, however, is exemplified by this legislation. There can be – and are – real cases of conflict between human rights and bat rights but it is bats, not humans, that now have the preferential option.

But what of the objection that such generous activity on a widespread scale, supported by a framework of law, would be detrimental to human interests? I think the answer has to be in the affirmative. The Generosity View rejects the idea that the rights and welfare of animals must always be subordinate to human interests, even when vital human interests are at stake. We must be quite clear about this. Acting out the Generosity Paradigm will cost human beings. In the short run the dismantling of unjust institutions such as animal experimentation, intensive farming, and the end to recreational practices such as hunting and shooting and angling for sport will involve some diminution of human pleasure or job prospects or even life chances (commonly understood). The question is, however, not whether we gain from these present practices but rather whether they are ill-gotten gains.

I state the issue plainly because there seems to be a general misconception that behaving morally to animals will not really involve humans in any fundamental change of life-style. Too many individuals want to speak generally about generosity to animals while still destroying their habitats, hunting them for sport, or consuming their flesh. To appreciate the moral gains to humanity from desisting from exploitation, we need to take the longer view. If we ask whether humanity has lost out because it no longer has access to the ill-gotten gains achieved through widespread slavery, racism or sexism, we can see immediately that though there were indeed gains – and still are for some – without these sacrifices moral progress would have been impossible. Whether we can now make moral progress in relation to animals is the question before us.

3

Humans as the Servant Species

The emphasis in the last chapter on the commonality of humans and animals may appear to obscure the traditional Christian claim concerning the uniqueness of humankind. It is frequently maintained that animal rightists see no real difference between animals and humans and try to put both on the same moral or theological level.[1] It is true that many animal rightists distrust the 'uniqueness claims' made for human beings and, as I go on to show, sometimes for good reasons. But does it follow that to endorse the ethical treatment of animals requires an abandonment of the traditional Christian view that humans are special or unique? I do not think so. In what follows, I try to show how the view that humans are morally superior is actually central to good animal rights theory. Drawing upon the idea of a God who suffers, I argue that human uniqueness can be defined as the capacity for service and self-sacrifice. From this perspective, humans are the species uniquely commissioned to exercise a self-sacrificial priesthood, after the one High Priest, not just for members of their own species, but for all sentient creatures. The groaning and travailing of fellow creatures requires a species capable of co-operating with God in the healing and liberating of creation.

Uniqueness Spotting

My starting point is a question: In what way, if at all, are human beings unique in creation? In the past, there have been almost too many answers to that question. A range of unique and crucial differences have been canvassed: humans alone have rationality, culture, language; humans alone are self-conscious and are solely capable of sentient existence. Humans alone are capable of praising God and entering into a relationship with the divine. There seems no end to the possibilities of uniqueness which humans can contemplate for themselves when they compare themselves to other species. The notion of the image of God has furthered an extensive uniqueness-searching anthropology which has dominated Christian tradition for centuries, irritating one distinguished Hebrew scholar, James Barr, into denying that the notion of the image refers to anything tangible at all, referring to such attempts as 'the blood-out-of-a-stone process'.[2]

There are at least three reasons why theology should be suspicious of this uniqueness-spotting tendency. The first and most obvious is that a good number of these differences have turned out to be not so unique after all. For example, few now share the conviction of Aquinas that only humans in creation are capable of rationality or intelligence in its broadest sense. Even fewer now share the enthusiasm of Descartes for the view that animals are automata, mechanisms devoid of self-consciousness, and seemingly incapable of feeling pain. An unmistakable sense of caution in this regard is registered by former Archbishop Robert Runcie. 'Both in theory and practice the boundaries of the human family are becoming unclear' he argues. Behind practical dilemmas

> there lies the theoretical difficulty of defining what it is that decisively distinguishes the human from the non-human – a difficulty that increases as, for instance, naturalists detect in non-human creatures subtleties of behaviour and complexities of communication which, until recently, would have been thought unique and exclusive of humans.[3]

Then there may be a question as to *why* humans find it necessary to place themselves in a distinct category from animals. One of the conclusions of Desmond Morris' popular book, *The Naked Ape*, which aroused most Christian commentators to complain, was his insistence that our desire to be placed above the animals was itself a sign of insecurity. 'Unfortunately, because we are so powerful and so successful when compared with other animals, we find the contemplation of our humble origins somehow offensive, so that I do not expect to be thanked for what I have done', he wrote. 'Our climb to the top has been a get-rich-quick story, and, like all *nouveaux riches*, we are very sensitive about our background. We are also in constant danger of betraying it.'[4]

To these suspicions needs to be added a third, namely that the distinctions we have drawn have been frequently and transparently self-serving, even selfish. For example, it seems to be altogether too convenient for Aristotle – to take simply one example – to suppose that since 'nature makes nothing without some end in view' it must follow that nature has made all animals 'for the sake of man'.[5] It has been so easy to turn this appeal to the purpose of nature, and in subsequent Christian centuries to 'divine purpose', into a justification for doing what we like to animals that we have come to suspect the opposite is the true sequence. As we have seen, Aquinas, following Aristotle, appeals both to the order of nature and also to divine providence to assure us that 'it is not wrong for man to make use of them, either by killing or in any other way whatever'.[6] The difference-finding tendency in Western tradition has undoubtedly served to minimize the moral standing of non-human creatures, and to enable us to exploit them with a clear conscience. One cannot be but bemused by the reference in the marriage service of the *Book of Common Prayer* to 'brute beasts that hath no understanding' since some, perhaps many, higher mammals seem to know more about monogamous relationships than at least some members of *homo sapiens*.[7] In short: much of our uniqueness-spotting within the Christian tradition has been linked directly or indirectly to the fostering of a low view of animality, the traces of which are still found in our language about 'brutes', 'beasts' and 'bestial'; even the word 'animal' has become a libel – and not just on human beings.

In a small but significant book of theological fantasy, entitled *Travels in Oudamovia*, John Austin Baker describes the traveller's reaction to Oudamovian life and worship which was characterized by a friendly non-exploitative relationship with animals:

> The truth they strove to bring home was that the world God has given to his creatures, the one world which they have to share, is in fact a different world to each one of them, but that the world each creature knows is equally true. We human beings, superior as we are, ought to be very humble because other creatures have other truths which we can only dimly grasp, worlds we can never fully enter.

He concludes with this question:

> And if this is so with regard to an ox or an ant, not to say a tree or a stone, how can we hope to comprehend the God who comprehends them all, to whom all worlds and truths are fully known because he made them?[8]

This interesting question leads me again to my starting point. Let me now frame the question in this way: Is it possible to have a theological understanding of humans as unique which avoids the suspicions and dangers of self-service, insecurity, and moral denigration of what is different – not to mention a view which might broadly be reconcilable with empirical evidence?

The Suffering God

I begin by laying some stress on this word 'theological'. Many of the
previous claims for human uniqueness have been essentially naturalistic
rather than theological. I mean by this that they have appealed to certain
abilities, qualities, or capacities, such as rationality, or power, or self-
consciousness, which are taken as determinative of what is uniquely
human. Such attempts are not theological in the strict sense of being
things which are grounded in the nature of God itself. Despite the
traveller in Oudamovia's not wholly unjust complaint that 'our understanding of God is even less adequate than our understanding of the life
of our cat',[9] it is here that there may be a way forward.

Attending seriously to the gospel narratives it may be that there is at
least one thing we can know. It seems appropriate to describe this truth
in the form of a story. It is from Helen Waddell's *Peter Abelard*. Peter,
you may recall, had been made to suffer a terrible injustice from people
who had taken the law into their own hands. In this passage, Peter is
walking close to a wood with his friend, Thibault.

> 'My God,' said Thibault, 'what's that?'
> From somewhere near them in the woods a cry had risen, a thin
> cry, of such intolerable anguish that Abelard turned dizzy on his feet,
> and caught at the wall.
> 'It's a child voice,' he said. 'O God, are they at a child?'
> 'A rabbit,' said Thibault. He listened. 'There's nothing worrying
> it. It'll be a trap. Hugh told me he was putting them down. Christ!'
> The scream came yet again.
> Abelard was beside him, and the two plunged down by the bank ...
> 'O God', (Abelard) was muttering. 'Let it die. Let it die quickly.'
> But the cry came yet again. On the right, this time. He plunged
> through the thicket of hornbeam.
> 'Watch out,' said Thibault, thrusting past him. 'The trap might
> take the hand off you.'
> The rabbit stopped shrieking when they stooped over it, either
> from exhaustion, or in some last extremity of fear. Thibault held the
> teeth of the trap apart, and Abelard gathered up the little creature in
> his hands. It lay for a moment breathing quickly, then in some blind
> recognition of the kindness that it met at the last, the small head
> thrust and nestled against his arm, and it died.
> It was that last confiding thrust that broke Abelard's heart. He
> looked down at the little draggled body, his mouth shaking.

'Thibault,' he said, 'do you think there is a God at all? Whatever has come to me, I earned it. But what did this one do?'

Thibault nodded.

'I know,' he said. 'Only – I think God is in it too.'

Abelard looked up sharply.

'In it? Do you mean that it makes Him suffer, the way it does us?'

Again Thibault nodded.

'Then why doesn't He stop it?'

'I don't know,' said Thibault. 'Unless – unless it's like the Prodigal Son. I suppose the father could have kept him at home against his will. But what would have been the use? All this,' he stroked the limp body, 'is because of us. But all the time God suffers. More than we do.'

Abelard looked at him, perplexed.

'Thibault, when did you think of all this?'

Thibault's face stiffened. 'It was that night,' he said, his voice strangled. 'The things we did to poor Guibert. He . . .' Thibault stopped. 'I could not sleep for nights and nights. And then I saw that God suffered too. And I thought that I would like to be a priest.'

'Thibault, do you mean Calvary?'

Thibault shook his head. 'That was only a piece of it – the piece that we saw – in time. Like that.' He pointed to a fallen tree beside them, sawn through the middle. 'That dark ring there, it goes up and down the whole length of the tree. But you only see where it is cut across. That is what Christ's life was; the bit of God that we saw. And we think God is like that, because Christ was like that, kind and forgiving sins and healing people. We think God is like that for ever, because it happened once with Christ. But not the pain. Not the agony at the last. We think that stopped.'

Abelard looked at him, the blunt nose and the wide mouth, the honest troubled eyes. He could have knelt before him.

'Then, Thibault,' he said slowly, 'you think that all this,' he looked down at the quiet little body in his arms, 'all the pain of the world was Christ's cross?'

'God's cross,' said Thibault. 'And it goes on.'

'The Patripassian heresy,' muttered Abelard mechanically. 'But, O God, if it were true. Thibault, it must be. At least, there is something at the back of it that is true. And if we could find it – it would bring back the whole world.'[10]

The point then so ably narrated by Waddell is this: God suffers. I shall not be concerned here with the precise theories about *how* God may be thought to suffer. Notwithstanding Abelard's 'mechanical' description of this view as 'the Patripassian heresy', it seems to me that there are a variety of ways in which we can understand God as suffering presence in the world that do not lose sight of divine omnipotence or indeed divine transcendence. Even so gospel-centred a scholar as Tom Torrance can be so nervous about an outright declaration of divine passibility that he resolves the problem by simply affirming the contradiction: God 're-deems our passibility in his impassability'.[11] But I want to leave that debate to one side, and suggest that the insight derived from God's self-definition in Jesus Christ leads inescapably to the view that God really and truly enters into suffering. This seems to me to be required by a fully incarnational theology in which God actually does what is claimed – namely enter into the awfulness of the human condition.

But like Thibault in the story, I want to go further. If it is true that God is the Creator and sustainer of the whole world of life, then it is inconceivable that God is not also a co-sufferer in the world of non-human creatures as well. Years of Christian tradition have obscured this basic implication of the gospel narrative for at least two reasons. The first is because the scholastic tradition in particular has denied to animals any moral standing so that even if they did suffer, such suffering was not regarded as morally significant. The second, and more obvious reason, is that later Christian tradition, especially manifest in Carte-sianism, simply denied that animals could feel pain at all. Even in this century notable theologians, such as Charles Raven, argued not just that animals did not suffer like humans but rather doubted that they suffered at all.[12]

And yet the idea that God is affected by the suffering of all creatures has not been lost on generations of saints and poets. 'Here I saw the great unity between Christ and us,' writes Julian of Norwich, 'for when he was in pain, all creatures able to suffer pain suffered with him.'[13] It is written of Margery Kempe that 'when she saw a crucifix, or if she saw a man had a wound, or a beast, or if a man beat a child before her, or smote a horse or another beast with a whip, she thought she saw Our Lord beaten and wounded'.[14] Perhaps the best known expression of this idea in poetry is found in Joseph Plunkett's *I See His Blood upon the Rose*:

I see His blood upon the rose
And in the stars the glory of His eyes,
His body gleams amid eternal snows,

His tears fall from the skies.

I see His face in every flower;
The thunder and the singing of the birds
Are but His voice – and carven by His power
Rocks are His written words.

All pathways by His feet are worn,
His strong heart stirs the ever-beating sea,
His crown is twined with every thorn,
His cross is every tree.[15]

More satisfying from a christological perspective is Edith Sitwell's *Still Falls the Rain* in which she pictures Christ's redeeming blood – like the rain – continuing to fall on the wounds of the suffering world.

He bears in his Heart all wounds, – those of the light that died,
The last faint spark
In the self-murdered heart, the wounds of the sad uncomprehending
    dark,
The wounds of the baited bear, –
The blind and weeping bear whom the keepers beat
On his helpless flesh ... the tears of the hunted hare.

Still falls the Rain –
Then – O I leape up to my God: who pulles me doune –
See, see where Christ's blood streames in the firmament:
It flows from the Brow we nailed upon the tree
Deep to the dying, to the thirsting heart
That holds the fires of the world, dark smirched with pain
At Caesar's laurel crown.

Then sounds the voice of one who like the heart of man
Was once a child who among beasts has lain –
'Still do I love, still shed my innocent light, my Blood, for thee.'[16]

This imaginative picture of Christ suffering all pain and violence in the universe that God has made conveys – it seems to me – a truth which has simply eluded the formal theorists and dogmaticians of the Christian tradition. Only very faintly, if at all, has the church allowed this truth to be expressed in its liturgy. For example, in the Byzantine rite for Holy Saturday it is held that 'the whole creation was altered by thy Passion; for all things suffered with thee, knowing O Lord, that thou holdest all things in unity'.[17] But this splendid example, I fear, is one of the comparatively few exceptions to an otherwise almost wholly monolithic anthropocentrism of East and West.

The recognition that suffering exists in the non-human world requires us to grapple with the problem of redemption for these spheres as well. If it is believed, in fidelity to the gospel story, that God truly enters into creaturely suffering, then there can be no good reason for excluding God's suffering presence from the realm of the non-human creation as well. Indeed quite the reverse. For the issue is not how much suffering or to what degree any being suffers, but *that it suffers at all* which is the underlying fact to be wrestled with. If as Bonhoeffer once remarked 'only a suffering God can help' it must follow that where there is suffering – no matter whatever the kind and to what degree – God suffers too.

Sacrificial Priesthood

You may recall Thibault's reaction to the question of suffering. Not only did he hold that God suffered in all suffering creatures, but also reflecting upon that suffering in both humans and animals, he had decided to become a priest. 'And then I saw that God suffered too,' he said, 'And I thought I would like to be a priest.' At first sight this might appear to be a rather unusual reaction. It has to be said that many prevailing notions of priesthood would find the relationship, if any, hard to fathom. Yet it seems to me that 'Thibaultian theology' (if I may describe it so) is altogether coherent. For if Christian priesthood derives its authority from Christ, as the focus of God's own self-definition, then it should also follow that priesthood is an extension of the suffering, and therefore also redeeming, activity of God in our world.

The one point I want to make here is this: The wider definition of God's presence, and therefore also of redeeming power, necessitates in turn a wider definition of priesthood. I am by no means the first person to think of priesthood in wider, we might say ecological, terms. Alexander Pope in his 'Essay on Man' describes the divine commission to have dominion and to look after the world in terms of Christian priesthood:

The state of Nature was the reign of God ...
Man walked with beast, joint tenant of the shade;
The same his table and the same his bed;
No murder cloth'd him, and no murder fed ...

Unbrib'd, unbloody, stood the blameless priest:
Heaven's attribute was Universal Care,
And Man's prerogative to rule, but spare.[18]

One of the first to use the phrase 'the World's High Priest' was Arch-bishop Leighton in the seventeenth century. He spoke of the priest in the psalmist's sense of offering the praises of all creatures to their God:

> All things indeed declare and speak His glory: the Heavens sent it forth, and the Earth and Sea resound and echo it back. But His reasonable creatures hath He peculiarly framed both to take notice of His glory in all the rest, and to return it from and for all the rest in a more express and lively way.
>
> And in this lower world it is Man alone that is made capable of observing the Glory of God, and of offering Him praises. He expresses it well who calls man 'the World's High Priest'.[19]

Such thoughts are similar to those expressed by Coleridge, who in his poem 'To Nature' anticipates some of the lyricism, if not the actual lyrics, of Teilhard de Chardin's 'Mass Upon the Altar of the World'.[20]

It may indeed be phantasy when I
Essay to draw from all created things
Deep, heartfelt, inward joy that closely clings:
And trace in leaves and flowers that round me lie
Lessons of love and earnest piety.
So let it be; and if the wide world rings
In mock of this belief, to me it brings
Nor fear, nor grief, nor vain perplexity.

So will I build my altar in the fields,
And the blue sky my fretted dome shall be,
And the sweet fragrance that the wild flower yields
Shall be the incense I will yield to Thee,
Thee only God! and Thou shalt not despise
Even me, the priest of this poor sacrifice.[21]

This notion of sacrifice is taken up by George Herbert in perhaps the best-known lines of all on this theme:

Man is the world's High Priest: he doth present
The sacrifice for all; while they below
Unto the service mutter an assent,
Such as springs use that fall, and winds that blow.[22]

Already we see the two familiar themes of Christian priesthood expressing themselves: the priest is the one who 'present(s)' or represents, and
also the one who offers up 'the sacrifice for all'. But what does it mean to
exercise a representative and sacrificial priesthood for the whole created
order? Who is representing whom and who is sacrificing what?

First, I want to suggest that the priest is the icon of Christ. The priest
is to present and represent the love of God focussed in Jesus Christ. If it
is true that the power of God is most authentically expressed in the form
of suffering service then we have to ask ourselves radical questions
about how we are to understand our own lordship or dominion over
nature in general and animals in particular. If we are to have among us
the mind of the one whose power is expressed in humility, in condescension, in reaching out to the least of all, has not our own relationship
to the suffering non-human got to undergo a fundamental re-
examination? Almost alone among contemporary theologians, Torrance
articulates the connection between the suffering world and the human
world of priestly redemption. Torrance holds to a high view of
humanity:

> From the perspective of theology, man is clearly made the focal point
> in the interrelations between God and the universe. He is given a
> special place within creation with a ruling and a priestly function to
> perform toward the rest of created reality. All lines of rationality and
> order, of purpose and fulfilment in the creation converge on him as
> man of God and man of science and depend upon his destiny.

But unlike others, Torrance does not stop here with the familiar theme
of theological self-congratulation. He couples his high view of humanity
with a strong view of human responsibility:

> this priestly role of man must take on a redemptive form – that is how
> we should view man's relationship to nature. It is his task to *save* the
> natural order through remedial and integrative activity, bringing back
> order where there is disorder and restoring peace where there is
> disharmony.[23]

In short: the representative function of priesthood is the presentation
and actualization of God's suffering service in the world.

Second, I want to suggest that Christ-like priesthood is necessarily
sacrificial. But what or whom is to be sacrificed? Archbishop Leighton,

and others before and after him, have understood this sacrificial work in terms of the offering of thanksgiving. 'In this lower world', writes Leighton, 'it is Man alone that is made capable of observing the glory of God, and of offering him praises.' John Zizioulas develops the point further when he describes the priest as the one who 'refers the world back to [its] Creator'.[24] Now I do not want to deny that the offering of thanksgiving, even on behalf of other creatures, is an important aspect of priesthood – though I would have to say that it is not clear to me that other creatures do not praise and commune with their Creator in their own way. But leaving that question aside, it seems insufficient to allow thanksgiving as the sole or major definition of what the priest has to offer.

Neither do I think that the sacrificial aspect of priesthood is adequately or properly characterized in terms of sacrificing other forms of life such as animals. 'The killing of animals,' writes Karl Barth, 'when performed with the permission of God and by His command, is a priestly act of eschatological character.'[25] But whatever may be the meaning and historical significance of the forms of animal sacrifice in the Old Testament, it seems very difficult indeed to reconcile the spirit of Christ-like sacrifice with animal sacrifice, and for reasons which I indicate elsewhere.[26]

The central point I want to make here is this: the priestly work of sacrifice is best characterized by the offering of self-costly love as exemplified by Christ himself. In Romans, the creation groans in travail because it is subject not by its own will to 'bondage to decay'. 'For the creation waits with eager longing for the revealing of the sons of God,' writes St Paul, 'because the creation itself will be set free ... and obtain the glorious liberty of the children of God.'[27] Here is supplied the decisive reference to those who ask 'What does it mean for humans to exercise a priestly role of redemption?' Quite simply: it concerns the releasing of creation from futility, from suffering and pain and worthlessness. This, I want to suggest, is the divine work of redemption to which humans are called by the power of the Spirit. It is the liberation of creation itself from decay and suffering – perhaps in some ways the most fundamental liberation of all. Such a perspective challenges at root the notion that human responsibility in the world extends only to serving and protecting our own species.

Strangely enough it is Nietzsche who in a most uncharacteristic piece of writing seems to point in my direction. 'The deeper minds of all ages have had pity for animals', he writes, 'because they suffer from life and have not the power to turn the sting of their suffering against themselves, and understand their being metaphysically.'[28] According to Nietzsche, nature needs the philosopher and the artist 'to strive thereby for the completion of nature'. But nature, according to Nietzsche, needs – not only the artist and the philosopher – but also the saint.

> In him the ego is melted away, and the suffering of his life is, practically, no longer felt as individual, but as the spring of the deepest sympathy and intimacy with all living creatures ... the attainment, at length, of the high state of man after which all nature is striving, that she may be delivered from herself.[29]

And it is concretely in the lives of many saints that we see prefigured this vision of the higher state of nature to which Nietzsche refers. Of the many examples one could give I choose this from St Isaac the Syrian. 'What is a charitable heart?' he asks, and replies as follows:

> It is a heart which is burning with love for the whole creation, for men, for the birds, for the beasts ... for all creatures. He who has such a heart cannot see or call to mind a creature without his eyes being filled with tears by reason of the immense compassion which seizes his heart; a heart which is softened and can no longer bear to see or learn from others of any suffering, even the smallest pain being inflicted upon a creature. That is why such a man never ceases to pray for the animals ... [He is] ... moved by the infinite pity which reigns in the hearts of those who are becoming united with God.[30]

Sensitivity to suffering (and with it compassion, empathy, mercy, loving forgiveness) are the hall-marks of priesthood. Only when we can say that we too have entered – however fleetingly – into the suffering of Christ in the suffering of all creatures can we claim to have entered into the priestly nature of our humanity. More even than that, for the goal of our priestly humanity is not, as St Isaac reminds us, simply passive. We are to be active in prayer and deed to ensure that we reflect not just Christ-like feeling for the suffering of the world but also Christ-like healing. We are not called to be mere spectators of the world of suffering but active co-participants with God the Holy Spirit in its redemption.

Service as Uniqueness

My starting point was the question: 'In what way, if any, are humans unique in creation?' The argument I have sketched has been as follows:

We need three shifts in our thinking. First, away from the idea that if God suffers at all, this suffering takes place solely within the human species, to the view that God suffers in all suffering creatures. Second, a shift away from a narrow conception of priesthood as largely or exclusively concerned with God and humanity – to the view that priesthood is a participation in God's redeeming presence in the world. And third, a shift away from the idea that the characteristics of priesthood – namely representation and sacrifice – can be detailed in a wholly human-centred way without involving the exercise of Christ-like power and service to the whole creation.

The answer I want to give then to my opening question is this: The uniqueness of humanity consists in its ability to become the servant species. To exercise its full humanity as co-participants and co-workers with God in the redemption of the world. This view challenges the traditional notions that the world was made simply for human use or pleasure, that its purpose consists in serving the human species, or that the world exists largely in an instrumentalist relationship to human beings. Only the most tenacious adherence to the possibility of God may be sufficient to redeem us from our own profoundly arrogant humanistic conceptions of our place in the universe.

It is important, however, to spell out the implications of the doctrine of priestly service which I have espoused. The first is that humanity can have no right to regard sentient creatures as simply means to their ends. Animals are not simply here for our use and to use animals at all incurs a very great responsibility. I agree with the principle commended by Stephen R. L. Clark that it is wrong to be the cause of 'avoidable ill'.[31] But I would, perhaps, go further. To make animals suffer for human purposes is not just morally wrong, it is an act of the gravest faithlessness. Humphry Primatt, who wrote the most impressive theological treatise on animals, got it right when he wrote that:

> The religion of Jesus Christ originated in the mercy of God; and it was the gracious design of it to promote peace towards every creature on earth, and to create a spirit of universal benevolence or goodwill in men. And it has pleased God therein to display the riches of his own goodness and mercy towards us; and the revealer of his blessed will, the author and finisher of our faith, hath commanded us to be merciful, as our Father is also merciful, the obligation upon Christians becomes the stronger; and it is our bounded duty, in an especial manner, and above all other people, to extend the precept of mercy to

every object of it. For, indeed, a cruel Christian is a monster of ingratitude, a scandal to his profession and beareth the name of Christ in vain ... [32]

That we now as a matter of course use sentient beings in ways that cause them harm and suffering as laboratory tools, as units of production in farming, as objects of sport and entertainment, are signs that we have lost not just a sense of our priestly humanity but a sufficient conception of the generosity of God revealed in Jesus Christ. All this is not to deny that we – indeed all nature – is caught up in the structures of disorder of which Torrance speaks.[33] Neither is it to suppose that we can easily turn to live in some Edenite harmony with other creatures. I accept that we are compromised and that we have difficult choices to make.

Nevertheless, it is precisely here where we may sense the impossibility of living other than we do, that we should reflect upon the fact that Christian priesthood is sacrificial, costly priesthood. It cannot be sufficient merely to have a negative vision of what we should do to prevent suffering in the world. We need positive vision of how we can take upon ourselves the suffering of the world and transform it by the power of the Holy Spirit. We need to experiment in ways of liberation rather than assuming that human interest, narrowly conceived, always comes first. All this has an urgency which in previous generations we failed to appreciate. For our ruthless, un-gentle treatment of the natural world has ushered in a cognizance of certain limits to exploitation. Extinct species, like dead nature itself, can no longer be exploited. It seems to me that Christians have an opportunity in the present circumstances to show what it means to live as though we believe in a generous loving God by living that generosity towards other non-human creatures.

Objections Considered

I now turn to briefly consider three objections to my argument.

The first queries my whole train of argument by suggesting that I have simply understated the powerful 'humans come first' tradition within Christianity. According to the Linzey view, it is claimed, we shall end up being more concerned about suffering hens than suffering humans.

I agree with this objection if it means that the suffering of humans – as well as the suffering of non-humans – should be the subject of the serving and sacrificial priesthood. Nothing in my argument should weaken concern for the healing of suffering humanity. Nevertheless, it is no longer clear that we can make an absolute distinction between one kind of suffering and another, either that of a member of another class, race, sex or – I would add – species. Neither is it obvious that we can in each and every situation claim that human suffering is more important than any other kind of suffering. Indeed I suggest that the attempt to place human well-being in a special and absolute category of its own is one of the reasons why other earthly creatures – indeed the earth itself – remains in a desperate state of travail, indeed a travail so great that its destruction, in part, if not as a whole, seems inevitable. In other words, exclusive moral preoccupation with our own species is part of the problem itself rather than its solution. We should face the fact that years of Christian anthropocentricity (of a bad sort) has helped lead us to the environmental crisis we now encounter. In short: we have to redress the balance and appreciate that humans are not just linked to nature, *we are part of* nature.

The second objection is that I have effectively reduced theology to ethics by simply redefining the essential characteristics of priesthood in ethical terms.

Some forms of this objection have my sympathy. John Zizioulas has recently stressed the limitations of a response to the ecological crisis which simply places all its hopes in ethics. 'Whether enforced by State legislation or taught or instructed by Churches, academic institutions, etc., it is ethics that seems to contain the hopes of humankind in the present situation,' he writes. And yet (he reminds us) 'ethics, whether enforced or free, presupposes other more existential motivations in order to function'.[34] It is difficult to deny that Zizioulas is right here. The appeal to ethics, by itself, is insufficient. Yet it is also very understandable. For centuries Christians have kept our relations with the non-human out of the ethical sphere and so it is perhaps not altogether surprising that their inclusion is now seen as a priority.

However, I am not one of those who think that salvation lies in ethics alone. Spiritually unenlightened humanity – especially one that is over-confident of its own humanism – can be a cause of moral darkness. The approach I have outlined is far from naive ethicism. But it may be construed as an attack upon what we have had a surplus of in the Christian tradition, namely non-ethical or anti-ethical theology. I suggest that we need a way of combining the two – theology and ethics – in a much clearer way than heretofore. Moral theology is a more acceptable term; ascetical or mystical theology even better.

But, at a deeper level, what this objection may signify is a divorce between divine activity and human response which is starkly perilous at the present time. The theological challenge is how we can understand the divine work of passibility and redemption *already operative* within creation through the work of the Holy Spirit. When we have such a conception we shall best be able to fully appreciate the necessity of human response to, indeed participation in, that work itself.

The third objection takes us back to my initial thesis concerning the passibility of God. How can God suffer eternally and also at the same time offer us liberation from suffering which is the central hope of the gospel? In short: if God suffers in creation, how can God also redeem us from that suffering?

Again, I have no little sympathy for this objection, which I once held and defended myself.[35] But the weakness of the argument – it now seems to me – is in its view that God cannot *both* suffer and redeem that suffering at one and the same time. The best, perhaps the only, model we can have is that of the incarnation itself. For if it is possible for God in Christ to enter into the suffering of the world, and yet transform that suffering into joy, why should this capacity be limited in time and space to one event only? I posit that Thibault was right: what is seen in Christ is one instance of the perpetual transformation of suffering happening throughout time.

In conclusion, you may recall Abelard's reaction to Thibault's doctrine of divine passibility. 'The Patripassian heresy', he recited 'mechanically.' 'But, O God, if it were true … It must be. At least, there is something at the back of it that is true.' Then Abelard went on: 'And if we could find it – it would bring back the whole world.'

At first sight it might seem an amazingly presumptuous claim that the recovery of the insight of divine passibility could lead to a recovery of the whole world. And yet it is purely co-incidental that its contrary view, namely the doctrine of divine *im*passibility, has triumphed and flourished in Christian centuries in which theology about the world – and especially our responsibility for it – seems to have almost entirely evaporated? It may be that here, as elsewhere, our doctrine of God has been much more significant for the salvation of the world than we might have thought possible. Abelard, I feel sure, would have approved of the mystical theology contained in these moving lines from Schweitzer's autobiography:

I could not but feel with a sympathy full of regret all the pain that I saw around me, not only that of men, but that of the whole creation. From this community of suffering I have never tried to withdraw myself. It seemed to me a matter of course that we should all take our share of the burden of suffering which lies upon the world.[36]

4

Liberation Theology for Animals

The idea that human beings are unique as a species in having the capacity to co-operate with God in the work of liberation and redemption leads us naturally to a consideration of liberation theology itself. As I show, however, liberation theology in no way fulfils its promise in relation to the oppression of animals. Instead of liberating theology from moral humanocentrism, these theologians appear to enslave us even more firmly to it. Their narrowness in this regard largely arises from a deficient christology. I try to show how – by recovering five basic christological connections – it is possible to construct a liberation theology which does – and inspires – justice to the suffering non-human creation.

The Dogma of Humanism

Observers of the theological scene over the past twenty years have witnessed the growth of what can only be described as a new way of doing theology. That theology, like all disciplines, should be subject to change and innovation is unsurprising; neither is it surprising that new fashions or movements should – to appropriate some words of John Clare –

> rise and vanish, an oblivious host ...
> into nothingness of scorn and noise ...[1]

What is surprising is that a way of theologizing which was at its inception at least a rather localized, particularized theology – related entirely to a given experience of injustice – should now have spurred on an international discussion about the nature of theology itself and how liberated, or liberating, it should be.

But what or whom is to be liberated? Gustavo Gutierrez in his pioneering work *A Theology of Liberation*, written in 1971 and first published in English in 1973, sketches 'three reciprocally interpenetrating levels of meaning of the term *liberation*'. First, liberation 'expresses the aspirations of oppressed *peoples* and social classes, emphasizing the conflictual aspect of the economic, social and political process which puts them at odds with wealthy nations and oppressive classes'. Second, liberation is a way of understanding history:

> *Humankind* is seen as assuming conscious responsibility for its own destiny ... In this perspective the unfolding of all the dimensions of *humanness* is demanded – *persons* who make themselves throughout their life and throughout history. The gradual conquest of true freedom leads to the creation of a new *humankind* and a qualitatively different society.

Third, in contrast with the word, development, the concept of liberation 'allows for another approach leading to Biblical sources which inspires the presence and action of *humankind* in history'.

> In the Bible, Christ is presented as the one who brings *us* liberation. Christ the Saviour liberates from sin, which is the ultimate root of all disruption of friendship and of all injustice and oppression. Christ makes *humankind* truly free, that is to say, he enables *us* to live in communion with him; and this is the basis for all *human* fellowship.[2]

I shall not be concerned here with the acceptability or otherwise of Gutierrez's biblical exegesis, nor with his understanding of concepts such as 'development' and 'history'. In contrast to what some may think are broad stroke definitions of liberation, I want to draw attention to what is in effect their narrowness. Liberation concerns oppressed 'peoples', 'humankind' growing in 'humanness'; Christ indeed is defined as the one who 'makes humankind truly free'. In short: the first major work of liberation theology espouses an uncompromisingly dogmatic humanocentricity.

Now it may be protested that a Bible-based theologian such as Gutierrez could not be so neglectful of the passages in the New Testament which speak of the meaning of Christ's work in terms of cosmic salvation. Indeed not. In his chapter on 'Liberation and Salvation', Gutierrez appears to follow the New Testament directly:

> The work of Christ is a new creation. In this sense, Paul speaks of a 'new creation' in Christ (Gal. 6. 15; II Cor. 5. 17). Moreover it is through this 'new creation', that is to say, through the salvation which Christ affords, that creation acquires its full meaning (cf. Rom. 8) ... This liberation fulfils in an unexpected way the promises of the

prophets and creates a new chosen people, which this time includes all humanity. Creation and salvation therefore have, in the first place, a Christological sense: *all* things have been created in Christ, *all* things have been saved in him (cf. Col. 1. 15–20).[3]

Despite the qualified humanocentric frame of reference here, the thrust is quite clear; '*all* things' are subjects of creation and salvation. The use of the word 'saved' here is not insignificant. For Gutierrez, like many other liberation theologians, salvation is closely linked with liberation, if not actually synonymous with it.[4] But Gutierrez does not maintain this emphasis upon the inclusive nature of cosmic redemption. He continues:

> Humankind is the crown and centre of the work of creation, and is called to continue it through its labour (cf. Gen. 1.28) ... To dominate the earth as Genesis prescribed, to continue creation, *is worth nothing if it is not done for the good of humanity*, if it does not contribute to human liberation, in solidarity with all, in history.

Here the underlying hermeneutic of liberation theology is exposed: All human endeavour is to be judged by this one moral maxim – the 'good of humanity'. Neither is there any attempt at qualification: any other endeavour is not only misdirected, it is 'worth nothing'.[5]

It is worth pausing for a moment, to take stock of the moral implications of this view. I shall not concern myself here with the wider green issues which this view inevitably eclipses, but rather focus on our treatment of animals. According to the view espoused here, our treatment of animals is not a *direct* moral issue at all. Only the good of humanity is acceptable as a criterion of moral worth. Indeed, implicitly by the total lack of reference to the world of animals we may judge that Gutierrez regards animals as without intrinsic worth – nothing in any of his works suggests otherwise. In practice this view means that we are right to treat animals as by and large we do treat them today: as resources, as commodities, as means, as tools, as food, as supplies or suppliers – all such actions are justified so long as the 'good of humanity' remains our aim.

It is important to understand that far from enumerating some radical humanistic principle, Gutierrez simply reinforces – almost by sleight of hand – the historic 'dismissal' of the claims of animals that has characterized both Christian and post-Christian Western societies.[6] Like all scholastic Catholic and Protestant thinking from St Thomas

Aquinas onwards, through the modern period up to and including Vatican II[7] and even including 'progressive' Roman Catholics such as Karl Rahner and Hans Küng, Gutierrez fails to envision the possibility of moral oppression beyond the sphere of human to human relations. It may be no accident that Gutierrez refers to God-given dominion over animals as the commission to 'dominate the earth'. Despite the fact that many biblical scholars have been at pains since 1970, and before, to stress that dominion does not mean 'domination' or 'despotism', Gutierrez links uncritically with scholastic tradition to justify his moral point which put strongly is this: only humans are worth anything.

Humanocentric Constriction

Some may think that while my interpretation of Gutierrez may be plausible, as a whole I am ungenerous to liberation theology. After all Gutierrez's book was written in 1971, and although I am using his expanded and revised version of 1988, it remains true that sensitivity to ecological questions was at that time at a comparatively embryonic stage. If fashions theological or otherwise, to quote Clare again – 'rise and vanish, an oblivious host ... into nothingness of scorn and noise' – it is hardly surprising that Gutierrez does not offer a full-blown doctrine of animal liberation. Peter Singer's own work *Animal Liberation* was not published until 1976, the same year as my own *Animal Rights*.

Anticipating this criticism, I want to turn to another major figure in liberation theology, namely Leonardo Boff. And the book I turn to is entitled – promisingly enough – *Saint Francis* – though with the potentially disquieting sub-title, *A Model for Human Liberation*. Written in 1981, ten years after Gutierrez's work, when at least ecological concerns were beginning to appear on the moral agenda of theology, it surely augurs well for a positive presentation of liberation theology and our treatment of animals.

And, sure enough, the opening chapter immediately picks up the contemporary theme. 'The crisis we are all suffering is structural in nature', begins Boff, 'and concerns the basics of our system of life together.'[8] Promising indeed. Brother Francis is presented as the one whose life of gentleness and care – what Boff calls 'the humanized eros' – is central for the creation of a 'civilization of conviviality'.[9] 'What most impresses modern humanity when faced with the figure of Saint Francis of Assisi', writes Boff, 'is his innocence, his enthusiasm for nature, his gentleness with all beings, his capacity for compassion with the poor and confraternization with all the elements, and even with death itself.'[10] Moreover Boff appears to recognize that the significance of Francis' appreciation of animals was not simply aesthetic but ontological. He quotes with approval St Bonaventure's well-known lines:

> He [St Francis] was filled with a greater gentleness when he thought of the first and common origin of all beings, and he called all creatures, no matter how small they were, by the name of brother or sister, *because he knew that they all had in common with him the same beginning.*[11]

So far, so good, we may think. But what is the moral lesson to be drawn from St Francis for animal liberation? Boff concludes: 'Modern humanity has forgotten that in our activity with nature we must deal *not only* with things, but *also with* something that *affects us* at *our* deepest level ... *We* cannot achieve *our identity* while denying a friendly and fraternal relationship with *our* natural world.'[12] The message therefore remains humanocentric – qualified to be sure, by an appreciation of how human identity and conviviality depend upon fraternity with nature, but still it is humanity, what constitutes human good, that remains the criterion of moral worth. This view is reinforced by the remaining chapters to the book. For subsequently Boff spells out the *real* message of Francis which is predictably concerned with *human* liberation, the poor in particular.[13]

Now interpreting St Francis, as Roger Sorrell's book shows,[14] is not without its difficulties and ambiguities. But one conclusion that can be safely drawn from what we know of his life and teaching is this: humanocentricity is deficient. Concern for animals, for all the aspects of the created world, is essential not because these things are pleasing to us humans (though pleasing, at least sometimes, they may truly be) but because they originate with the Creator. The line from St Bonaventure is much more revealing than Boff admits. It is precisely because of the 'common origin' of all beings with God, that all creatures have value and may therefore be termed 'brothers' and 'sisters'. Now it would be difficult to claim St Francis as a modern day thoroughgoing animal liberationist. Most animal liberationists, myself included, would make a distinction between concern say for brother cauliflower and sister ape. Nevertheless, as I have written elsewhere:

> We need to remember that the challenge of so many saints in their love and concern for even the most hated of all animals, was in almost

all cases *against* the spirit of their times. Christian authorities have been forgetful or indifferent to the claims of animals, or perhaps more accurately, simply misled by *ad hoc* theological speculations ... We do well to remember that God has other interests in the world apart from the human species ... This leads us to perhaps the most revolutionary thought of all. St Francis sought to petition the Emperor to protect the birds for the sake of 'the love of God'. In other words, he knew that however they may appear to us, all creatures have some standing in the sight of God. From our human perspective, some animals may appear terrible or frightening or demonically possessed or all of these things, but from God's point of view every creature is a blessed creature or it is no creature at all. What so many of the saints force us to wrestle with is the idea that we must view creation from God's own perspective and not our own. The worth of every creature does not lie in whether it is beautiful (to us) or whether it serves or sustains our life and happiness. Only if we can save ourselves from an exaggerated anthropocentricity can we begin to construct an adequate theology of animals. Only God, and not man, is the measure of all things.[15]

In short, Gutierrez and Boff, dissimilar though they may be in some ways, represent a theology of liberation which has radically failed to grapple with the possibility of oppression and injustice beyond the sphere of human to human relations. Even when confronted – in the case of Boff – with evidence in the form of St Francis of Assisi and his extension of the moral community to include animals – and even other beings – the result is still humanocentrism, albeit qualified and seemingly sympathetic to environmental concerns. But the criticism that should be made of this liberation theology is not only that its concept of *liberation* is too narrow, ineluctably it follows that such narrowness results itself from a constricted and exclusive *theology*.

Recovering Christological Connections

In order to substantiate this charge, it is necessary to show that there is a theological basis for animal liberation, indeed that liberation theology itself, properly interpreted, provides it. One way forward could be to show that, without forcing their texts, liberation theologians frequently define the oppressed in terms that could well apply to animals. If the biblical meaning of the poor, for example, is 'one who does not have what is necessary to subsist'[16] – as Gutierrez suggests – it would not be difficult, within the terms of this definition, to find many non-human animals whose lives are deformed, stunted and deprived of their natural capacities to exist – among whom, incidentally, should be counted the 45 million laying hens in this country kept permanently on sloping wire mesh, unable to spread even a wing and confined in conditions of semi-darkness.[17] Another way forward could be to show how a frequently-used concept like 'neighbour' includes what its biblical sense intends, namely those who exist *alongside us*, and it is not infrequently that non-human animals are our neighbours, or more precisely our conscripted companions, in this sense.

But I turn to the central theological deficiency in liberation theology, namely its christology. Our starting point here is Gutierrez's insistence that christology *is* anthropology. 'The God of Christian revelation is a God incarnate,' he argues, 'hence the famous comment of Karl Barth regarding Christian anthropocentrism, "Man is the measure of all things, since God became man."'[18] Whether such a one-line quotation adequately characterizes Barth's theology is a moot point. I am re-minded of the equally famous remark about Barth to the effect that since he wrote so much, no view attributed to him is entirely falsifiable. But there is no doubting that Gutierrez has picked up what we have already noted: a strain in Barth's own thinking, a regrettable tendency to reduce christology to anthropology and to view the created world merely as backdrop or theatre to the 'real revelation' which happens purely in the human sphere.[19] But is this definition of christology as anthropology itself sufficient theologically? Are liberation theologians – such as Gutierrez in his *A Theology of Liberation*, Jon Sobrino in his *The True Church and the Poor*, or even Leonardo Boff in his magisterial work on christology, namely *Jesus Christ Liberator* – right to follow Barth to the extent that in their books, the world of creation barely merits a few pages and the plight of animals not even a footnote? In order to rectify this deficiency, we need to recall five christological connections, most of which we have discussed already. I restate and summarize them here:

1. *Christ as co-Creator.* There needs to be a renewed vision of Christ as *Logos* through whom *all things* come to be. The *Logos* is the source and destiny of all that is. Athanasius writes of how the Word 'orders and contains the universe' illuminating 'all things visible and invisible, containing and enclosing them in himself'.[20] But if this is true, Christ is not only of significance to human beings but as *Logos* the decisive fact of

being for all creatures. It becomes impossible to separate the human and non-human worlds of creation as though they were absolutely distinct. Of course different creatures have differing capacities, qualities and relationships, but radically, absolutely distinct, none of them can possibly be. If 'all things were made by him, and without him was not anything made that was made', as St John claims,[21] what is of primary significance is not the distinctions between creatures but their common origin.

2. *Christ as God-incarnate*. There needs to be a new perception of the assumption of materiality in the incarnation. Of course the incarnation is God's Yes to human beings – their life, welfare and destiny – but so often Christians have understood this divine Yes as an absolute No to the rest of creation. Neither is this mistake limited to liberation theologians. Hans Küng, who has justifiably an international reputation in theology, is able to posit that the welfare of humans is God's sole concern.[22] 'For the Word spread himself everywhere', writes Athanasius, 'above and below and in the depth and in the breadth, *in the world*',[23] The Yes of God the Creator extends to all living, especially fleshly, beings: the *ousia* assumed in the incarnation is not only specifically human, it is also creaturely. If we ponder this fact we shall be released from *hubris* in our relationship with other non-human beings. It is important to understand that an exclusivist, overly particularist, understanding of the incarnation, if held to rigidly, excludes not only animals, but also women; not only women but all Gentile, uncircumcised men.

3. *Christ as the new covenant*. It is often practically overlooked by theologians even of the stature of Karl Barth that the Noahic covenant includes all living things. God 'elects' (to use Barth's language) not only human beings but also all living creatures, indeed the earth itself. The question we must therefore ask is: What must follow for our human relations with other creatures if God the Creator willed to love, actualize and establish them in a covenant with himself or herself which is inseparable from the covenant with humanity itself established in Jesus Christ? The scholastic theology – which still seems to live on in liberation theology – has denied that humans have any moral duties *to* animals (only duties *concerning them* – often construed as property[24]) and therefore excluded them from the bounds of human fellowship. Here as elsewhere liberation theology is not radical enough. It has only echoed the prevailing Thomist scholasticism which still finds a voice today, for example in this line from Bernard Haring: 'Nothing irrational is capable

of the beautifying friendship with God.[25] In opposition we need to posit
the appropriateness and spiritual significance of God's all-embracing
covenant. An understanding of the mystery of God's love which
excludes in principle all other life forms is profoundly impoverished.
Father Zossima's advice in Dostoyevsky's *The Brothers Karamazov* is a
good antidote:

> Love all God's creation, the whole of it and every grain of sand. Love
> every leaf, every ray of God's light. Love the animals, love the plants,
> love everything. If you love everything you will perceive the divine
> mystery in things. And once you have perceived it, you will begin to
> comprehend it ceaselessly more and more every day. And you will
> come to love the whole world with an abiding, universal love.[26]

4. *Christ as the reconciler of all things*. Although Barth does not go as far
as Athanasius in his significant claim that Christ is the 'Saviour of the
Universe',[27] there is even in Barth at least one enlightened moment
when he seems to claim something very similar. 'The truth is', he writes,
that 'He is Lord and Servant who lives, not for Himself, but for the sake
of *the creaturely world and humanity*, for their deliverance', and thus the
'order of reconciliation' is also 'the confirmation and restoration of the
order of creation'.[28] To be fair, so also does Leonardo Boff pick up
this theme expressed in the well-known lines from Ephesians and
Colossians concerning the unity of all things in Christ. He writes:

> Affirmations of such grave theological import are possible and
> comprehensible only if we admit, with the New Testament, that the
> resurrected Jesus revealed in himself the anticipated goal *of the world*
> and the radical meaning *of all creation*. If Christ is the end and the
> Omega Point, then everything began in function of him and because
> of him everything was created.[29]

The deficiency in Boff's thought here lies not so much in failing to see
the connection as failing to recognize its moral dimension.

5. *Christ as our moral exemplar*. It is here that we reach the crux of the
matter. Liberation theologians are keen to see Jesus Christ as the
liberator *par excellence*. Jesus takes sides with the poor and the oppressed.
He 'makes his own the interests of … the poor, the sick, the lepers, the
sinners, the tax-collectors, the Samaritans', argues Sobrino.[30] 'The
Crucified in these crucified persons weeps and cries out, "I was hungry
… in prison … naked" (Matt. 25.31–46)', argues Boff.[31] It is difficult to

dispute the force of the connection made here. Gutierrez writes poignantly of how those who live in squalor and poverty 'feel keenly' that believers 'cannot claim to be Christian without a commitment to liberation'.[32]

In the light of this, we have to ask again the central christological question: if the ominipotence and power of God is properly expressed in the form of *katabasis*, humility and self-sacrifice, why should this model not properly extend to our relations with creation as a whole and animals in particular? If liberation theologians are right in locating concern for the poor, the captive and the vulnerable as the especially right concerns of those who follow Christ, then why is it that the suffering of non-human animals should be regarded as a matter of so little consequence? In short: If we are to ask how it is that we humans are to exercise our dominion or God-given power over non-human animals, then we need look no further than to Jesus as our moral exemplar: of power expressed in powerlessness and of strength expressed in compassion. If self-costly, generous loving is the hallmark of true discipleship, then we have to ask what grounds we have for excluding animals from this proper exercise of Christian responsibility.

This last point highlights the striking failure of liberation theology. It is humans who are capable, indeed I would say commissioned, to liberate God's creation. The old view is expressed by Keith Ward in his paraphrase of Genesis 1. He argues that 'man' is made a 'god' in creation and that creatures 'should serve him'.[33] The new view should be significantly different: given our God-given power and lordship over creation it is *we* who should *serve creation*. The inner logic of Christ's lordship is the sacrifice of the higher for the lower; not the reverse. If the humility of God in Christ is costly and essential, why should ours be less so?

In arguing in this way I continue to draw on the vision of St Paul that the non-human creation groans in suffering awaiting its liberators. Though it may well be that Paul did not fully appreciate the implications of the view he was expounding, it seems entirely in accordance with the spirit of the teaching of Jesus that the non-human creation should look to those described as the 'sons of God' to rescue them from the 'bondage to decay' to which they are now subject. Not only do I suggest that we ourselves achieve redemption by becoming redeemers but also that all theological talk of liberation can only properly take place within the context of the 'bondage to decay' or subjection to futility, that is the oppression that characterizes the created world as a whole. In short: there can be no liberation theology without the liberation of creation itself; no liberating theology without a God determined to liberate every being suffering oppression.

Three Objections

I want now briefly to consider three objections to my argument.

The first objection argues that far from liberating us from humano-centrism I have rather enslaved us even more firmly to it. For according to the Linzey thesis humankind is essential in order to liberate animals, and therefore some kind of humanocentricity, however enlightened, is inevitable.

I must plead guilty here. My attack of course was principally directed against a particular kind of humanocentricity, one that not only views humankind as important but also sees it as the only criterion of moral good. That kind of Christian humanism I want firmly to reject while accepting that a new form of humanism – what I would call the suffering servant humanism – is not only defensible but practically essential if the created world is to become – as Paul calls it – liberated by the sons of God. The new kind of humanism we need has to reject absolutely the idea that human beings are the measure of the worth of other creatures. Our task is to perceive that what we are and what other beings are is really creation: the result of a loving generous God who creates freely, who allows what has been called 'the risk of creation', but who does not fail to enable redemption and liberation. As I see it therefore it is the Spirit of God in Christ who is the true liberator; humans are called to become agents of that liberating Spirit for which all creation longs. The sighs of the suffering creation are indeed interpreted to us through the Holy Spirit. The charge then of humanocentricity of a specific kind should stand, but to be precise theologically, it is as Spirit-filled sons and daughters of God who hold before themselves the model of Christ as the suffering yet glorified servant.

Yet it may be protested that our scriptures, our tradition and our history are uniform in offering us the old view of humanism. How can one explain the colossal emphasis upon human beings in the history of salvation? From my perspective, without undue difficulty. For it is precisely because humans have been so awful, so unaware of their redemptive task and so unthoughtful of their Creator God, that it is not surprising if biblical theology is overwhelmingly concerned with the creation of a new humanity in Christ. For it may be that Paul was right that humans in some sense hold the moral key to the whole show of creation. It may be that only when humans can liberate themselves into a new life of self-sacrifice, moral generosity and practical humility that the future of the created world can be assured. It cannot escape us at the present time that, like it or not, the destructive capacities of humankind threaten not only ourselves but the integrity of creation itself.

The second objection finds the language of oppression and liberation used with regard to animals strained and inappropriate. Is the language of oppression such as may be used in relation to slaves, blacks, Jews, gypsies, gays, or women really appropriate for dogs and cats, let alone battery hens or laboratory rats?

I use the word 'oppress' in precisely the way suggested by *The Oxford Dictionary*: to 'overwhelm with superior weight or numbers or irresistible power … [to] govern tyrannically, keep under by coercion, subject to continual cruelty or injustice'. This I contend is precisely what we do to animals since we hunt, ride, shoot, fish, wear, eat, cage, trap, exhibit, factory farm and experiment upon billions of animals every year. Those who wish to deny that such treatment is oppressive have to deny that our treatment of animals is a moral issue at all. If animals are as Descartes seemed to think simply machines, incapable of self-consciousness and sentiency, then it might be an option to suppose that what we did to them caused them no injury. But biology and ethology can leave little room for doubt that pain and suffering and deprivation are felt by animals only to a greater or lesser degree than by humans. Given this knowledge, we are without moral excuse. This is not to foreclose the issue as to whether or not the infliction of some forms of pain, suffering and deprivation may be justifiable, but the essential point in both the case of humans as well as animals is that such injury requires moral justification. We reserve our highest condemnation in the law courts not for individuals who perceive the wrong they do and are sorry for it, but rather for those individuals who do not see that they do any wrong.

For some the idea that humans have treated animals tyrannically may still appear fanciful, especially since human well-being – at least in one sense – has so greatly benefited from it or because normal human life appears so impossible without it. I sometimes share these senses that *homo-tyrannicus* cannot reform itself, and am indeed sometimes dismayed by the lack of sensitivity shown to animal suffering. On the other hand, a moment of reflection will help us to appreciate that for centuries so-called civilized cultures have oppressed other humans – usually the most vulnerable – and also that a not insignificant number of human beings seem to care for neither battery hens nor battered children.

The third objection picks up my view about the liberation of creation and asks *what it must mean* to posit the liberation of mice and hedgehogs, let alone ants and cauliflowers. Are not liberation theologians right in agreeing with the main teaching of the Christian tradition that liberation only arises as a concept within the human sphere?

In order to answer this question we need to continue to hold before ourselves what St Paul envisons as the *prima facie* evidence of 'bondage to decay'. It is the 'groaning and travailing' of the non-human creation that most impresses him. And should impress us too, I want to argue. For although non-human animals are not capable of claiming their right of liberation (a characteristic, we may note, they also share with some humans – comatose patients, newly-born children, the mentally deficient – for example), and while it is true that not all non-human animals do express their existential predicament precisely through groans and sighs, it is nevertheless true that all such non-human animals here envisaged are capable of injury. That stones can be injured seems highly improbable. The breaking of one large stone creates other stones. The breaking of stone may not be aesthetic, indeed it may be dangerous to the operator of the hammer, but it is not wrong in any conceivable sense because in no conceivable sense can we speak of it being injured by such a process. But can we not injure plants, some might protest? Konrad Lorenz recommended suicide for 'any man who finds it *equally* easy to chop up a live dog and a live lettuce'.[35] Lorenz may overstate the case. But what is important is that lettuce do not possess responding capacities for self-awareness and are therefore not capable of being injured as we know to be true in the case of mammals and humans to say the least. This of course does not answer the problem of all the grey areas, slugs, snails, earthworms and the like. I have no immediate answer to these cases. I would oppose the gratuitous slaughter of any of them, but whether any are 'subjects of life' as Tom Regan puts it[36] – that is, beings capable of knowing that they are being harmed and suffering because of it – is an open question. But what is not an open question is that the groaning and travailing of monkeys, sheep, pigs, horses, cattle, dogs, and cats and the rest – are, as far as these things can be settled at all, beyond reasonable doubt.

There is another more startling interpretation of St Paul worth considering. It is not only that non-humans should be liberated from their groans and pains, but also that animals will in some sense be saved from their parasitical existence in which such sighs and pains are inevitable. Understood in this light, and I am certainly not the first to understand Paul in this way,[37] we are invited to extend our imagination towards another world order altogether, one indeed in which there is no life living at the expense of another and in which humankind lives perfectly in companionship with the animals whose sighs are no longer necessary. Such you may protest is the stuff of dreams and visions. St Paul indeed may well have understood his writing as precisely that: vision-like possibilities of a world in which the Spirit of God is fully operative; a new creation indeed. But it may be that our dogged and persistent humanocentrism has prevented us from listening seriously to those other voices within our tradition that do indeed suggest a transformed world order.

Shifts of consciousness, sometimes gradual, sometimes dramatic, are not beyond the wit of the human species. What is significant is that sometimes dream-like, visionary hypotheses suddenly acquire a powerful hold on the collective imagination and release new bursts of moral energy. The divine right of humans may be an idea whose time has gone. That humans should use their power in defence of the weak, especially the weak of other species, and that humans should actively seek the liberation of all beings capable of knowing their oppression and suffering may be an idea whose time has come.

5

Animal Rights and Parasitical Nature

The preceding chapters have assumed that God's will is a redeemed creation freed from parasitism. This is an unfashionable view in modern theology which has accepted, almost as a matter of course, that God's redemption will be limited to the human sphere in the next world or at least that God's will is ecological parasitism in this. Here, I defend the world-transforming designs of the Deity I see revealed in Jesus Christ, and also suggest that the urge to behave 'unnaturally' in respect of our carnivorous habits can be a sign of grace. Living without killing sentients wherever possible is a theological duty laid upon Christians who wish to approximate the peaceable kingdom. Here, as elsewhere, I perceive a major cleavage between those who advance an 'ecological ethic' and those who advocate a creation-based liberation theology.

The Vampire's Dilemma

Imagine that you are a twenty-five year old living in New Orleans, called Louis. The date is 1791. You suffer a terrible bereavement in the untimely death of your brother, a death for which you blame yourself. You spend nights drinking in New Orleans in a state of near despair. One night just a few steps from your door, you are attacked by an unknown assailant. To experience family bereavement, to be consumed by guilt and remorse, to verge on the abyss of despair – surely these are terrible things. Even more terrible when one is violently attacked – without provocation – to boot. And yet such is the way of life that as terrible things are happening to us, even more terrible things are just round the corner.

In the case of Louis, he woke up, not only battered and bruised, but bled – almost to death. The assailant was not just an ordinary eighteenth-century New Orleans mugger, but a vampire, and what is more, a vampire-making-vampire. Louis regained consciousness not as an ordinary mortal but as a member of an immortal species. Some of you of a more enquiring disposition may be curious as to how one vampire propagates its species. Alas I cannot claim any expertise in vampirology, but I am led to believe that the process happens like this: the propagating vampire sucks the blood from his or her would-be progeny almost to the point of death but then instead of letting him or her actually die, fills the person with blood mingled from his own. Looked at purely dispassionately, we could liken the process to a blood transfusion with a certain extra factor supplied. For ease of reference I shall refer to this in due course as the 'X' factor.

Doubtless you will be aware that one salient feature of a vampire's existence is the need to kill for food or, to be more precise, to suck blood. It is important to understand that this is no optional gastronomic extra but essential for vampire life. Indeed, technically, I was wrong to describe Louis as a vampire made so simply by the process of transfusion. Louis became a vampire only as he recognized the deep hungering thirst for blood and in particular learned how to kill. Lestat, his propagator, had to teach him. As the deep hungering thirst grew within Louis he finally consented to drink human blood. A victim was selected, Lestat completed the preparatory work, and Louis was invited to drink from the victim's wrist. This is how Louis relates this first experience:

> I drank, sucking the blood out of the holes, experiencing for the first time since infancy the special pleasure of sucking nourishment, the body focused with the mind upon one vital source.

As Louis drew blood, he heard sound:

> A dull roar at first and then the pounding like the pounding of a drum, growing louder and louder, as if some enormous creature were coming up on one slowly through a dark and alien forest, pounding as he came, a huge drum. And then there came the pounding of another drum, as if another giant were coming yards behind him, and each giant, intent on his own drum, gave no notice to the rhythm of the other. The sound grew louder and louder until it seemed to fill not just my hearing but all my senses, to be throbbing in my lips and fingers, in the flesh of my temples, in my veins. Above all in my veins, drum and then the other drum ... I realized that the drum was my heart, and the second drum had been his.[1]

I venture to relate this first experience, not in any way for ghoulish purposes, but in order that we may understand Louis' predicament correctly. Those who are apt to be rather superior in their attitude to vampires frequently forget that sucking blood was no mere satisfaction of the appetite, rather it was a profound life-engaging experience involving not inconsiderable ecstasy.

Now I have called this predicament 'the Vampire's dilemma'. But some of you may legitimately query whether Louis' new situation should be classed in these terms. After all a vampire is a vampire. He or she does what he or she does, notwithstanding mystical ecstasy, because of necessity. No blood, no vampire. And yet Louis' experience is rather unusual in this regard. He certainly needs blood, indeed without it he would die. He even craves for it, and like all vampires, is physically distraught without at least one such blood-sucking encounter every day. And yet through some fortuity of circumstance, Louis is not happy about being a vampire. Not that he feels nostalgic for his mortal origins, after all he was desperately unhappy at least immediately prior to his vampire-hood. Neither is Louis' unhappiness principally because of his lack of vampire colleagues. It is certainly true that his one close vampire acquaintance, even would-be friend, Lestat, is not always charming company, and yet solitude for a vampire may not be the grievous blow it is for us simple mortals. Vampire life, and especially its increased powers of movement, perception, sensibility – not to mention flight – does have some compensating factors. It would be wrong, as some high-minded vampire commentators have suggested, to suppose that immortality under such conditions is necessarily disagreeable.

Nevertheless, Louis is unhappy. We should allow him to describe his sorry predicament in his own words:

> Am I damned? Am I from the devil? Is my very nature that of a devil? I was asking myself over and over. And if it is why then do I revolt against it ... turn away in disgust when Lestat kills? What have I become in becoming a vampire? Where am I to go? And all the while, as the death wish caused me to neglect my thirst, my thirst grew hotter: my veins were veritable threads of pain in my flesh: my temples throbbed and finally I could stand it no longer. Torn apart by the wish to take no action – to starve, to wither in thought on the one hand; and driven to kill on the other – I stood in an empty, desolate street and heard the sound of a child crying.[2]

For those who are already wondering what happened to the child and what Louis decided to do, I should report that Louis bled the mother of the child and made the child a vampire. Together they travel the world, ostensibly in search of other vampires who will help them to understand why they are as they are.

By now the point to which this elaborate metaphor is leading must be becoming increasingly obvious. But before I state the point – or dilemma – I must acknowledge my debt to Louis and in particular his literary creator, Anne Rice. For it is from her book, *Interview with the Vampire*, that I have taken the basic plot. This book, I understand, is only the first of three volumes which explore the nature of contemporary vampire-hood.[3] I cannot claim to have read the other volumes but it is clear from what I have read that the human species is in debt to Anne Rice's imagination. If, as Charles Morgan once remarked, there is no failure except failure of the imagination, Rice's work richly deserves both her reputation and her readership, the latter of which I am assured runs into tens of thousands.

Parasitical Predicaments

The full extent of Louis' dilemma should now become clear. Should he go on living at the expense of other, mortal creatures? Does it matter that he kills to live, and if it does not matter why should he feel so stricken about it? Likewise we may ask does it matter that the human species exists today only by the mass slaughter of billions of other creatures as food? Six to nine billion non-human animals are slaughtered in the United States every year; approximately 500 million in the United Kingdom. In comparison with this annual carnage, consumption even by the most rapacious of all vampires is rather slight. The average American eats more than the average vampire.

If we return to Louis' story for a while, we find that some features of his predicament show uncanny similarity to our own. In the first place, almost all Louis' fellow vampires do not see that there is a moral problem at all. When he raises with his propagator, Lestat, whether there might be something less than desirable about sucking blood, Louis is chided for his emotional immaturity. He was simply chasing the 'phantoms of [his] former self'. 'You are in love with your mortal nature,' argues Lestat. In other words, Louis had not yet grown up. He did not yet see that the issue of killing was no moral issue at all. As Lestat puts it:

> Vampires are killers ... Predators whose all-seeing eyes were meant to give them detachment. The ability to see human life in its entirety not with any mawkish sorrow but with a thrilling satisfaction in being the end of that life, in having a hand in the divine plan.[4]

Although Lestat here seems to suggest that killing is actually to be commended theologically, I think it is fairest to characterize Lestat's overall view of killing as amoral. Since death for each mortal individual is inevitable, the process of hastening that inevitability is as devoid of moral significance as is the blowing of the wind or the pouring of the rain.

And it is this idea that brings us to the second, and by far the most significant, similarity between almost all vampires and almost all humans. Eating animals by humans is thought to be as natural as sucking blood is for vampires. The argument is quite explicit: 'Do what it is your nature to do,' argues Lestat: 'This is but a taste of it. *Do what it is your nature to do.*'[5] This claim seems to sum up the dilemma of both vampires like Louis and mortal vegetarians like myself who would rather live without killing. Are we not simply opposing the nature of things as given, or indeed our own natures? Are not non-blood-sucking vampires and non-meat-eating humans similarly anomalous in the history of our respective species? Is it not true that both are seemingly incapable of facing the world as it is without emotion or moral squint?

Considerations such as these lead Louis and his child colleague to a series of journeyings, one might even say pilgrimages, in search of knowledge both of how they came to be and more decisively still to the Creator of all things which be. In the middle of his European voyage by ship, Louis nurtures the hope that somewhere in this new continent he might find 'the answer to why under God this suffering was allowed to exist – why under God it was allowed to begin, and how under God it might be ended'.[6]

Rethinking Natural Law

In the same way that Louis was led to God in order to explain and understand the 'X' factor that makes vampires blood-sucking or humans carnivorous, so too have many previously wrestled with the morality of killing in the sight of God. Louis is by no means alone in the history of moral deliberation. Plato seems to have envisaged a world, almost a Golden Age, in which all creatures lived harmoniously, and only after humans had been given God-like power over animals, did those harmonious relationships degenerate into strife and violence.[7] Genesis 1 similarly depicts a state of perfect Sabbath harmony within creation where humans and animals are both prescribed a vegetarian diet.[8] This fundamental insight that parasitical existence is incompatible with the original will of God has to be grasped if we are to understand the subsequent attempts in Genesis both to limit and accommodate killing. The Fall and the Flood are the great symbols of why humanity can no longer live at peace either with themselves or with other creatures.

And yet the insight that parasitical existence is incompatible with the designs of the Creator still does not answer the problem of how vampires or carnivores must live today. If God can tolerate such a system are we not in the end to resign ourselves to it, or abandon the notion of a holy, loving Creator altogether? Most humans have followed the reasoning of Samuel Pufendorf who argued in 1688 that

> it is a safe conclusion from the fact that the Creator established no common right between man and brutes, that no injury is done brutes if they are hurt by man, since God himself made such a state to exist between man and brutes.[9]

At first sight religious people would appear to be impaled on the horns of a dilemma. Either they accept that God did not ordain a just state of affairs, in which case we can no longer postulate a loving, just deity; or otherwise they have to accept that God is not – as claimed – the sovereign Creator of all things. But are Christians obliged to take either of these two options? I think not. There is a third and theologically much more satisfying option. It begins by asking us to consider that the world really is *creation*. It is the work of a loving and holy God – yes – but it is also creation, and not Creator. Because the world is creation and not Creator, it cannot be anything other than less than divine. To be a creature is necessarily to be incomplete, unfinished, imperfect. If creation was wholly perfect it would have to be like God, perfection itself. From this standpoint the very nature of creation is always ambiguous; it points both ways; it affirms and denies God at one and the same time. Affirms God because God loves and cares for it but it also necessarily denies God because it is not divine. It follows that there can be no straightforward moral or theological appeal to the way nature is. Note the way in which Pufendorf deliberately takes the state of nature as a yardstick or measure of what God wills or plans for creation. I argue rather that the state of nature can in no way be an unambiguous referent to what God wills or plans for creation.

The issue may be clarified by reference to the traditional theological notion of natural law. We turn to what has been one of the most enlightened of attempts to rehabilitate natural law theory. In his essay, 'Rethinking Natural Law', John Macquarrie argues that it is essential to

distinguish natural law as an ethical concept from any scientific law of
nature:

> The expression 'natural law' refers to a norm of responsible conduct,
> and suggests a kind of fundamental guideline or criterion that comes
> before all rules or particular formulations of law.[10]

Now at first sight such a redefinition would seem to support Louis'
position. After all does not Louis experience a pre-rational, intuitive
conception of what is right? Something parallel to what Macquarrie calls
a 'norm of responsible conduct' – a 'criterion' that comes before all
formulations of law? The problem is, however, that Macquarrie – like so
many ethicists before him – is unable to develop and justify such a notion
of natural law without reference to what he calls 'the way things are'.

> Natural Law too claims to be founded in *'the way things are'*, in
> ultimate structures that are explicitly contrasted with the human
> conventions that find expression in our ordinary rules and customs.[11]

Again:

> [Natural law] safeguards against moral subjectivism and encourages
> moral seriousness by locating the demand of moral obligation in *the
> very way things are.*[12]

In contrast, I suggest that if we can use the term 'natural law' at all in this
context – it can properly, perhaps only, be discovered *not* in *'the way
things are'* but in the sense of *what should be*. In short: So much natural
law theory rests upon an unqualified 'naturalism'. What we have
witnessed almost by sleight of hand is a developing 'naturalism' within
moral theology which fundamentally limits the redeeming capacities of
God to what humans perceive to be 'the way things are' in nature itself.
The result has been an almost total failure to grasp the possibility of
redemption outside the human sphere.

One example must suffice: John Armstrong in a sensitive and perceptive discussion of Hebrew attitudes to animals nevertheless castigates
the Isaianic vision of the lion lying down with the lamb as an attempt 'to
get rid of the beasts of prey or change their nature beyond recognition'.[13]
He appears not to see the point of Isaiah's vision which is not that
animality will be destroyed by divine love but rather that animal nature is
in bondage to violence and predation. The vision of Isaiah is directly
relevant here: It invites us to the imaginative recognition that God's

transforming love is not determined even by what we think we know of elementary biology.

Trans-Natural Moral Imperative

If there can be any rehabilitation of natural law we must reiterate that we are speaking neither of 'law' or 'nature' in any recognizable sense. There is nothing in creation which of itself can give us an unambiguous understanding of the moral purposes of God. To return to Louis' dilemma for a moment, I am suggesting that he is right to be vexed and troubled. He is right to rail and thunder against a kind of nature which forecloses on the moral option. Louis is right to seek a way out; even against all appearances of necessity he is right to go on searching, and not least of all, he is right to place a question mark alongside God him/herself. Louis' deep pre-rational intuitive sense that sucking blood is not right is what we should call not 'natural law' but rather 'trans-natural moral imperative'. To have grasped such an insight is an implicitly theological act; the world does not explain itself, either there is explanation outside creation or creation remains enigmatic and inexplicable.

But if it is right that Louis should strive even against all odds to realize this moral imperative, even more should the human species seek to live without killing animals to eat. This is the obvious direction of my argument. The vampire has a dilemma because it seems – at least at present – that he cannot choose to live without recourse to blood, but we humans do now have such a choice. Whether humans have always been so free is something which at worst I am doubtful about, at best I have an open mind. When that theologian, Dean Inge, deeply committed to animal rights as he was, argued as recently as 1926 that we could not give up flesh because 'we must eat something',[14] I do not believe that he was being disingenuous. Inge really believed, as did many of his compassionate forebears, that one could not live without eating animals. Rumours of vegetarians existed but like the rumours themselves they did not – it was thought – persist. Most people until comparatively recently were incredulous that real vegetarians both existed *and* flourished. Despite all the vegetarian literature produced by George Bernard Shaw, popular commentators still claimed that only secret consumption of liver kept him alive. Again only comparatively recently have dietitians accepted that vegetable protein is, like meat, 'first class protein', and even now it seems there are some nutritionists determined to expose what they see as the dangers of veganism. For the first time in the history of the human race vegetarianism has become a publicly viable option, at least for those who live in the Western world. This is not of course to overlook all the many pioneers and prophets, but all of these have been just that: pioneers, protesters and prophets against the stream. But that mainstream has now to contend – in the United Kingdom at least – with something approximating four million vegetarians, demi-vegetarians and vegans. For humans there is now no dilemma compounded through ignorance. We can live free of meat; there are now numerous examples of people who do so and who are alive and well. When we know that we are free to do otherwise eating meat constitutes what Stephen Clark calls 'empty gluttony'.[15]

Objections to Vegetarianism

To this conclusion, I anticipate four objections.

Creation not Fallen

The first argues that my insistence upon the 'fallen' nature of creation, and its inherent ambiguity, mitigates against contemporary environmental ethics and with it an increased respect for animals in particular. After years in which nature and materiality have been devalued within Christian theology do we not need a new theology of the inherent goodness of all creatures? Was Gerard Manley Hopkins wrong when he claimed that the 'world is charged with the grandeur of God'?[16]

It is true that in recent years observers of the theological scene will have witnessed the growth of a body of writing concerned to reestablish what is called the 'sacralization of nature'. Such writing must be construed as a valuable protest against the kind of unqualified appeal to human supremacy articulated by, for example, Charles Davis, in 1966. Davis argues that nature is no longer regarded by 'scientific man' as 'sacred and untouchable' and he proclaims that such a view of nature is in full harmony with the Christian faith indeed required by it. 'Any other view of nature is, in the sight of Christian teaching, idolatrous, superstitious or magical.'[17] Davis may well have reason to regret his utterances at a time when it is precisely unremitting human domination of the earth that seems to threaten even human survival. It is not difficult to see how in the light of contemporary environmental destruction that individuals want to posit a relocation of value which includes all natural objects. Slogans such as 'the world is all good' or 'the earth knows best' are quite understandable as protests to the massive contemporary devaluing of creaturely life.

And yet understandable as this protest is, when it is combined with a view that all 'natural' structures of life are themselves good or perfect in every way, the whole possibility of a theological ethic is eclipsed. Certainly we need to recover a sense of the original blessing of creation, but if we suppose that all in creation is indiscriminately good, then we have no room left to establish the best. One may be forgiven for thinking that the task left to humanity is – on some ecological accounts – simply to emulate the structures of parasitical existence. We are supposed to glory in the economy of existence whereby one species devours another with consummate efficiency. It may not be surprising then that some recent commentators have seen a potentially sinister relationship between far right philosophy and some forms of green political theory. Whether such a connection can be responsibly made is a matter I cannot pursue here, but it cannot be doubted that an appeal to pure 'naturalism' opens up a pathway to a rebirth of brutalism in which humans are invited not morally to transform the cosmos but to imitate its worst manifestations. If the legacy of Genesis is sometimes thought to be disadvantageous to animals, even more so some aspects of the contemporary legacy of Darwinism.

And yet some may surely question whether we now have gone too far on the other side. Are we not to celebrate the life of creation with all its beauty, magnificence and complexity and therein with Hopkins to perceive signs of the grandeur of God? Is not the biblical material right to point us to the ways in which some animals at least appear to provide moral examples for our own behaviour? Is not the story of Balaam's ass a sign of how morally advanced are the beasts compared to the mindless Balaams of our world? I have no desire to deny the force of any of these arguments. Karl Barth is right to speak of how creation should be construed as 'justification', that is, as divine beneficence, benefit, grace.[18] That there is beauty, value, goodness in the created order is judicious Christian doctrine; that the whole creation is right as it is, or in the way it is, that it is in no way incomplete or unfinished, is not. To maintain that creation is *all* all right is to make God the Redeemer redundant. In short: 'the earth is all good' slogan fails to recognize the 'X' factor.

Jesus and Parasitism

The second objection is that Jesus was – as far as we know – no crusading vegetarian. While there are no precise biblical accounts of him eating meat, the canonical Gospels leave us in no doubt that he ate fish. And if this is true on what grounds can we claim him as the revelation of an alternative non-parasitical existence?

At first sight this appears a pretty cast-iron objection. As Stephen Clark asks: 'Shall not the Judge of all the earth do right?'[19] There seem, however, to be two principal grounds on which this argument founders. The first is in its implicit assumption that the demands of contemporary Christian discipleship can be met simply by the imitation of the Jesus of first-century Palestine. If this is really taken to its limit, there would be hardly any scope for moral theology at all. The purpose of ethical reflection would be invalid. Ethical striving would simply centre upon the need to imitate Jesus as he then was in that situation. In contrast, what Christian discipleship requires is summed up well by John Macquarrie:

> The Christian ... defines mature manhood in terms of Jesus Christ, and especially his self-giving love. But Christ himself is no static figure, nor are Christians called to imitate him as a static model. Christ is an eschatological figure, always before us; and the doctrine of his coming again 'with glory' implies that there are dimensions of christhood not manifest in the historical Jesus and not yet fully grasped by the disciples. Thus discipleship does not restrict human development to some fixed pattern, but summons into freedoms, the full depth of which is unknown, except that they will always be consonant with self-giving love.[20]

The second way in which this argument founders is in failing to grasp the necessary particularity of the incarnation. To be God incarnate as a human being does not mean being some kind of Superman. The traditional affirmation about Jesus is not that he is God, but that he is God and human. The point is no mere technicality. God incarnates himself or herself into the limits and constraints of the world as we know it. It is true that one of the purposes of the incarnation was to manifest something of the trans-natural possibilities of existence, but no one human life can demonstrate, let alone exhaust, all the possibilities of self-giving love. To those who argue that Jesus was deficient or limited either in his lack of crusading power for feminism, for the abolition of slavery, or for veganism – not to mention home rule – miss the central point that to confess Christ crucified is to confess a Christ inevitably and profoundly limited by the fact of incarnation. To be in one place at one time means that one cannot be everywhere.

In the light of this it is all the more significant that early reflection upon the work and person of Christ is determined to spell out its eventual cosmic dimension and meaning. The line from Ephesians expresses it well:

> [God] has made known to us his secret purpose, in accordance with the plan which he determined beforehand in Christ, to be put into effect when the time was ripe; namely that the universe, everything in heaven and on earth, might be brought into a unity in Christ.[21]

And likewise in Colossians where God chose Christ

> and through him to reconcile all things to himself, making peace through the shedding of his blood on the cross – all things, whether on earth or in heaven.[22]

This concept of cosmic reconciliation provides the framework in which we may grasp the trans-natural moral imperative glimpsed in the actual historical life of Jesus. For the revelation of God in Jesus is such as to intensify rather than diminish the puzzle of the created order. For Jesus stands against as much as for the order of nature as we now know it. The natural processes of sickness and death and disease, even indeed the vagaries of the weather, are subject to the power of God in Jesus Christ. If we follow Jesus we are set upon a course of trans-natural transformation whereby the sick do not suffer and die but are healed and restored; the poor are not downtrodden but become the first among equals; and even the winds which blow us to the four corners are gathered together. The so-called 'nature miracles' of Jesus are signs among many that in Jesus is a birth of new possibilities for all creation. I suggest that what we have in Jesus is a model not of the accommodation of nature but rather of the beginning of its transformation. Not that all things were transformed by Jesus, nor that all of his life in every aspect was so transforming, nor that every part has even yet been transformed, but that to follow Jesus is to affirm, and seek to actualize, the fundamental possibility of world transformation.

Psychological Bondage

The third objection to my thesis is that even if eventual peace and harmony is God's will in Christ for all creation, we cannot achieve it now. Humans do face a dilemma. Even if there is no natural law requiring us to eat flesh, there is a psychological one. Humans cannot be expected to forego the enormous pleasure of consuming flesh. Gluttony it may be, but we humans can do no better. As vampires need their mystical fix of blood, so we humans need our 'finger-lickin good' chicken or juicy steak.

Some may think that I have already caricatured this objection, but I have put it in such a crass form because in this way it expresses a fundamental kind of despair about moral self-improvement which is a great deal more widespread than is often supposed. There are all kinds of reasons why Christians should be wary of schemes for moral perfectionism. Grandiose moral and social hopes often create incapacitating disappointment when it is discovered that they cannot be realized. In particular it follows from my overall argument that humans are themselves simply creatures: limited, finite, incapable of seeing things whole, incapable indeed by themselves of becoming whole. Moral burdens incapable of being relieved can create anger, frustration, even violence.

We do well to realize what a frail and limited vessel the human creature is. If we cannot prevent greed, stupidity, cruelty, deceit, violence, envy, hatred, culpable acts of wickedness performed by members of our own species against other members of our species, what chance can we have of behaving any better to other, non-human, creatures?

Those of us who may sometimes feel encouraged to an optimistic view of life need to take cognizance of the lyrical protest of the political philosopher, William Godwin:

Let us not amuse ourselves with a pompous and delusive survey of the whole, but let us examine parts severally and individually. All nature swarms with life. This may in one view afford an idea of an extensive theatre of pleasure. But unfortunately every animal preys upon his fellow. Every animal however minute, has a curious and subtle structure, rendering him susceptible, as it should seem, of piercing anguish. We cannot move our foot without becoming the means of destruction. The wounds inflicted are of a hundred kinds. These petty animals are capable of palpitating for days in the agonies of death. It may be said with little licence of phraseology that all nature suffers. There is no day nor hour, in which in some regions of the many peopled globe, thousands of men, and millions of animals, are not tortured to the utmost extent that organized life will afford. Let us turn our attention to our own species. Let us survey the poor; oppressed, hungry, naked, denied all the gratifications of life and all that nourishes the mind. They are either tormented with the injustice or chilled into lethargy. Let us view man writhing under the pangs of disease, or the fiercer tortures that are stored up for him by his brethren. Who is there that will look on and say 'All is well; there is no evil in the world'?[24]

Notwithstanding the beauty and goodness and magnificence of the created world, no sane person it seems to me could simply say 'All is well; there is no evil in the world.' And I agree with Godwin that the 'creed of optimism', as he puts it, 'has done much harm in the world'.[25] But it seems precisely because one cannot say in truth that all is well with the world, and further that the creed of optimism speaks truthfully of how the world is, that the case for believing in world-transforming Christian theism is so strong. The choice is clear: either there is at the heart of being unredeemed or unredeemable suffering and misery and death, or there is actually a pattern of transformation, glimpsed in Christ, which is actually capable of bringing about a new world order.

Now there can be little doubt that such a perception is demanding and burdensome and itself flies in the face of not inconsiderable evidence. But it should be clear that such a perception is consistent with, even required by, the Christian faith. To the objection that this invites otiose, even harmful, perfectionism, there can only be one answer. The God who demands is also the God who enables. Even by the power of the Holy Spirit it may be that the world cannot be made well at a stroke given the necessary self-limitations imposed by the Creator. Nevertheless, it is possible and credible to believe that by the power of the Spirit new ways of living without violence can be opened up for us even within a world which is tragically divided between the forces of life and the forces of death. We should celebrate the possibility that through the Spirit we can today live in some way freer of the 'X' factor with regard to animals than many of our forebears. Optimism may well be facile. Despair, however, is not a Christian option.

Self-Evident Imperative?

The fourth and last objection questions the rational and theological basis for obeying this pre-natural intuition in what I have called the trans-natural moral imperative. Is it self-evident that we should live in peace, or that peace is itself better than violence? Can anything be self-evident in our confused and contradictory creaturely world? I do not suppose that my own tentative answer will satisfy all, as explanations of moral imperatives seldom do. But I suggest that there may be one sense in which the notion of so-called 'natural law' can help us. It is found in the notion of Heraclitus that 'all human laws are nourished by the one divine law; for this holds sway as far as it will, and suffices for all and prevails in everything'. This law is identified by Heraclitus with the *logos*, 'the primordial word or reason in accordance with which everything occurs'. Before it is protested that I am merely returning to a notion of natural law previously rejected, let it be clear as one commentator makes explicit:

> A 'law of nature' is merely a general descriptive formula for referring to some specific complex of observed facts, while Heraclitus' divine law is something genuinely normative. It is the highest norm of the cosmic process, and the thing which gives the process its significance and worth.[26]

It will not be overlooked that the concept of *logos* here defined in a Greek context has obvious affinities with Jewish and Christian ones. It is, I suggest, in the doctrine of Christ as the *Logos*, that we are given the revelatory principle that peace is better than violence and that reconciliation is better than disintegration. The Cosmic Christ through whom all things come to be is the source and destiny and well-being of all creatures. To affirm the Cosmic Christ is to embrace a new possibility of existence within our grasp now. It will be clear that this view gives a high place to humans in nature; not because they are so worthy in themselves but because they are as no other species – as far as we know at least – capable of focussing the forces of life and death, of becoming vampires or vegetarians.

It is for this reason that I also want to conclude that vegetarianism – far from being some kind of optional moral extra or some secondary moral consideration – is in fact an implicitly theological act of the greatest significance. By refusing to kill and eat meat, we are witnessing to a higher order of existence, implicit in the *Logos*, which is struggling to be born in us. By refusing to go the way of our 'natural nature' or our 'psychological nature', by standing against the order of unredeemed nature we become signs of the order of existence for which all creatures long.

I end as I began by asking you to consider the plight of our morally stricken vampire called Louis. I am sorry to say that I cannot report a happy ending. Despite his searches all over the world and his encounter with fellow vampires older and wiser than himself, and despite all his moral strength, he is unable to free himself from his own parasitical nature. There is one saving grace for Louis, however. His story will not have been told in vain if it has helped us to recover a sense of the responsibility of our own moral freedom.

Part Two

Challenging Ethical Practice

6

Animal Experiments as Un-Godly Sacrifices

The idea that animals are here for our use has a long history. The new idea that there are moral limits to what we should do to animals has been a long time coming and in its practical implications will appear radical and uncompromising. Nowhere is this clearer than in our use of animals in scientific research. In this chapter, I begin by picking up the theological notion that animals have an irreducible non-utilitarian value and I try to show how this insight is grounded in the traditional doctrine of God as Father, Son, and Holy Spirit. I then move on to eek out the precise moral implications of this insight, and to show how in practice such implications require the moral rejection of animals as sacrificial subjects in pursuit of human advantage.

The Theological Basis of the Value of Creation

It [creation] exists for God's glory, that is to say, it has a meaning and worth beyond its meaning and worth as seen from the point of view of human utility. It is in this sense that we can say that it has intrinsic value. To imagine that God has created the whole universe solely for man's use and pleasure is a mark of folly.

These words come from the Report of a Working Group set up in 1971 by the then Archbishop of Canterbury 'to investigate the relevance of Christian doctrine to the problems of man in his environment'.[1] The Report's affirmation of the 'intrinsic' value of creation is so traditional that it may be interpreted as theologically unexceptional. It is, after all, quite central to Christian doctrine that the creation made by God is good. But could it be that this affirmation, commonly held by Judaism and Islam as well as Christianity, has implications for our moral treatment of animals that have hitherto largely been unseen? In what follows I hope to indicate something of the minimum that can be deduced from this insight from a Christian perspective and to consider how morally significant that minimum might be.

To begin with, it is important to see how it is that the affirmation of the intrinsic value of the world is inseparable from the Christian doctrine of God. It is not sufficient to say that the creation made by God must necessarily be good. It is important to indicate *how* the goodness of creation is constituted and *how* the creativity of God is related in Christian doctrine to the further works of incarnation, reconciliation, and redemption.

God the Creator

God can be defined in classical terms as 'infinite, self-existent, incorporeal, eternal, immutable, impassible, simple, perfect, omniscient and omnipotent'.[2] God is the source of all being, life, energy and movement – everything. The Creator brings into being another reality that is objectively distinct from him/herself. God does not need creation. The created world exists both as a manifestation of divine love and the Creator's intention to manifest his/her love within it. The created order is dependent upon God not only for its creation but also for its continued existence. Everything that exists therefore does so in a relationship with the Creator to which it belongs. From this straightforward statement, the value of creation may be perceived by implication in the following ways:

1. It has its origin with God, who is by definition holy and perfect. Because it is ontologically distinct from God, creation occupies a separate sphere of existence and possesses its own separate identity.

2. It cannot exist and continue to exist without God's express approval and will. It cannot within the limits of divine purpose be other than it is or cease to be without God.

3. It exists meaningfully, that is, with purpose, in so far as its Creator confers purpose upon it.

4. It exists within a relationship of grace, that is, an unconditional beneficent attitude on the part of the Creator.

Viewed against this larger backdrop we see that the creation and its order, character and design, in so far as they reflect the Creator's intention, must be objects of value. The question must inevitably be raised as to how far the creation as we now see it faithfully reflects the designs of the Creator. Classical Christian theism teaches the fallenness of human nature, a state that in principle affects at least the whole of the created world. As Eric Mascall writes, 'Like a microscopic crack in a china vase, it [i.e., our fall from grace] initiated a process of disintegration and corruption whose consequence spread far beyond the area of their origin and affected the whole subsequent history of the human race and of the material realm.'[3] This means that any reading off from the created world to the realm of moral imperatives must be highly suspect at best. For the laws of nature, operative in this fallen world, may not be the absolute or initially chosen laws of God. This does not mean that Christians cannot learn from nature or marvel at it, only that we cannot assume that the creation as we now know it is a textbook of moral reference. The fallenness of creation aside, however, the doctrine of creation maintains the intention of God to create all things good and so that all things must be objects of value.

God Incarnate

The doctrine of the incarnation may be taken as affirming, in the classical formulation of Chalcedon, that the Second Person of the Trinity took human flesh at a particular moment in history.[4] Much that is affirmed in the doctrine of creation is necessary for this affirmation to make sense:

1. There must be an objective reality, distinct from God, with which God can have a providential relationship.

2. This objective reality must be such that God can participate within it and do so in such a way that this purpose may be fulfilled.

3. This objective reality, presupposed by the incarnation, must be such that the divine presence can incarnate itself within it.

Point three requires some elaboration. The incarnation must presuppose that creation is open to God and that human creation in particular is compatible with the being of God so defined. The incarnation must therefore imply that the world is valuable to God and – not withstanding its inherent ambiguity as creation – that it is the appropriate medium for self-revelation. As Mascall writes: 'By their very dependence upon God, finite beings are inherently open to him; an absolutely autonomous and incapsulated finite entity would be a contradiction in terms. A created universe ... is necessarily not only a finite but an open one.'[5] In other words, unlike some other world religions, incarnational theology pre-supposes what can be called a high doctrine of matter. Material substance, that is, flesh and blood, which is what humans share in particular with much of the animal kingdom, is the pivot of God's redeeming purposes.

It is often suggested as we have seen that the incarnation underlines the special value of humans in creation. And there can be little doubt of this. But it is a mistake to assume that the incarnation does not also reinforce the value of matter and living beings in particular. There is a long tradition of Byzantine theology that emphasizes the inter-connectedness of humans and creation and also of creation and incarnation.[6] As Brian Horne explains: 'The Jesus who is crucified is also the Logos of God: through him all things come into being, in him all things are "summed up", and by him all things are sanctified by the presence of the Spirit. In taking man to himself, he takes all nature to himself'.[7] To say the very least: It is not a *necessary* implication that the incarnation is the sole affirmation of the worth of humankind.

God the Reconciler

I shall not be concerned here with the various theories of atonement (propitiation, substitution, ransom, and so forth) but with the idea presupposed by the doctrine (about which there is scarce dispute) that Christ reconciled fallen creation to God the Father by his life and (especially) his death. Again I shall not explore the precise grounds for affirming the fallen nature of creation. Many theories have been expounded but no one explanation has found complete assent within the Christian tradition.[8]

The striking point here is that the act of reconciliation must, logically, include *all* that is fallen, *all* that was previously unreconciled. Does this involve the non-human creation? The answer we give to this question will depend in turn upon the further question of whether animals and plants are already reconciled to God by their act of creation or whether in some moral sense they are capable of falling or being influenced by the fall of other beings from divine grace. Christian theology has normally been reluctant to relate the reconciling work of Christ to animals because they are not seen as capable of sin in the traditional sense. But because they are affected by human sin, is it possible that they might be freed from its consequences by the power of the cross? Though theologians have often doubted this, Paul Tillich, for example, sees the possibility of incarnation and reconciliation in non-human worlds. He writes: 'Incarnation is unique for the special group in which it happens, but it is not unique in the sense that other singular incarnations for other unique worlds are excluded. Man cannot claim', argues Tillich, 'that the infinite has entered the finite to overcome its existential estrangement in mankind alone'.[9]

The point seems to be supported by the report of a working party set up by the Board for Social Responsibility of the Church of England in 1970. It concluded: 'Both the sufferings of animals and the sufferings of Christ could lead to cynicism if considered in isolation. But in the context of Easter and Pentecost the suffering of Christ takes on new meaning and this new meaning gives point to the groaning and travailing of all creation.'[10] There seem to be three possibilities, all of which are compatible with orthodox Christian belief: (1) that animals are not capable of sin or estrangement and therefore are not able to be included in the saving work of Christ; (2) that if they have sinned or fallen from grace it may be possible for the Son of God to become incarnate in their nature in order to reconcile them, or (3) that 'by becoming incarnate in one rational species, the Son of God has *ipso facto* become the redeemer of all'.[11]

My preference, as already shown, is for option three, but I propose to leave this question generally open. For its resolution in no way affects what is certainly implied in the affirmation of the atonement. No less than with the doctrine of the incarnation, we are again led inescapably to the notion that creation has value. God, so Christians affirm, is determined to bind him/herself to creation in order to save it from the worst possibilities (largely, though not exclusively, represented by humankind) of self-destructiveness.

God the Redeemer

The doctrines of reconciliation and redemption are, of course, essentially different sides of the same activity of God. One may be taken as pointing to the work of Christ in obedience to God the Father in history, the other to the consummation of this work at the end of time. For among all orthodox theologians there is both the affirmation of what has been done up to the present and what needs to be done in the future to fulfill God's purposes.

It is at this point, when we are asked to affirm the world-transforming nature of redemption, that we see clearly the significance and worth of all creation. For nothing that God has made can be omitted in the moment of completion. Christians may be questioning and agnostic as to the precise details of this hope, but it cannot but follow from a God who creates, incarnates, and reconciles that *everything* will be made new. The Archbishop's Working Group concludes:

> To speak thus of the restoration of all things involves the whole creation and not mankind alone. On any interpretation of the classical Christian teaching about the resurrection of the body, it is difficult to see how man's bodily life can enter into eternity ... without in some sense involving that world in which we have rejoiced and of which the human body is a part. Nothing which God has made will ultimately be lost. All the splendour of the natural world and the creative achievements of man, however transitory and easily destructible they may appear, have eternal significance.[12]

It must also follow that each and every hurt and harm in creation (both human and animal, in so far as each is capable of being hurt or harmed) will be made good, and that all the suffering of the present time is not worth comparing to the glory as yet unrevealed. Keith Ward makes this point emphatically:

> If it is necessary that each sentient being must have the possibility of achieving an overwhelming good, then it is clear that there must be some form of life after earthly death. Despite the many pointers to the existence of God, theism would be falsified if physical death was the end, for then there could be no justification for the existence of this world. However, if one supposes that every sentient being has an endless existence, which offers the prospect of supreme happiness, it is surely true that the sorrows and troubles of this life will seem very small by comparison. Immortality, for animals as well as humans, is a necessary condition of any acceptable theodicy; that necessity, together with all the other arguments for God, is one of the main reasons for believing in immortality.[13]

Not all Christians will go as far as Ward,[14] though it cannot be overlooked that some form of eternal life for animals has found serious advocates within Christianity.[15] Whatever the precise ramifications, one simple point needs to be stressed. It is inconsistent with the thrust of all the previous doctrine considered that what has been made, sustained, and loved will not be completed according to the Father's purposes. From this perspective, whatever the precise spiritual status of animals in redemption, God is to them Creator and Redeemer.

I would not want to argue that the particular way in which I have presented these central doctrines would be agreeable to all Christians.

But I hope I have shown enough for it to be clear that the appeal to the value of creation can be supported by orthodox Christian belief and indeed, that these doctrines taken together require such an affirmation. It will be seen that I have not based this conclusion on any particular strand within the biblical tradition, or upon exegesis of particular texts, or on one or more characterizations of theological work. Rather, in taking the nexus of doctrines together, each one relating to and informing the other, we are on much surer grounds, I judge, in claiming to interpret accurately mainstream Christian orthodoxy.

Moral Implications

But the central question is: If we accept such a theological notion of the worth of creation, what follows from it and what are the moral implications in particular? There are, I suggest, four implications of direct moral relevance:

1. If creation has value to God, then it should possess value to human beings.

2. The theological value of creation thus elaborated should be seen to be distinct from humans' estimation of their own value and utility as this may be variously defined from time to time.

3. The theological purpose of creation should also be seen to be distinct from humans' estimation of the purpose and significance of creation.

4. If creation has value and should have value for humans, it should follow that humans cannot claim a right to absolute value within creation.

This first point may appear elementary, and in one sense it is, but it has immense significance. The affirmation of the value of creation is first and foremost an affirmation of its worth to God. The claiming of value for creation is not some kind of more sophisticated moral judgment; it is perception of worth that stems from what Christians believe to be true about the nature and work of God. It is not some kind of optional possibility for those who are Christians; it is inseparable from the confession of God as creator, incarnate, and redeemer. In accepting this implication, however, we are not committed to the view that all creation has the same or equal value. It is still possible (and I think desirable) within the general perception of the value of creation that we should distinguish between, say, the value of stones and the value of sentient beings. Again how we interpret the value of respective parts of creation subsequently is a matter of discernment and judgment. How we should articulate the respective value of different life forms within the range of inter-related theological themes is a question I hope to raise shortly. At this point, I want to suggest that there is prima facie an obligation to value the creation that God so values.

I am not suggesting in point two that God's estimation of the value of creation and humans' own evaluation may not sometimes agree or overlap; indeed it would be a poor theology that held the two at a permanent distance. But whatever convergence there may be, it is a mistake to refuse the distinction. Humans cannot simply take as God's view their own evaluation of themselves in the cosmos. So much in the Christian tradition testifies to this distinction in the case of the individual's estimate of his or her value in relation to other humans that it only makes sense to insist upon this same principle of distinction here. Because of this, it must also follow that humans cannot claim to be the only measure of good as regards their fellow creatures. In all cases sentients have their own individual lives, their own needs, and their own pattern of behaviour. Of course human interests are morally important, but they cannot claim to be the only morally important interests.

Regarding point three, the same must be said about the notion of purpose, which often underlies claims about the nature of value. As the Archbishop's Report indicates, 'It [creation] has meaning and worth beyond its meaning and worth from the point of view of human utility'.[16] This point is unaffected by how far and how much can be known in theological terms about the purpose of God in the mysterious activity of sustaining creation. What has to be held on to is the distinction between God's purposes and humans' purposes. Again we may hope and believe that they meet and converge, but we cannot always resolve the tension in our favour with assurance. The knowledge of God as presupposed in Christian doctrine, even the *saving* knowledge of God in orthodoxy, is not such that we can claim a knowledge of divine purpose in all things. This point is aptly made by Karl Barth: 'We do not know what particular attitude God may have to them [non-human creatures], and therefore what might be their decisive particularity within the cosmos ... We can and must accept them as our fellow-creatures with all due regard for the mystery in which God has veiled them.'[17] This point is certainly not new. Christians have often wondered why it is that we do not know more theologically about the life and status of animals. For myself, I am inclined to believe that we can know by implication a great deal more than Barth suggests, but whatever view is held, it must also be appreciated that there can be no straightforward deduction from silence to human *gnosis*, even when humans' vital interests are at stake.

The fourth point may be seen as a simple underlining of the previous three, except in one regard. It is sometimes claimed that the traditional affirmation of the special place of humans in creation is such that it resolves any consideration of the value of other life forms in our favour. But even if we accept a hierarchy of valuable beings in God's sight, as some Christians have traditionally posited, it does not follow that either we must ascribe absolute value to humans or absolutely none to animals. We may say that certain forms of life have less value to God than humans, and human beings may (and often do) judge according to the hierarchy of values they perceive. But it cannot be claimed that creation is of little or no account. This simple point cannot be stressed too strongly, because in a rush to affirm the truth of one aspect of moral theology it is only too easy to lose sight of another. Human beings cannot affirm their own value within the created order without at the same time affirming the value of all created beings. This is not an independent value judgment; it is an implication deeply embedded in the nature of the affirmation itself. This point is well summarized by the *Animals and Ethics* Working Party report convened by the then Dean of Westminster in 1977:

> On a theistic understanding of creation, such as the Christian entertains, it is a mistake to suppose that all animal life exists only to serve humankind; or that the world was made exclusively for man's benefit. Man's estimate of his own welfare should not be the only guideline in determining his relationship with other species. In terms of this theistic understanding man is custodian of the universe he inhabits with no absolute rights over it.[18]

Animals as Sacrificial Victims

At this stage I want to anticipate one major objection to the position I have advanced so far. This objection does not deny that creation has value, even that there are circles of closer proximity to humans within creation, but maintains that it is right that the lower creation should serve the higher creation, as is witnessed in the sacrificial tradition of the Old Testament.

At first sight this objection has considerable force. Is it not true that to some degree the Old Testament sanctions the use of animals in ways that are instrumental to the spiritual welfare of human beings? Does not God as revealed by the Old Testament require sacrifices of animals to appease divine wrath and judgment? 'Then Noah built an altar to the Lord, and took of every animal and of every clean bird, and offered burnt offerings on the altar. And when the Lord smelled the pleasing odour, the Lord said in his heart, "I will never again curse the ground because of man ... neither will I ever again destroy every living creature as I have done"' (Gen. 8.20–22). If this *is* indeed taken to be the real meaning of animal sacrifice, then there can be very little doubt about the low value of animals so envisaged. But is this the right interpretation? How could it be that a God who out of love creates animals would delight in their gratuitous destruction? Unsatisfied with this interpretation, many scholars have questioned its theological basis. As early as 1965, Eric Mascall wrote that

> there has ... been a tendency, which has had the most unfortunate consequences, to assume that the essence of sacrifice consists in the destruction of some valuable object, preferably a living one, in order to honour or to propitiate a deity, a destruction which in the case of an animal victim, will involve its slaying ... It has obtained a firm foothold even in the Christian Church and has provided the guiding concept for many doctrines of the Atonement.

Reviewing early scholarship, Mascall continues: 'It is therefore a matter for deep satisfaction that in recent years there has come to the fore a wider and more positive notion of sacrifice which, while finding a real place for the insights of what might be called the established view, altogether avoids its weaknesses.'[19] This work, principally by Eugene Masure and R. K. Yerkes, has insisted that the basic significance of sacrifice is not the destruction of the creature but its offering to God. Writes Masure, the substance of sacrifice

> is ... the return of the creature to him who has made it for himself so that it may find its end and therefore its happiness in him and for his glory ... Sacrifice is the movement or action by which we try to bring ourselves to God, our end, to find our true beatitude in our union with him. *To sacrifice a thing is to lead it to its end.*[20]

The crucial point here is that far from reinforcing the low value of the sacrificial victim, the ritual actually (though I accept in practice para-doxically) underlines the value of the animal slain and also its acceptance and transformation by God. 'Even here', Mascall explains, 'there is no suggestion that God is glorified by the destruction of his creature, for if it could be literally destroyed there would be nothing left for him to accept and transform.'[21] In short, therefore, the tradition of sacrifice is best seen as the freeing of animal life to be with God, an acknowledgment that it (as with all creatures) belongs not to humans but to God and that God is able to accept and transform its life. Puzzling though this interpretation may be, it is the one most consistent with the other biblical threads concerning the value of animal life and our responsibility for it. Even in the Genesis passage recently recalled, the sacrifice of animals led to the resolve to secure the value of human *and* animal life more firmly (8.20–22).

Within the Jewish tradition, however, the practice of animal sacrifice and its efficacy did not pass without question and protest. 'What to me is the multitude of your sacrifices?' says the Lord in the book of Isaiah. 'I have had enough of burnt offerings of rams, and the fat of fed beasts … I will not listen; your hands are full of blood. Wash yourselves; make yourselves clean; remove the evil of your doings from before my eyes; cease to do evil' (1.11f.; cf. Ps. 50.7 f.). Although many scholars believe that the basis of this objection was cultic rather than ethical, it is not altogether inconceivable that this cultic objection had a moral dimension.[22] Very few if any Christians, however, would find the practice of animal sacrifice acceptable at this present time. This is not because they would wish to deny its historical importance or because they would necessarily find any interpretation of the practice indefensible, but because they believe that the sacrificial tradition has reached its ultimate point and climax in the sacrifice of Christ. He, Jesus Christ, in the true sense offering, acceptance, and transformation, is our sacrificial victim that leads us to God.[23] It is through him, and not through the sacrifices of animals, that we are able to find ourselves in our Father's presence.[24]

It is this point more than any other that needs to transform the Christian understanding not only of sacrifice but of our relationship with the order of creation itself. It is here that we reach a distinctive Christian interpretation. Many theologians have laid great stress upon the transformation of the notion of sacrifice in Christ, but few if any have drawn out its radical implications for our relationship with animals. For what is involved in the life of Christ is both a different order and nature of sacrifice.

In the first place, the inner logic of the sacrifice of Christ is not the sacrifice of the lower to the higher but the higher to the lower. The power of God is expressed in the notion of 'lordship', but the nature of this lordship in the incarnation involves humility, the surrender of absolute power, self-costly loving, a preparedness to suffer, and active compassion towards the weak and helpless. Many strands in the New Testament speak of the condescension, the *katabasis*, of God in taking flesh and experiencing for the sake of love the weakness and frailty of the creature (e.g., Mark 8.32f.; John 13.2f.; II Cor. 8.9). Second, the nature of the sacrifice is not simply that of blood (though Good Friday is real enough) but of life and love. It is pre-eminently the sacrifice of God's love for us wrought mysteriously in the acts of incarnation and atonement.

If this is true, then it must follow that the nature of human dominion or lordship has to be quite different from what we take it to be at present. We must ask again the central christological question: If the omnipotence and power of God are actually expressed in the form of loving condescension towards humans, should we not take this attitude as the model by which we should express ourselves towards the non-human world? If, as Christians have traditionally affirmed, in Christ God was truly reconciling the world through the power of love, should not our exercise of power towards creation be shaped and motivated by this example? This christologically based notion of love in action is so central to orthodox formulations and indeed is cited so often as an exemplar for our relations with our fellow humans that we may be perplexed to know why it has taken Christians so long to see the force of this example as a model for their relationship with the natural world. We may put the matter like this: Under the dispensation of the Old Covenant it was clear that God allowed humans rights to use creation, even though the precise limits of these prerogatives were interpreted ambiguously and differently. But it is not at all clear, as defined under the New Covenant, that humans have these same rights and can use their power with the same confidence. For if full weight is given to the moral exemplar of Christ, then it can be validly held that the unique moral capacities of humans demand of them a loving and costly relationship with the natural world. As we have already argued, our distinctive contribution within the purposes of God the Creator is to make actual and real God's loving design within it.[25]

A Critique of Animal Experiments

We are now in a position where we can confront our question directly: Practically and morally, how should the insight of the worth of creation and of animals in particular help to shape and determine our use of them in science? Three broad conclusions should be reached:

1. *Animals are not expendable for humans.* I mean by this that animals must not be viewed simply as raw materials for our designs, no matter how morally laudable. Animals are not things. They are not simply objects of humans' use or pleasure. They cannot be used in such a way without infringing on the right of their Creator, whose will is such that they should exist as they are within their own terms and limits of existence. Whenever human beings take to themselves the use of animals, they incur great responsibility. I do not conclude that animals may *never* be used in any way that betters humankind. There are a variety of ways in which humans can live in a symbiotic relationship with animals that benefits both parties. But that is surely the point. When animals are used so that their own lives are enhanced, supported, or protected in some way, the motivation is often more than simple human self-seeking. What is not justifiable is the intention to so use and take over the natural life of animals that its reward for humans is seen as its only reason for existing. The doctrine of creation will not allow us unrestricted and unrestrained use of the animal world for human purposes.

In the interdependent creation where, to the naked eye, each species appears to make its way at the expense of others, and where the apparent needs of humans and animals can conflict, our moral uncertainty is likely to be great. I do not wish to evade this point and suppose that conflicts do not occur and that the resolution of them is an easy matter. In this sense it must be clear that neither humans nor animals can possess absolute rights. But, on the other hand, to cause animals avoidable injury, either through death, deprivation, or suffering, must be seen as morally wrong. This at least should, I judge, be the moral norm. I do not say that realizing this norm will be easy, or that it will not require us to make some real sacrifices, or that individuals should not be free to exercise their own consciences within a framework of law. But I hold that we need fresh conviction and moral energy to realize this norm, socially and individually, as a recognition of the value of animals and therefore their moral claim upon us.

The question may be asked, however, whether it is a *necessary* implication of the doctrine of creation and the value of life presupposed by it that harming creation is, when avoidable, wrong? Is it not possible to admire creation as if it were a work of art, for its aesthetic value, without subscribing to a theory of moral limits? Such a view misses the point that humans have responsibility for animals in a way that simply does not pertain to works of art. Animals are valuable *in themselves* by virtue of their creation by God. It is not just that injury to animals reinforces a low view of their value (though it certainly does that) but that it is a practical denial of their intrinsic value. Animals belong to God in a way that makes their significance and value more fundamental even than human artistic creations, inspiring though the latter may be.

2. *Animals are not instrumental to humans.* I mean by this that animals must not be viewed simply as a means to human ends, no matter how morally laudable. Animals are not laboratory tools. Their purpose for existing is not simply to serve the human species. They do not simply exist in some utilitarian relationship to humans whereby they can be seen as fodder for furthering human purposes of life enhancement or enjoyment or happiness. The doctrine of creation stands in opposition to all such wholly humanocentric notions. Humans, as we have indicated, cannot claim to be the total measure of good as regards other living creatures. Again this is not to deny that humans may sometimes use animals for their purposes so long as these purposes are consonant with the theological good of the individual creatures themselves. What they cannot do is assume that their purposes of betterment are always God's purposes. Humans cannot take their needs as always absolute and primary.

I do not want to oversimplify what is clearly a complex area of human/animal interaction. In many areas we do not know the precise significance and purpose of sentient beings. Through ignorance we may do enormous damage; through inactivity we may precipitate adverse conditions for many living beings; and we may often have to judge on what we take to be insufficient or largely intuitional evidence. The effects of what we do to animals in terms of their long-term conditions of life or survival may not be clear to us. All this needs to be granted. But where we have the will and the freedom to do so, it must be wrong to subordinate animal life to human purposes without any regard for their intrinsic value. We need to remind ourselves that in theological terms our use of animals has the nature of trust; we are accountable to God. Animals do not belong to us.

The use of animals for experimentation poses another considerable problem for Christian moralists. For how are we to evaluate the routinized and institutionalized use of millions of animals, bred, reared, and destroyed for experimental purposes annually? Even if some use of animals for experimental purposes were justified, how in turn could this justify the whole institutionalized subjugation of animal life for human purposes on such a vast scale? It is not only the scale but the intention behind such enormous institutional activity that must make us question the disregard for animals implicit in such trade and business. There is an important distinction to be drawn between individual use of animals sometimes prompted by necessity and the subjugation of animals on a huge scale on the assumption that they can be used solely for human ends. I have made this point before, but it is one that cannot be made too strongly. It is clear to me that the value of animals, as understood from the perspective of Christian doctrine, cannot be subordinated, as many scientists appear to believe, at each and every point to some human good, whether it is imagined, hypothetical, or real. Christian moral theology can never be happy with ethical thinking given over entirely to human-centred utilitarian calculation. Some element of calculating the good as we see it is inevitable in moral evaluation, but when that evaluation is dominated by the supposed absolute good of humankind, theological insights are only too easily pushed aside in favour of some supposed common sense humanitarianism.

One further point in this vein needs to be noted. Although the benefits of knowledge gained through much animal experimentation are indeed great (and much anti-experiment propaganda has been sadly misleading on this point I fear), it is by no means clear to me that it can qualify, even in terms of a utilitarian calculus, to be the absolute good. Raising an issue of this kind invites the charge of insensitivity to human sickness and the appalling effects of disease upon human beings, but it has to be disputed whether knowledge, even such beneficial knowledge that can save or prolong human life, has priority over all other kinds. Knowledge of ourselves as moral and spiritual beings is also a moral good. It matters as much that we have knowledge of our ultimate life and destiny and indeed of our moral relationship with the natural world as it does that we have knowledge that will prevent death and alleviate pain. The scientific attempt to absolutize beneficial scientific knowledge over all other forms of knowledge may be regarded as no less excessive than previous theological attempts to fill that category. As Patrick Corbett writes:

> The intellectual founders of the modern world, men like Bacon and Descartes, correctly interpreting the scientific and technological revolution which has eventually produced the industrial societies in which we now live, laid great emphasis on what may be called

analytical or conceptual intelligence, the kind of intelligence which works experience up into explicit concepts and tested propositions, as opposed to the imaginative intelligence displayed, for example, by cats, mothers and poets. In a sense they were right to do so; the development of analytical intelligence is a wonderful and admirable thing and its practical application has yielded many wonderful and admirable results. But we are now coming to realize in many different ways that the emphasis laid upon it in Western thought has been exaggerated. No matter how fascinating it is in itself and how gratifying the power it gives us, to let it dominate our vision of the world is to lose sight of ourselves. The things that make life valuable – love, friendship, strength, dexterity, imagination, peace of mind – owe little to analytical intelligence and are often undermined by intensive cultivation of it.[26]

3. *Animals are not to be sacrificed for humans*. I mean by this that animals must not be seen as lesser beings which while valuable can be traded in for some kind of greater advantage to humans. The historical language of sacrifice is doubly inappropriate when applied to laboratory animals. In the first place, as we have seen from a theological perspective, sacrifice takes place as an offering to God, not to human beings. It is a practice that does not involve the destruction of a being but its liberation and transformation. It can be justified in retrospect on that strict understanding alone. Second, the specifically Christian view of sacrifice must necessarily preclude any offering to God that is not freely given. The sacrifice of Christ was not a propitiation demanded of Christ by an angry God. On the contrary, it was the free offering to God the Father in the cause of love for fellow creatures. It is the sacrifice of love freely given, and not the sacrifice of blood required, that is the distinctly Christian understanding of this matter. In this sense to speak as some scientists still do of 'sacrificing' animals for human well-being is erroneous if not slightly disingenuous. If we are to speak of sacrifice at all in this context it must be the sacrifice of human beings who, in accordance with the moral will of God, freely forego immediate gains for the sake of others.

It is for this reason especially that the direction of this argument moves inexorably against the legalization of experimental procedures on animals. I cannot persuade myself that the *institutionalization* of this practice is compatible with the moral norm I have outlined. This norm is already enshrined in a principle concerning experimentation on human subjects. Article 1.5 of the Declaration of Helsinki adopted by the World Medical Assembly in 1964 (and revised by the same body in 1975) reads: '... concern for the interests of the subject [in human experimentation] must always prevail over the interest of science and society,' and article 111.4 (the final provision of the Declaration) reads: 'In research on man, the interest of science and society should never take precedence over considerations related to the well-being of the subject.'

This Declaration is in turn a development of the Nuremberg Code of 1947 'which was a by-product of a trial of physicians for having performed cruel experiments on prisoners and detainees during the Second World War'.[27] The Code states as its first principle: 'The voluntary consent of the human subject is absolutely essential.' It continues: 'The person involved should have the legal capacity to give consent; should be situated as to be able to exercise free power of choice, without the intervention of any element of force ... or other ulterior form of constraint or coercion.'[28]

Animals, of course, cannot give their consent to scientific procedures performed upon them. But this makes the infliction of injury upon them not easier but equally difficult, if not harder to justify. As Tom Regan explains: 'Risks are not morally transferable to those who do not voluntarily choose to take them.'[29] If the Helsinki principle is valid, I cannot see any good theological grounds for including humans within its provision and not other sentient beings which, while arguably less valuable, are objects of special moral responsibility. The subjugation of any being, human, foetal, or animal, to experimental procedures against its own interests must be morally wrong. This principle needs to be enshrined in law for both humans and animals.

I reach this conclusion with some reluctance. This is not because I am in serious doubt about the rightness of the principle, but for three practical reasons. In the first place, the enhanced awareness of the value of creation and of animals in particular is not simply a matter of law. Obedience to law *per se* is a dubious moral good and may not increase real respect for animals. As I have already argued, law at best can only prevent the worst and protect the weakest.[30] In the second place, there must be some recognition that some, perhaps many scientists, at least in the United Kingdom, dislike experimenting upon animals, and more importantly, a growing number of them are seeking ways to reduce the number they use or find alternative ways of pursuing the same research. Many scientists are more deeply troubled by the use of animals than absolutist animal literature would suggest. When Hans Ruesch, for example, writes, 'Greed, cruelty, ambition, incompetence, vanity, callousness, stupidity, sadism, insanity are the charges that this treatise [his book] levels at the entire practice of vivisection,' I can only bewail his lack of charity.[31] I have no desire to be part of unrestrained attacks on science or scientists, even in the cause of moral principles that I share. In the third place, moral absolutism can often spill over into legalism or self-righteousness. Some people enjoy a good moral condemnation the way others enjoy a good dinner. When we reach strongly held principles that are implicitly critical of the actions of our fellow humans, then we always need to look at ourselves and take stock. As for myself, I see no grounds for self-righteousness in this general area of our treatment of animals. Western society is so bound up with the use and abuse of animals in so many fields of human endeavour that it is impossible for anyone to claim that they are not party, directly or indirectly, to this exploitation either through the products they buy, the food they eat, or the taxes they pay.

Nevertheless, having stated these reservations boldly, it is inevitable that it is to the law that we must turn if we are to prevent the routinized and institutionalized abuse of animals in experimentation. The law should defend the interests of those who are weakest in this matter. People, however, must be free to disagree about the appropriate strategy for that end, and the appropriate methods that should be employed in order to advance it, but it is clear that the aim *should be* the end of institutionalized animal experimentation.

I realize that this whole way of approaching the matter may appear strange to many Christians who have been led to believe that the notion of dominion gave humans exclusive rights over the animal world. There is, it is true, a whole tradition of Christian theology that has advanced itself by putting stress upon human uniqueness and thereby separating responsibilities to humankind from responsibilities to creation.[32] Something in this tradition has value, but much of it we can now see was vitally flawed by its extreme emphasis on the prerogatives of humans without a sufficient appreciation of our responsibility towards creation. I can only plead for an increased appreciation that theological work is in part at least the result of experience and interpretation. At one time and in one place one insight may be pressed to the reduction or exclusion of another; for a time one vital insight may be lost or buried under erroneous interpretation. Theology is ever working towards holding together a range of insights, the full development of which always lies in the future. As one theologian wrote as early as 1977:

In the past theology has often been slow to respond to new points of insight and sensitivity – though later both its own vision and its own heart have been enlarged by them: to sensitivity, for instance, about the iniquity of slavery and the rights of coloured people. Perhaps the theology of our own age will be convicted of myopia if it does not spend serious reflection upon the new kind of reverence for nature which is appearing among us. The present seems an opportune time for reflection. For the wholly anthropocentric theology of the last 15 or 20 years has clearly run out of inspiration and is degenerating towards triviality.[33]

I want to conclude, therefore, by suggesting that the minimum we have sought to deduce from the concept of the value of creation, considerable though that minimum is, cannot be theologically sufficient. The notion of moral generosity previously elaborated[34] is indispensable here. Too many moralists in the animal field (myself included), eager to delineate some minimum moral status for animals in the hope of protecting them from unnecessary ill, have failed to lay before themselves the full positive weight of the value of creation. To recognize the value of creation we have not only to prevent evil but also to promote good. Therefore in each and every situation we must ask what good our presence can bring, and what care, aid, and protection we can offer to the created world. Not just how far or in what circumstance we can prevent the worst possible happening, but rather how we can express in a positive way the very highest moral behaviour of which we are capable towards animals. In this regard we must question whether our relationships with animals should be rightly influenced by straightforward utilitarian calculations of the human good presupposed, for example, by animal researchers. We need to be careful lest our own exalted moral and theological reasoning gives us a basis for the justification of a spirit of moral meanness towards the created world.

7

Hunting as the Anti-Gospel of Predation

Allied to the view that animals are here for our use is the idea that animals are here for our enjoyment. It is astonishing to think that this idea should have had such widespread currency within the Christian tradition that St Francis de Sales, to take only one example, could have supposed that hunting was one of those 'innocent recreations' which we 'may always make good use of' in developing our spiritual life.[1] Far from being 'innocent' or morally neutral, I argue that hunting represents the anti-gospel of Jesus our Predator. Few, I think, have really grasped what it means theologically to justify the destruction of sentient life simply for the sport involved in it. Only if parasitical nature is to be celebrated as divinely-purposed existence can hunting for amusement be justified. Whatever the difficulties in conceiving of a world without predation, to intensify and heighten – without any ethical necessity – the parasitical forces in our world is to plunge creation further into that darkness from which the Christian hope is that we shall all, human and animal, be liberated.

Hunting with Jesus

Imagine you are a hunter – with a difference. A Bible-believing, God-fearing, Christian hunter. You are up at 4.30 a.m. in your hunting cabin. Your day begins with some self-examination. 'Who are you today?' you ask yourself. You are aware that not all Christians will approve of your planned activities. But not only do you love hunting, you also love the Lord. You know God loves you and blesses you. You are assured that if you can 'hunt with Jesus, it doesn't matter what anyone else says or believes'. 'I hunt with God as my companion,' you say to yourself, 'knowing He will direct me and keep me safe.'

As you get dressed, you spiritually prepare yourself. Nothing can be done right, you think to yourself, 'unless I include God in it and that applies to hunting too'. 'Remember, in the woods, Satan has a gun!' When you sit eating your breakfast, you put your Bible and the state game laws in front of you and 'you vow to obey them both that day'. The Christian hunter obeys both the 'law of God' and the 'law of man'. Moreover, before you leave your cabin, you write out lines of scripture on individual pieces of card to memorize at certain times in the day.

As a Christian hunter, you abhor the 'slob' hunters. Slob hunters are those who shoot indiscriminately and without regard to property rights. You used to be one of these, but now you have seen that it is impossible to testify to Jesus on the hunting field and also to be a slob hunter. Jesus, you see, demands the best. While as a Christian hunter you love hunting, you also admit to an element of 'sadness' in being responsible for the death of another creature. You comfort yourself with the thought that death is not an 'end' for the animal but a 'glorious beginning'.

As a Christian then, you kill carefully, not like the slobs. You handle your rifle with care and caution always, doing your best to shoot cleanly with the first bullet. What you kill will always end up as meat in your freezer. As you wait patiently on your tree stand for the Lord to send you a legal buck, you draw inspiration from eternal verities:

> you think a lot while you're blending in. You memorise the Bible verse you've propped behind a twig ... Maybe you even wonder what God thinks of you right now. He could spook every animal in the forest any-time he wanted to, but right now everything seems to be pretty cool with him. It's not too hard to know what God expects, if you know your Bible. The Bible never changes, because God never changes.

When it comes to the kill, you pray that the Lord will position the buck precisely to enable a clean shot. The Lord obliges. When its all over, 'you take a minute to thank Him for sending you this animal'.

Some of you may think that the conscientious Christian hunter here described is a figment of my imagination. Not so. The narrative is taken from an unusual book entitled *The Christian Hunter's Survival Guide* published as one of a series of 'Power Books'.[2] The author is himself a clergyman, Pastor William H. Ammon. Pastor Ammon resides in Pennsylvania and is executive director of an organization called Sportsmen for Christ.

Conscientious Christian Killing

How are we to evaluate morally and theologically the activity of this Christian hunter? I have chosen to concentrate on Pastor Ammon quite deliberately because those of us opposed to hunting have the unfortunate tendency to choose the worst possible examples among the hunting fraternity. The tendency to misrepresent, to overstate, to present the opponent in the worst possible light, is of course present on both sides of this debate. When Pastor Ammon, for example, cites Cleveland Amory as applauding the harm done to hunters themselves in 'hunting accidents' – and therefore of valuing animal life over human life – I doubt whether he has fully and properly represented Amory's position.[3] Notwithstanding this little exaggeration, Ammon is clearly a conscientious Christian. Those of us having a non-fundamentalist view may smile from time to time at what appears to be the naivety of some of his biblical interpretations – each chapter of his book is concluded with a list of 'memory verses' many of which seem to bear little or no relation to the issue in hand – but it would be impossible to doubt the obvious sincerity of the position he advocates.

Neither can we deny the moral seriousness and probity of the narrative presented to us. Unlike many, Pastor Ammon has pondered the morality of hunting. However defensive some of his arguments may appear, he admits that all is not well on the hunting field. 'It's disturbing to realize', he writes, 'that many hunters are as every bit as bad as the public thinks they are.'[4] He recommends strict observance of game laws including respect for quotas, and suggests that hunters should 'police' their own ranks. 'A real hunter won't hunt with a slob,' he maintains. Ammon converted from such slobbery. He feels sure that Jesus would agree with the line of Peter Singer that 'If a being suffers there can be no moral justification for refusing to take that suffering into consideration.'[5] Ammon is in favour of reducing wherever possible the suffering which hunting inevitably entails for the animals concerned.

Neither is Ammon a sport hunter in a way that many of his colleagues are. Of course he loves hunting and finds it thrilling. But whereas previously he shot indiscriminately, he now only shoots legally and only what is edible. 'If I am not going to eat it, I don't shoot it,' he maintains.[6] He honestly acknowledges that his moral scruples are not widely shared. For example: 'Some hunters justifiably argue my buck-only principle is poor deer management – they're right; it's just the way my conscience leads.'[7]

Moreover, Ammon is, despite what he says, sensitive to criticism by fellow Christians. He is aware of how a 'good percentage of the Christians he desires fellowship with would consider him a blood-thirsty Bambi killer if he told them of his hunting'.[8] Because of this resentment, some Christian hunters – we are told – hardly ever talk about their pursuits after church and some desist from going to church at all. Ammon very frankly describes how he felt guilty emerging from his parsonage house in hunting clothes and how he went to elaborate lengths to avoid being seen in camouflage gear by members of his congregation. But sensitivity has its limits and Ammon now feels that the time has come to testify both to Jesus and to the moral acceptability of hunting.

I do not want in any way to laugh or sneer at Pastor Ammon. Although I regard his moral and theological positions as naive and untenable, until hunting is finally abolished, I wish there were more conscientious people like Pastor Ammon on the hunting field. None of us, it seems to me, should shun moral sensitivity from any quarter, remembering especially that however morally advanced we may think we are, it is probably the case that each of us still has moral blindspots on one issue or another.

Given this weight of self-disclosed moral and religious sensibility, is there a decisive theological critique to be mounted against him? I think there is.

Our critique should properly begin not by disputing Ammon's seriousness, sensibility or sincerity, but rather by recalling his words on the subject of death. 'As a Christian,' he writes, 'I see death as a glorious beginning, not an end.'[9] In one sense Ammon is of course right. Christian belief is marked by a refusal to see life as terminated by physical death. However difficult this belief may be for many living in the post-Christian West, it is inconceivable that historical Christianity could have survived – and still survive – without such a belief. And yet this belief has not altered the fact that this tradition has also been characterized at one and the same time by an intense valuing of each and every human life, so much so that nowhere is human murder countenanced within moral theology. Seeing death as a 'glorious beginning' has not prevented Christianity from opposing murder to humans; why should it do so in the case of animals? Ammon interestingly (and, in my opinion, rightly) asks whether: 'If life is eternal for a saved man, why not for a creature who never sinned against the nature God gave him?'[10] Leaving aside the question of animal immortality, if we ask why it should be that the death of an innocent – possibly mortal yet certainly sentient – creature should not be inimical to the Creator of that life, we are, it seems, left with a void. How are we to reconcile the recognition and celebration of this God-given sentient life with its summary destruction?

One answer that Ammon may give is that such killing is not 'wanton'.

'A person who kills an animal and then lets it lie and rot or throws it away is wasting God's creation,' argues Ammon, 'and he continues: 'That turns hunting into wanton killing which is a sin.'[11] I agree with Ammon that wantonness is indeed a sin but then so is *all* hunting for sport or meat. Since there is no strict necessity in either (we can live perfectly healthy and happy lives without both) it is difficult to avoid the conclusion that the sheer wantonness represented by the unnecessary activity of hunting constitutes nothing less than an offence to God.

Ammon avoids this conclusion by looking in two directions. The first is to biblical authority. 'Thou shalt not kill' he argues applies only to humans. In context, there is no doubt that he is right. In *this* context at least it is safe to assume that the divine command properly concerns human beings alone. But if we are to appeal to biblical evidence, we cannot properly let the matter rest there. Whilst it is true that at one stage some biblical writers saw meat eating as a divine permission (due to human weakness say some biblical scholars), it is also the case that later reflection – represented in Genesis and the prophetic books such as Hosea and Isaiah – held that meat eating was contrary to God's original will and/or was to be transformed into a higher state of peaceful existence in the future.[12] To overlook these varied but consistent passages is to play false to the complexity of theological reflection as represented in the Old Testament. We can admit of course that different views can be held about the authority of these later reflections. We can admit to the plausibility of divergent views. But what we should not do is to ignore or silence contrary views, or worse still, to present the ambiguity of the biblical material as though while God's mind may not change the biblical writers changed theirs. I shall return to the question of biblical perspectives before I conclude.

Jesus our Predator

The second direction in which Ammon looks is to some sense of human primacy in creation and that therefore eating animals is God's will. 'God meant man to be different from the earth's animals, over which he was to be dominant. A hunter doesn't go out and kill a "brother animal" when he hunts; he takes game that God has provided for his table ...'[13] It is this appeal to the dominance of humankind and therefore to the legitimization of the predator/prey relation that I now wish to turn. For it is this perception that theology must underwrite such a relationship that I most want to question.

Ammon is certainly not alone in his view that predator/prey relations are compatible with, or are sanctioned by, Christian theology. Ammon occupies a place which is also cohabited by what seems an increasing number of eco-theologians. Two examples must suffice. The first is from the work of Richard Cartwright Austin, a prolific writer on environmental theology with no less than five books to his credit. He writes perceptively about the need to be sensitized to nature and to avoid cruelty. In the context of a moving meditation on a fish eagle taking its prey, Austin extols the beauty of predation:

> Now I think that death may be part of the goodness of God's creation, so long as death and life remain in balance with each other. To eat, and finally to be eaten, are part of the blessing of God.[14]

In case it is thought that this is an eccentric view, I choose as my second example that well-known theologian and exponent of creation spirituality, Matthew Fox. In a recent interview with Jonathon Porritt, he is asked why he ascribes both equality and intrinsic value to *all* species. While he argues that 'the being of the whale is just as sacred as the being of the Queen of England', he also insists that

> the other reality is that one of the laws of the Universe is that we all eat and get eaten. In fact, I call this the Eucharistic law of the Universe, even Divinity gets eaten in this world. And so the key is not whether we are going to be doing some dying in the process of being here, but whether we kill reverently. And that, of course, means with gratitude. You know, in the Christian tradition, it's interesting that the sacrifice of Divinity is called eucharist, that is, 'thank you', gratitude. Gratitude is, I think, the test of whether we are living reverently this dance of the equality of being on the one hand, but also the need to sacrifice and be sacrificed on the other.[15]

Notice how in all three writers, Ammon, Austin and Fox, though especially in Fox, our perception of God's will is tied to what seems God's intended order of things, even to what 'the laws of nature' supposedly reveal. A 'good' theology, it is supposed, will conform itself to these 'laws' of nature, and – in the case of Austin at least – perceive God's blessing in them. In short, the gospel of 'hunting with Jesus' is a gospel of Predation. Life eating life is not some unfortunate aspect of the natural world to be tolerated in the meantime between creation and consummation. Rather, God actually wills and blesses a self-murdering system of survival. God's will *is* death.

The first thing that should be said in response to this view of nature is that it is by no means certain that it is the whole picture. Whilst it is true that there seems to be cruelty, aggression and violence in the natural world (humans included) it is also true that there is cooperation, mutual aid, even possible altruism between species, animal as well as human. It seems to me that the challenging view of Peter Kropotkin that co-operation as much as competition characterizes the natural order has never really been met.[16] At the very most the predator/prey view of nature has only half of the truth.

Nevertheless, I will stay with the pessimistic view of nature for the sake of argument. For if it was really true that predation is God's will, it would have to follow for Christians that the life of Jesus – what after all is the self-disclosure of God – manifested and vindicated this predator/prey relationship.

Such a gospel would be substantially different from the one we currently have. Jesus would not just be eating some fishes, but feasting on calves and lambs. Jesus, according to the Predator Gospel, would be the butcher *par excellence*. He would be the one who far from desisting from animal sacrifice actually encouraged his disciples to excel in it. Instead of driving out the sacrificial animals from the Temple, the Jesus of the Predator Gospel would drive them in. The line that most characterizes his ministry would not be 'the good shepherd lays down his life for the sheep' but rather 'the good shepherd slaughters – with gratitude – as many sheep as he can'. Far from beginning his ministry, according to Mark (1.13), 'with the wild beasts' and thereby symbolizing reconciliation with nature, the Predator Jesus would be 'with the wild beasts' with bow and arrow. Instead of commending the rescuing of a fallen animal from the pit, Predator Jesus would point to the inevitability of God's far-reaching plan of death, disease and decay.

Indeed, since predation is God's 'blessing' – and we are assured by Fox that all species have equal value from whales to the Queen of England – the Predator Jesus would offer a singular example in the human realm too. Far from consorting with sinners or excusing prosti-tutes, the Predator Jesus would be the first to cast the stone. Instead of healing the sick, the Predator Jesus could only approve of the efficiency of God-given ecological systems. Instead of raising Lazarus from the dead, the Predator Jesus could only comment that death is God's blessing. Instead of preaching the good news of the coming kingdom of God, the proclamation would run: 'Eat and be eaten'.

And as for all the stuff about the primacy of love, the value of humility, and the power of forgiveness, another commandment would be given to us: 'Obey the Law of Death' or simply: 'Love Death'. Remember, killing is spiritual experience. When performed with thanksgiving, you are only God's priestly agent in the cosmic forces of renewal and sacrifice.

I have allowed myself some literary licence in reconstituting the gospel of Jesus our Predator only to show the incontestable incompatibility between such a gospel and the real gospel of liberation offered by Jesus Christ. Now I do not deny that there are one or two problems here to be ironed out. Did Jesus really eat fish and if he did were they sentient creatures? Did Jesus really send the demons into the Gadarene swine? And what about the plight of the fig tree who seems to have been rather severely punished for what may well have been poor human cultivation of its affairs?

I do not deny the difficulty and ambiguity in these stories within the Gospels, and since we are dealing with documents themselves written some thirty to sixty years after the events described, we should not be surprised if some details of understanding are no longer recoverable. But overall, and without the faintest fear of contradiction, we can with confidence proclaim that the Predator view of Jesus is untenable.

The Sacrifice for All

What are we to make then of Matthew Fox's interpretation of the eucharist as a vindication of predation? According to Fox 'even Divinity gets eaten in this world'. Leaving aside for a moment whether holy communion can be quite understood in these literal terms, what Fox fails to indicate is that divinity *allows itself* to be eaten. I do not dispute that Jesus' death on a cross is a real sacrifice, even that the eucharist is a means of participating in the renewing power of this sacrifice, but we need to distinguish between being prepared to die and being murdered. God is no murderer. Jesus chooses the cross rather than betray God. But God does not murder Jesus. Fox fails to comprehend the fundamentally most significant point of all which is this: Humans are the species that can and sometimes should sacrifice themselves for God's cause whereas precisely because they cannot choose to sacrifice themselves, the sacrifice of animals is always murder. I mean by murder here the involuntary, unsought death of any sentient creature.

It is a fundamental, possibly disingenuous, mistake to associate the free sacrificial offering of Christ with the enforced killing of other creatures. It is a double mistake because Christians actually came to see the sacrifice of Christ as that which made the former sacrifices of animals redundant, even theologically perverse. The significance of the eucharistic meal, therefore, is not the perpetuation of the old world of animal sacrifice but precisely our liberation from it. As the well-known lines from the Easter Anthems (recited daily in Anglican Evening Prayer) put it:

> Christ our Passover has been sacrificed for us:
> so let us celebrate the feast,
> not with the old leaven of corruption and wickedness
> but with the unleaven bread of sincerity and truth ...
> See yourselves therefore as dead to sin
> and alive to God in Christ Jesus our Lord.[17]

What the sacrifice of Christ, represented in the ritual of the eucharist, is seen to effect is a new possibility and order of creation in which we can be free from our 'old natures' – indeed nature itself – and live together in a spirit of humility and self-sacrifice. In short: the eucharist is not an invitation to sacrifice but to be sacrificed. It is here that I find myself in agreement with Ammon that humanity can and must be distinguished from animals, not because of some supposed right to kill, but rather because we humans have the power to serve creation. The hope for humanity is that one day they might indeed recognize that they are made in God's image and learn self-sacrifice for the rest of the created world.

A further connection should be made. The eucharist has been traditionally regarded as the messianic feast *par excellence*, even a foretaste of heaven. As the first Christians shared the cup and broke the bread they became convinced that in Christ a new order of creation was made possible. Because of this they also shared the Jewish hope that one day all creation would be free from predation and violence and that even and especially non-human animals would share what St Paul calls 'the freedom of the children of God' through 'deliverance from bondage to decay' (Rom. 8.18–24, RSV). This hope that a new beginning was possible for all nature was born in them because of the realization that even the sinful nature of human beings could be transformed. Thus Christian eschatology developed its own notion of a transfigured new heaven and earth. Some of the earliest eucharistic prayers in, for example, the Apostolic Constitutions are characterized by a conviction concerning the eventual restoration and completion of all things – indeed one of those prayers specifically offers the eucharist for 'all things'.[18]

Deliverance from Bondage

As is so often the case, the problem with biblical fundamentalists is that they are not actually biblical enough. What overwhelmingly characterizes both the Old and the New Testaments is the view that creation is not yet finished; it is still in the process of being made. What God wants us and creation to be is a hope as yet unfulfilled. Almost all New Testament scholars agree that the thrust of Jesus' teaching was eschatological, that is, concerned with the eventual fulfilment of God's purposes on earth. 'On earth as it is in heaven' is, after all, the prayer Jesus taught to his disciples. The biblical orientation is not to baptize the 'laws of the universe' as the purposes of God but rather to look to their transformation and fulfilment. If we are to appeal to the life and teaching of Jesus as the revelation of God, we cannot avoid the fact that so much of his life challenges, if not contradicts, the order of the world as we know it.

From this standpoint, to be involved in wanton killing can only be judged deplorable. It is, in the words of Edward Carpenter, 'to fall back into that bondage, into that predatory system of nature, from which the Christian hope has always been that not only [humanity] but the natural order itself is to be released and redeemed'.[19] That the natural order is characterized – to some degree – by predatory forces will always present for Christians a problem and a mystery though some plausible explanations may be possible.[20] But one thing is certain. Since in Christ there is a new creation, there can be no justification for humanity to increase, exacerbate and intensify that predatory system itself. The truth is that, whatever may have been the situation for our forbears, we can live differently, and we should. The Christian view has frequently been focussed on the centrality of humanity in creation. It may yet be possible, in ways we scarcely understand, for creation to free itself from bondage by humans releasing themselves from their own.

For those who regard this possibility as rather improbable, I advocate some reflection upon the methods frequently employed in some forms of hunting: in fox, otter, mink and deer hunting, beagling, hare coursing, bear and badger baiting, cock-fighting, and even some forms of shooting with dogs, 'sportsmen' devote themselves to intensifying any natural antipathy between one species and another. Hounds are taught how to chase and kill with consummate ruthlessness or else they themselves are punished or killed. Cocks are drugged and given artificial spurs in order that they may fight with greater wounding power. Terrier dogs are trained to terrorize and mutilate other animal species. In these and other ways humans do not simply 'imitate' (as some hunters claim) the fallen order of creation. On the contrary, in these examples humans concentrate, heighten and intensify whatever violent propensities there may be in animals to their quintessential point of refined and maximum cruelty. Hunters do not 'imitate' the cruelties of nature: they create them.

Pastor Ammon writes movingly of the day when God saved him from being 'king of the slobs':

> It was a boring day, with no game birds and no rabbits, and my Dad and I had sunk to shooting squirrels and pigeons – anything that moved. Suddenly there was a fluttering on the ground to my left. My heart sank when I saw a beautiful little white fantailed pigeon lying there, a victim of my boredom. You call yourself an animal lover? I heard my heart say. Look what you've done! I looked inside myself that day and truly hated what I saw: selfishness, greed, irresponsibility, and a lot more that terrified me. My life changed that day because of that pigeon; God used death to bring me to Him and deliver me from being a slob hunter.[21]

It may not be inconceivable that the same God who can bring Pastor Ammon to desist from shooting pigeons may well have greater conversions in mind for the future.

8

Vegetarianism as a Biblical Ideal

Of all the ethical challenges arising from animal theology, vegetarianism can arguably claim to have the strongest biblical support. Even the acceptance of the minimalist principle of avoiding injury to sentients wherever possible renders killing for gastronomic pleasure unacceptable. In this chapter, I chart the outline of the argument drawn from Genesis and Isaiah while also taking account of the fact that Jesus is not depicted as a vegetarian in the canonical Gospels. Even if we accept that Genesis 9 permits meat-eating as a special concession to human sinfulness, it still remains an open question as to whether carnivorousness can be justified as a matter of principle.

Food of Paradise

And God said, 'Behold, I have given you every plant yielding seed which is upon the face of all the earth, and every tree with seed in its fruit; you shall have them for food. And to every beast of the earth, and to every bird of the air, and to everything that creeps on the earth, everything that has the breath of life, I have given every green plant for food' (Gen. 1.29–30, RSV).

And God blessed Noah and his sons, and said to them, '... Every moving thing that lives shall be food for you; as I gave you the green plants, I give you everything' (Gen. 9.1–4, RSV).

At first glance, these two passages may be taken as epitomizing the difficulty of appealing to scripture in the contemporary debate about animal rights. The sheer contradictoriness of these statements presses itself upon us. Genesis 1 clearly depicts vegetarianism as divine command. Indeed 'everything' that has the breath of life in it, is given 'green plant for food'. Genesis 9, however, reverses this command quite specifically. '[A]s I gave you the green plants, I give you everything' (9.3). In the light of this, the question might not unreasonably be posed:

Cannot both vegetarians and carnivores appeal to scripture for justification and both with *equal* support?

In order to unravel this conundrum we have first of all to appreciate that the community whose spokesperson wrote Genesis 1 were not themselves vegetarians. Few appreciate that Genesis 1 and 2 are each the products of much later reflection by the biblical writers themselves. How is it then that the very people who were not vegetarian imagined a beginning of time when all who lived were vegetarian (herbivore to be precise) by divine command?

To appreciate this perspective we need to recall the major elements of the first creation saga. God creates a world of great diversity and fertility. Every living creature is given life and space (Gen. 1. 9–10, 24–25). Earth to live on and blessing to enable life itself (1.22). Living creatures are pronounced good (1.25). Humans are made in God's image (1.27), given dominion (1.26–29), and then prescribed a vegetarian diet (1.29–30). God then pronounces that everything was 'very good' (1.31). Together the whole creation rests on the sabbath with God (2.2–3). When examined in this way, we should see immediately that Genesis 1 describes a state of paradisal existence. There is no hint of violence between or among different species. Dominion, so often interpreted as justifying killing, actually precedes the command to be vegetarian. Herb-eating dominion is hardly a license for tyranny. The answer seems to be then that even though the early Hebrews were neither pacifists nor vegetarians, they were deeply convicted of the view that violence between humans and animals, and indeed between animal species themselves, was not God's original will for creation.

But if this is true, how are we to reconcile Genesis 1 with Genesis 9, the vision of original peacefulness with the apparent legitimacy of killing for food? The answer seems to be that as the Hebrews began to construct the story of early human beginnings, they were struck by the prevalence and enormity of human wickedness. The stories of Adam and Eve, Cain and Abel, Noah and his descendants are testimonies to the inability of humankind to fulfil the providential purposes of God in creation. The issue is made explicit in the story of Noah:

> Now the earth was corrupt in God's sight, and the earth was filled with violence. And God saw the earth, and behold, it was corrupt; for all flesh had corrupted their way upon the earth. And God said to Noah, 'I have determined to make an end of all flesh; for the earth is filled with violence through them' (Gen. 6.11–14, RSV).

The radical message of the Noah story (often overlooked by commentators) is that God would rather not have us be at all if we must be violent. It is violence itself within every part of creation that is the pre-eminent mark of corruption and sinfulness. It is not for nothing that God concludes that: 'I am sorry that I have made them' (Gen. 6.7).

Ambiguous Permission

It is in *this* context – subsequent to the Fall and the Flood – that we need to understand the permission to kill for food in Genesis 9. It reflects entirely the situation of the biblical writers at the time they were writing. Killing – of both humans as well as animals – was simply inevitable given the world as it is and human nature as it is. Corruption and wickedness had made a mess of God's highest hopes for creation. There just had to be some accommodation to human sinfulness. 'Every moving thing shall be food for you; and as I gave you the green plants, I give you everything' (Gen. 9.3). For many students of the Bible this seems to have settled the matter of whether humans can be justified in killing animals for food. In the end, it has been thought, God allows it. And there can be no doubt that throughout the centuries this view has prevailed. Meat eating has become the norm. Vegetarians, especially Christian vegetarians, have survived from century to century to find themselves a rather beleagued minority. The majority view can be summed up in this beautifully prosaic line of Calvin:

> For it is an insupportable tyranny, when God, the Creator of all things, has laid open to us the earth and the air, in order that we may thence take food as from his storehouse, for these to be shut up from us by mortal man, who is not able to create even a snail or a fly.[1]

What Calvin appears to overlook, however, as do many in the Christian tradition, is that the permission to kill for food in Genesis 9 is far from unconditional or absolute:

> Only you shall not eat flesh with its life, that is, its blood. For your lifeblood I will surely require a reckoning; of every beast I will require it and of man ... (Gen. 9.4–5, RSV).

Understanding these lines is far from straightforward. At first sight these qualificatory lines might be seen as obliterating the permission itself. After all, who can take animal life without the shedding of blood? Who can kill without the taking of blood, that is, the life itself? In asking these questions we move to the heart of the problem. For the early Hebrews life was symbolized by, even constituted by, blood itself. To kill *was* to take blood. And yet it is precisely *this* permission which is denied.

It is not surprising then that commentators have simply passed over these verses suggesting that some ritual, symbolic significance was here entertained but one which in no way substantially affected the divine allowance to kill. But this, I suggest, is to minimize the significance of these verses. Re-reading these verses in the light of their original context should go rather like this: The world in which you live has been corrupted. And yet God has not given up on you. God has signified a new relationship – a covenant with you – despite all your violence and unworthiness. Part of this covenant involves a new regulation concerning diet. What was previously forbidden can now – in the present circumstances – be allowed. You may kill for food. But you may kill only on the understanding that you remember that the life you kill is not your own – it belongs to God. You must not misappropriate what is not your own. As you kill what is not your own – either animal or human life – so you need to remember that for every life you kill you are personally accountable to God.[2]

If this reading is correct, and I believe few scholars would now dissent from this interpretation, it will be seen immediately that Genesis 9 does not grant humankind some absolute right to kill animals for food. Indeed, properly speaking, there is no *right* to kill. God allows it only under the conditions of necessity. A recent statement by the Union of Liberal and Progressive Synagogues expresses it this way: 'Only after the Flood (contends Gen. 9.3) was human consumption of animals permitted and that was later understood as a concession, both to human weakness and to the supposed scarcity of edible vegetation.'[3] John Austin Baker similarly concludes: 'The Old Testament... does nothing to justify the charge that it represents an exploitative, humanly egoistical attitude to nature. Although it recognizes man's preying on nature as a fact, it characterizes that fact as a mark of man's decline from the first perfect intentions of God for him.'[4]

To give a more complete account of biblical themes requires us to move on from Genesis 1 and 2, to Isaiah 11. We need to appreciate that while killing was sometimes thought to be justifiable in the present time, biblical writers were also insistent that there would come another time when such killing was unnecessary. This is the time variously known as the 'future hope of Israel' or the 'Messianic Age'. Isaiah speaks of the one who will establish justice and equity and universal peace. One of the characteristics of this future age is the return to the existence envisaged by Genesis 1 before the Fall and the Flood:

> The wolf shall dwell with the lamb, and the leopard shall lie down with the kid, and the calf and the lion and the fatling together, and a little child shall lead them. The cow and the bear shall feed; their young shall lie down together; and the lion shall eat straw like the ox. The sucking child shall play over the hole of the asp, and the weaned child shall put his hand on the adder's den. They shall not hurt or destroy in all my holy mountain; for the earth shall be full of the knowledge of the Lord as the waters cover the sea (Isa. 11. 6–9, RSV).

It seems therefore that while the early Hebrews were neither vegetarians nor pacifists, the ideal of the peaceable kingdom was never lost sight of. In the end, it was believed, the world would one day be restored according to God's original will for all creation. Note, for example, how the vision of peaceable living also extends to relations between animals themselves. Not only, it seems, are humans to live peaceably with animals, but also formerly aggressive animals are to live peaceably with other animals.

We may sum up the main elements as follows: Killing for food appears essential in the world as we now know it influenced as it is by corruption and wickedness. But such a state of affairs is not as God originally willed it. Even when we kill under situations of necessity we have to remember that the lives we kill do not belong to us and that we are accountable to God. Moreover, God's ultimate will for creation shall prevail. Whatever the present circumstances, one day all creation, human and animal, shall live in peace. As Anthony Phillips writes: 'While the Old Testament recognizes that this is not an ideal world, and makes concessions until the messianic kingdom comes, it remains man's duty to do all in his power to reverence animal life.'[5]

Living without Violence

It should now be seen that far from being confused and contradictory, biblical narratives on killing for food have not only internal integrity but also relevance to the contemporary debate about animal rights and vegetarianism. There are three ethical challenges in particular that we should grapple with.

The first thing that should be noted is that these biblical perspectives do not minimize the gravity of the act of killing animals. So often in our heavily industrialized societies we think of animals, especially farm animals, as merely food machines or commodities that are to be bought or sold for human consumption. This presumed, institutionalized *right* does not fit easily alongside the covenant of grace. Genesis 1 specifically speaks of animal life as that which 'has the breath of life' (1.30). This life is a gift from God. It does not belong to human beings. It may be used only with the greatest reserve and in remembrance of the One from whose creative hands it comes. Those who wish to use animals frivolously or with no regard for their God-given worth cannot easily claim Genesis in support.

Karl Barth is instructive on this point and deserves to be read in full:

> If there is a freedom of man to kill animals, this signifies in any case the adoption of a qualified and in some sense enhanced responsibility. If that of his lordship over the living beast is serious enough, it takes on a new gravity when he sees himself compelled to express his lordship by depriving it of its life. He obviously cannot do this except under the pressure of necessity. Far less than all the other things which he dares to do in relation to animals, may this be ventured unthinkingly and as though it were self-evident. He must never treat this need for defensive and offensive action against the animal world as a natural one, nor include it as a normal element in his thinking or conduct. He must always shrink from this possibility even when he makes use of it. It always contains the sharp counter-question: Who are you, man, to claim that you must venture this to maintain, support, enrich and beautify your own life? What is there in your life that you feel compelled to take this aggressive step in its favour? We cannot but be reminded of the perversion from which the whole historical existence of the creature suffers and the guilt of which does not really reside in the beast but ultimately in man himself.[6]

The second challenge is that we have no biblical warrant for claiming killing as God's will. God's will is for peace. We need to remember that even though Genesis 9 gives permission to kill for food it does so only on the basis that we do not misappropriate God-given life. Genesis 9 posits divine reckoning for the life of every beast taken even under this new dispensation (9.5). The question may not unnaturally be asked: How long can this divine permission last? Karl Barth writes that 'it is not only understandable but necessary that the affirmation of this whole possibility (of killing for food) should always have been accompanied by a radical protest against it'. And yet he concludes: 'It may well be objected against a vegetarianism which presses in this direction that it represents a wanton anticipation of what is described by Isa. 11 and Rom. 8 as existence in the new aeon for which we hope.'[7] Whatever may be the merits of Barth's arguments here, it should be clear that Barth cannot and does not claim that killing is God's will. On the contrary it stands in direct contrast to the 'new aeon for which we hope' or, as he puts it elsewhere, 'under a caveat'.[8] In short: even though killing may be sometimes permissible, God will not tolerate it for ever.

In this respect it is interesting that one highly regarded Talmudic scholar, Abraham Isaac Kook, maintains that the most spiritually satisfying way of reading the practical biblical injunctions concerning killing is in terms of preparation for a new dawn of justice for animals. 'The free movement of the moral impulse to establish justice for animals generally and the claim for their rights from mankind', he argues, 'are hidden in a natural psychic sensibility in the deeper layers of the Torah.' Given the corruption of humankind, it was natural and inevitable that moral attention had first to be paid to the regulation of human conduct towards other humans. But in Kook's view the various injunctions concerning the selection and preparation of meat (in for example Lev. 17.13; Ezek. 16.63; Lev. 22.28 and Deut. 22.26–27) were commandments 'to regulate the eating of meat, in steps that will take us to the higher purpose'. And what is this higher purpose? None other it seems than universal peace and justice. Kook maintains that just as the embracing of democratic ideals came late within religious thinking 'so will the hidden yearning to act justly towards animals emerge at the proper time'.[9]

The third challenge to be grasped is that those who wish now to adopt a vegetarian or vegan life-style have solid biblical support. Biblical vegetarians will not say, 'It has *never been* justifiable to kill animals.' Rather they should say, 'It is *not now* necessary to kill for food as it was once thought necessary.' The biblical case for vegetarianism does not rest on the view that killing may never be allowable in the eyes of God, rather on the view that killing is always a grave matter. When we have to kill to live we may do so, but when we do not, we should live otherwise. It is vital to appreciate the force of this argument. In past ages many – including undoubtedly the biblical writers themselves – have thought that killing for food was essential in order to live. But as I pointed out in chapter 5, we now know that – at least for those now living in the rich

West – it is perfectly possible to sustain a healthy diet without any recourse to flesh products. This may not have always been true in the past. Until comparatively recently conventional wisdom was always that meat was essential to live well.

Those individuals who opt for vegetarianism can do so in the knowledge that they are living closer to the biblical ideal of peaceableness than their carnivorous contemporaries. The point should not be minimized. In many ways it is difficult to know how we can live more peaceably in a world striven by violence and greed and consumerism. Individuals often feel powerless in the face of great social forces beyond even democratic control. To opt for a vegetarian life-style is to take one practical step towards living in peace with the rest of creation. One step towards reducing the rate of institutionalized killing in the world today. One less chicken eaten is one less chicken killed.

Nevertheless, we do well to appreciate the biblical perspective that we do not live in an ideal world. The truth is that even if we adopt a vegetarian or vegan life-style, we are still not free of killing either directly or indirectly. Even if we only eat beans and nuts and lentils, we have to reckon with the fact that competing animals are killed because of the crops we want to eat. Even if we decide not to wear dead animal skins, we have to face the fact that alternative substances have frequently been tested for their toxicity on laboratory animals. Even if we only eat soya beans we do well to remember that these have been forced fed to animals in painful experiments. As I have written elsewhere, there is no pure land.[10] If we embark on vegetarianism, as I think we should, we must do so on the understanding that for all its compelling logic, it is only *one* very small step towards the vision of a peaceful world.

Prince of Peace

There is, however, one major – and some would say conclusive – objection to my pro vegetarian thesis that should be considered. We have previously encountered it: Jesus was no vegan and probably no vegetarian. There are no recorded examples of Jesus eating meat in the Gospels. The only possible exception is the Passover itself, but it is not entirely clear that Jesus ate the traditional passover meal.[11] Jesus did, however, eat fish if the Gospel narratives are to be believed. How are we to reconcile this to the established Christian view of Jesus as the Prince of Peace? There are four possible answers to this question.

The first is that the canonical Gospels are mistaken and Jesus was actually a vegetarian. However implausible this view may appear, among those who are pro animals there have always been a number who have never believed that Jesus ate the flesh of other living creatures.[12] Those who take this view argue that 'fish' in the New Testament did not actually mean fish as we know it today.[13] Moreover it has been argued that Jesus was really an Essene, albeit an unusual one, a member of the sect who were strict vegetarians.[14] Indeed there are various 'Essene gospels' in which Jesus is depicted as a vegetarian but all of these are, I think, of comparatively modern invention.[15] However there are some fragments of some early gospels, such as the Gospel of the Ebionites, which do depict Jesus as a vegetarian though one suspects for reasons of their own.[16] What I think is much more interesting is the quantity of apocryphal material which in various ways does describe Jesus as having a special concern for, and affinity with, the animal world.[17] How much, if any, of this material is historically reliable is highly questionable but in an area where we know so little it is probably unwise to be dogmatic. It is just conceivable that some of this material does contain genuine historical reminiscence of some kind but that has to be a remote possibility. What may be significant is that this material, historical or not, exhibits a sensitivity to animals which some in the Christian community felt at one stage or another was – or rather should be – characteristic of the historical Jesus.

There is one other question which should perhaps be pondered and it is this: What would it have *meant* for Jesus to have been a vegetarian in first-century Palestine? In context, it could well have meant associating himself with a Manichaean philosophy of asceticism which would have been inimical to his teaching as a whole. Since the Manichaeans were almost all vegetarians – largely on ascetical grounds – it may be pondered whether Jesus was ever confronted with ethical vegetarianism such as we know it today.

The second possible answer is that Jesus was not perfect in every conceivable way. Jews and Muslims would, of course, have no difficulty with this proposition but orthodox Christians would surely find this idea difficult. After all, traditional Christian belief has always been that Jesus Christ was truly God and truly human. Most Christians would hold that being sinless was an essential part of being God incarnate. Those who argue that Jesus was not wholly perfect, however, are not, of course, wholly without biblical support. The question of Jesus: 'Why do you call me good?' and his answer: 'No one is good but God alone' is recorded in all three Synoptic Gospels (Luke 18.19; Matt. 19.17; Mark 10.18).

Moreover, it is not inconceivable that Jesus could have been *both* God incarnate and less than morally perfect in every way. Some scholars, such as John Robinson, have maintained this.[18] Perhaps it could be argued that while Jesus committed no sins of commission (deliberate wrongdoing), of necessity every human being commits some sins of omission (things left undone). However, such a view falls short of traditional Christian doctrine and biblical texts such as Hebrews 4.15 which argues that Jesus 'was tempted as we are, yet without sin'. Though, even here, it is possible that Hebrews is describing ritual purity rather than ethical perfection.

The third answer is that the killing of fish is not a morally significant matter or, at least, not as significant as the killing of mammals. There is something to be said for this view. Even those who argue rigorously for animal rights sometimes do so on the basis that animals as God's creatures are 'subjects of a life' – that is they have sensitivity and consciousness and the ability to suffer – but it is not clear that *all* fish do actually possess *all* these characteristics. In many cases we simply do not know. This must mean, I think, that their moral status is somewhat different from those animals where self-consciousness and sentiency can reasonably be taken for granted. Nevertheless, do not fish merit some benefit of the doubt? Are they not also fellow creatures with some God-given life and individuality which means that wherever possible their lives should be respected?

Approximating the Peaceable Kingdom

The fourth answer is that sometimes it can be justifiable to kill fish for food in situations of necessity. Such a situation, we may assume, was present in first-century Palestine where geographical factors alone seem to suggest a scarcity of protein. Such a view would on the whole be more consistent with the biblical perspective that we may kill but only in circumstances of real need. Hence we may have to face the possibility that Jesus did indeed participate in the killing of some life forms in order to live. Indeed we may say that part of his being a human being at a particular stage and time in history necessitated that response in order to have lived at all.

Of all the four possible responses, I find this last one the most convincing. As I have indicated before, the biblical view is not that killing can never be justified and ought to be avoided at all costs. There are times, for example, when euthanasia may well be the most compassionate response to an individual being undergoing unrelievable suffering. But even if we accept that killing for food may be justified in those situations of real necessity for human survival, such as may be argued in the case of Jesus himself, this in no way exonerates us from the burden of justifying what we now do to animals in circumstances substantially different. This last point is centrally important and must not be obscured. There may have been times in the past or even now in the present where we have difficulty imagining a life without killing for food. But *where we do have the moral freedom* to live without recourse to violence, there is a prima facie case to do so. To kill without the strict conditions of necessity is to live a life with insufficient generosity.

It would be wrong, however, to give the impression that the life and teaching of Jesus is a disappointment as far as the enlightened treatment of animals is concerned. While it is true that there is a great deal we do not know about Jesus' precise attitudes to animals, there is a powerful strand in his ethical teaching about the primacy of mercy to the weak, the powerless and the oppressed. Without misappropriation, it is legitimate to ask: Who is more deserving of this special compassion than the animals so commonly exploited in our world today? Moreover, it is often overlooked that in the canonical Gospels Jesus is frequently presented as identifying himself with the world of animals. As I have written elsewhere:

> His birth, if tradition is to be believed, takes place in the home of sheep and oxen. His ministry begins, according to Mark, in the wilderness 'with the wild beasts' (1.13). His triumphal entry into Jerusalem involves riding on a 'humble ass' (see Matt. 21.b–6). According to Jesus it is lawful to 'do good' on the Sabbath, which includes the rescuing of an animal fallen into a pit (see Matt. 12.10b–12). Even the sparrows, literally sold for a few pennies in his day, are not 'forgotten before God'. God's providence extends to the entire created order, and the glory of Solomon and all his works cannot be compared to that of the lillies of the field (Luke 12.27). God so cares for his creation that even 'foxes have holes, and birds of the air have nests; but the Son of man has nowhere to lay his head' (Luke 9.58).[19]

The significance of these and other verses may be much more than had previously been thought. One small example must suffice. Mark describes Jesus' ministry as taking place firstly within the context of wild animals (1.13). Richard Bauckham has recently argued that the context in which this verse should be understood is messianic in orientation.

Jesus is shown to be in continuity with the Isaianic tradition in seeing the messianic age as bringing about a reconciliation between nature and humanity.[20] If this is true, it may be that Mark is seeking to demonstrate how the gospel of Jesus has implications for the whole of the created world and harmony within the animal world in particular. Those who follow Jesus might argue that in seeking to realize what can now be realized in our own time and space of the messianic age is to live now in conformity with the Spirit of Jesus itself.

In conclusion, reference has already been made to how vegetarians have formed a rather beleagued minority in times past. But it is worth recalling that not a few of the great figures in Christendom have adopted a vegetarian diet. Among these should not go unnoticed the wide variety of saints who have expressed a particular regard for animals and opposed their destruction. 'Poor innocent little creatures', exclaimed St Richard of Chichester when confronted with animals bound for slaughter. 'If you were reasoning beings and could speak you would curse us. For we are the cause of your death, and what have you done to deserve it?'[21] There has always been an ascetical strand within Christianity which has insisted that humans should live gently on the earth and avoid luxury food. The rule of life penned by St Benedict for his religious community, for example, expressly forbade the eating of meat. 'Except the sick who are very weak, let all abstain entirely from the flesh of four-footed animals.'[22] Moreover, it often comes as a surprise for Christians to realize that the modern vegetarian movement was strongly biblical in origin. Inspired by the original command in Genesis 1, an Anglican priest, William Cowherd, founded the Bible Christian Church in 1809 and made vegetarianism compulsory amongst its members. The founding of this church in the United Kingdom and its sister church in the United States by William Metcalfe, effectively heralded the beginning of the modern vegetarian movement.[23]

The subsequent, if rather slow, growth of vegetarianism from 1809 to 1970, and its rapid and astonishing growth from 1970 to the present day is testimony that Cowherd may have been right in his view that mainstream biblical theology has overlooked something of importance in Genesis 1. It may be that when the history of twentieth-century cuisine is finally written, the radical changes in diet which we are currently witnessing will be found to be due more to the rediscovery – by Cowherd and his modern descendants – of two biblical verses (Gen. 1.29–30) than anything else. These two verses, we may recall, came into existence by people imagining possibilities in the light of their belief in

God the Creator. By rekindling the same vision in our own time, we may be enabled to realize – at least in part – those possibilities which our forebears could only imagine. Forward, we may say, not backward to Genesis.

9

Genetic Engineering as Animal Slavery

This chapter rejects absolutely the idea that animals should be geneti-cally manipulated to provide better meat-machines or laboratory tools. According to the perspective embraced by animal theology, to refashion animals genetically so that they become only means-to-human-ends is morally equivalent to the institutionalization of human slavery. There is, therefore, something morally sinister in the untrammelled develop-ment of genetic science which admits of no moral limits save that of the advancement of the controlling species. Nothing less than the dismantling of this science as an institution can satisfy those who advocate moral justice for animals. We reach here the absolute limits of what any reputable creation theology can tolerate.

Animal Revolution

Imagine a place called Manor Farm. The farmer, Mr Jones, has retired for the night. Quite an ordinary farm of its type with a wide variety of animals: cart-horses, cattle, sheep, hens, doves, pigs, pigeons, dogs, a donkey and a goat. The only difference with this farm is that the animals can talk to one another. And in the dead of night when the farmer is sound asleep, the Old Major, a prize Middle White Boar, addresses a secret meeting in the barn. He begins:

> Now, comrades, what is the nature of this life of ours? Let us face it: our lives are miserable, laborious, and short. We are born, we are given just so much food as will keep the breath in our bodies, and those of us who are capable of it are forced to work to the last atom of our strength; and the very instant that our usefulness has come to an end we are slaughtered with hideous cruelty. No animal in England knows the meaning of happiness or leisure after he is a year old. The life of an animal is misery and slavery: that is the plain truth.

The Old Major continues his oration with increasing passion:

> But is this simply part of the order of nature? Is it because this land of

ours is so poor that it cannot afford a decent life to those who dwell upon it? No, comrades, a thousand times no! The soil of England is fertile, its climate is good, it is capable of affording food in abundance to an enormously greater number of animals than now inhabit it ... Why then do we continue in this miserable condition? Because nearly the whole of the produce of our labour is stolen from us by human beings. There, comrades, is the answer to all our problems. It is summed up in a single word – Man. Remove Man from the scene, and the root cause of hunger and overwork is abolished for ever.

Man is the only creature that consumes without producing. He does not give milk, he does not lay eggs, he is too weak to pull the plough, he cannot run fast enough to catch rabbits. Yet he is lord of all the animals. He sets them to work, he gives back to them a bare minimum that will prevent them from starving and the rest he keeps for himself ... and yet there is not one of us that owns more than his bare skin.

Finally the oration reaches its crescendo to gladden the animal hearts that hear it:

What then must we do? Why, work night and day, body and soul, for the overthrow of the human race! That is my message to you comrades: Rebellion! I do not know when that Rebellion will come, it might be in a week or in a hundred years, but I know, as surely as I see this straw beneath my feet, that sooner or later justice will be done. Fix your eyes on that, comrades, throughout the short remainder of your lives! And above all, pass on this message of mine to those who come after you, so that future generations shall carry on the struggle until it is victorious.[1]

By now, of course, you will have guessed the location of Manor Farm – in the *Animal Farm* of George Orwell's imagining. We all know that Orwell intended his book not as a satire on the oppression of pigs and horses but on the oppression of working-class humans by their indolent and unproductive bosses. Nevertheless, it could not have escaped Orwell's attention, as it may not have escaped ours, that there is indeed a similarity between the arguments used (so brilliantly summarized and rebutted by the Old Major) for the justifying of oppression of humans and animals alike.

And if we see this similarity we shall also have grasped something historically quite significant.[2] For the two arguments, or rather assumptions, alluded to in the rousing polemic of the Old Major, namely that one kind of creature belongs to another and exists to serve the other, have not been confined to the animal sphere. Earlier we have made reference to how Aristotle – typically or untypically – held that animals were made for human use. 'If then nature makes nothing without some end in view,' he argues, 'nothing to no purpose, it must be that nature has made all of them [animals and plants] for the sake of man.'[3] Notice that Aristotle is not claiming here that we may sometimes make use of animals when necessity demands it, rather he is asserting that it is in accordance with nature, indeed it is *by nature*, that animals are humans' slaves. And if we ask how Aristotle knows that animals are by nature slaves the answer seems to be that if they were not they would 'refuse' but since they do not, it obviously follows that it is natural to enslave them. It is crucial to appreciate, however, that this ingenious argument does not stand alone in Aristotle's *The Politics*. When Aristotle comes to considering the right ordering of society, based in turn on the pattern of nature, he uses the example of animal slaves to underline and justify the existence of *human* slaves as well:

> Therefore whenever there is the same wide discrepancy between human beings as there is between soul and body or between man and beast, then those whose condition is such that their function is the use of their bodies and nothing better can be expected of them, those, I say, are slaves by nature.[4]

In a notorious section, Aristotle describes human slaves as 'tools' and none other than pieces of property. 'A slave is not only his master's slave but belongs to him *tout court*, while the master is his slave's master but does not belong to him.'[5] In short: Aristotle does not demur from using the same two arguments, namely that one creature belongs to another and one kind of creature exists to serve the other – to justify both animal and human slavery. As for women, incidentally, they appear to stand somewhere in between, possessing some soul, that is reason, but not as much as men, and having a kind of half status depending upon their rationality.[6]

Belonging to and Existing for

Aristotle represents what we may call the 'belong to and exist for' element within the Western intellectual tradition which Christianity in particular has taken over and developed to the detriment of slaves and women as well as animals. In Aquinas, for example, a few centuries on, we find this same argument repeating itself. 'There is no sin in using a thing for the purpose for which it is,' he argues.[7] Also with women, though to a lesser degree, we may observe a similar logic. Men, not men and women, are made in the image of God and thus only males possess full rationality. Women are half way between men and the beasts. 'In a secondary sense the image of God is found in man, and not in woman,' argues Aquinas, 'for man is the beginning and end of woman.'[8] Some of us may not fail to see an echo of Aristotle in these words.

Now the simple point I want to make is this: the debate about slavery, human or animal, is not over. Let us take human slavery first. Most of us think that the battle about human slavery was fought and won two hundred or more years ago. If we think that we are simply mistaken. The Anti-Slavery Society exists to combat slavery which continues to exist in many parts of the world, albeit under different guises and in different forms.[9] But if we stay with the issue of slavery and the slave trade of less recent history and go back about two hundred or more years, we will find intelligent, respectable and conscientious Christians supporting almost without question the trade in slaves as inseparable from Christian civilization and human progress. The argument is not an exact repeat from Aristotle, but one that may owe something to his inspiration. Slavery, it is argued, was 'progress' – 'an integral link in the grand progressive evolution of human society' as William Henry Holcombe, writing in 1860, put it. Moreover, slavery was a natural means of 'Christianization of the dark races.'[10] Slavery was assumed to be one of the means whereby the natural debased life of the primitives could be civilized. And in this it may not be too far-fetched to see at least a touch of the logic of Aristotle, who defended human slavery on the basis that domestic tame animals were better off 'to be ruled by men, because it secures their safety'.[11] As David Brion Davis points out: 'It is often forgotten that Aristotle's famous defence of slavery is embedded within his discussion of human "progress" from the patriarchal village, where "the ox is the poor man's slave", to the fully developed polis, where advances in the arts, sciences, and law support that perfect exercise of virtue which is the goal of the city state'.[12]

If slavery then was frequently defended on the basis of 'progress', on which basis, we may ask, did its opposers oppose it? We know that individuals – like Shaftesbury, Wilberforce, Richard Baxter and Thomas Clarkson – opposed the trade in slaves because they regarded it as cruel, dehumanizing and the source of all kinds of social ills. But one argument we find them using time and again, namely that 'man' had no right to absolute dominion over other 'men'. According to Theodore Weld's influential definition, slavery usurped 'the prerogative of God'. It constituted 'an invasion of the whole man – on his powers, rights, enjoyments, and hopes [which] annihilates his being as a MAN, to make room for the being of a THING'.[13] In other words, humans cannot be owned like things or as property. This argument was not peculiar to Weld and Wilberforce and the other reformers in the eighteenth century. Nearly fourteen hundred years before Wilberforce was born, St Gregory of Nyssa made the first theological attack on the institution of slavery itself. His argument is simple; man is beyond price. 'Man belongs to God; he is the property of God'; he cannot therefore be bought or sold. St Gregory was arguably the first to break decisively with that 'belong to and exist for' element within the Western tradition.[14]

And yet St Gregory's argument contains a twist in its tail. For Gregory argues that humans cannot have dominion over other humans and therefore possess them, because God gave humans dominion not over other humans but over the world and animals in particular. In other words, humans belong to God and are therefore beyond price but the animals, since they belong to humans, can be bought and sold like slaves![15] One kind of slavery is therefore opposed on the grounds that another is self-evident.

We are now in a position to confront the second kind of slavery I want to consider, namely the slavery of animals. When it comes to animals we find almost without exception the kinds of arguments used to justify human slavery also used to justify the slavery of animals. Animals, like human slaves, are thought to possess little or no reason. Animals, like human slaves, are thought to be 'by nature' enslaveable. Animal slavery, like human slavery, is thought to be 'progressive', even of 'benefit' to the animals concerned. But two arguments are used repeatedly, and we have already discovered them: Animals belong to humans and they exist to serve human interests. Indeed Brion Davis describes what is meant by a slave in a way that makes the similarity abundantly clear:

> The truly striking fact, given historical changes in polity, religion, technology, modes of production, family and kinship structures, and the very meaning of 'property', is the antiquity and almost universal acceptance of the *concept* of the slave as a human being who is legally owned, used, sold, or otherwise disposed of as if he or she were a domestic animal.[16]

It may be asked: what has all the foregoing to do with the issue of genetic engineering? The answer is this: Genetic engineering represents the concretization of the *absolute* claim that animals belong to us and exist for us. We have always used animals, of course, either for food, fashion, or sport. It is not new that we are now using animals for farming, even in especially cruel ways. *What is new is that we are now employing the technological means of absolutely subjugating the nature of animals so that they become totally and completely human property.* 'New animals ought to be patentable', argues Roger Schank, Professor of Computer Science and Psychology at Yale University, 'for the same reason that new robots ought to be patentable: because they are both products of human ingenuity.'[17] When technologists speak, as they do, of creating 'super animals'[18] what they have in mind is not super lives for animals so that they may be better fed, lead more environmentally satisfying lives, or that they may be more 'humanely' slaughtered; rather what they have in mind is how animals can be originated and exist in ways that are completely subordinate to the demands of the human stomach. In other words, animals become like human slaves, namely 'things' – even more so in a sense since human masters never, to my knowledge, actually consumed human slaves. Biotechnology in animal farming represents the apotheosis of human domination. In one sense it was all inevitable. Failing to have respect for any proper limits in our treatment of animals always carried with it the danger that their very nature would become subject to a similar contempt. Now animals can be not only bought and sold, but *patented*, that is owned, as with human artefacts, like children's toys, cuddly bears, television sets, or other throwaway consumer items, dispensed with as soon as their utility is over.

Again we are not, even at this point, as far away from Aristotle as some might suppose. For in an uncanny, prophetic-like part of his work, Aristotle seems to anticipate a time when human slaves would be automated, being slaves of their own nature, rather than by Nature or the will of their masters. 'For suppose', he muses, 'that every tool we had could perform its task, either at our bidding or itself perceiving the need ... then master-craftsmen would have no need of servants nor masters of slaves.'[19] Some might argue that biotechnology has transformed this ancient dream into a present nightmare.

Patenting and Creation Doctrine

The nightmare intensifies when we look further into the concept of patenting. In 1992, the European Patent Office in Munich actually granted a patent for the oncomouse, the first European patent on an animal. The controversy over this has not unnaturally focussed on the issue of suffering to animals and whether genetically-engineered animals (in this case a mouse genetically designed to develop cancer) are likely to lead to an increased level of suffering among laboratory animals. This is an important consideration, but the one which requires even more attention is whether the granting of patents for genetically-engineered animals is acceptable in principle. Such a step would, in my opinion, reduce their status to no more than human inventions, and signifies the effective abdication of that special God-given responsibility that all humans have towards the well-being and autonomy of sentient species. Animal patents should not be given; not now, not ever.

We should be clear what the full granting of a patent will mean. A patent confers the legal status of ownership. For the first time – in a European context at least – animals will be classed legally as property without any duty of care; animals will become human artefacts or inventions. If the application for this patent withstands opposition, it will mark the lowest status granted to animals in the history of European ethics. While historically animals have sometimes been thought of as 'things' – beings without rights or value – the patenting of animals will mark their *enduring legal classification* in these terms. I have, I hope, said enough in this and previous chapters to demonstrate that such a use and classification of animal life is not compatible with the Christian doctrine that animals are God's creatures. The Christian doctrine of creation requires us to grasp the fact that human estimations of our own worth and value cannot be the sole grounds for evaluating the worth of other creatures.

Allied to the debate about whether and in what ways humans may use animals is the debate about how far humans are justified in changing the nature of created beings, including their own. It would not be possible to argue that humans must not interfere with any part of nature as it now is, either animate or inanimate. According to traditional Christian belief, creation is 'fallen', in a state of 'bondage', and therefore – from the Creator's perspective – unfinished. It follows that there is scope for human development of nature, and the notion of dominion in particular presupposes an *active* role for humans in the care and management of the planet.

That accepted, such empowerment to 'better' creation carries with it some strict limits. In the first place, the empowerment presupposed in Genesis is the power to do good in accordance with God's will. It is not a commission to do with creation willy nilly as one wishes. Second, in each and every case it must be shown that such 'alteration' of nature is consistent with the designs of the Creator and not simply the pursuance of human avarice and self-advantage.

Here we reach the nub of the matter. Is the created nature of animals 'bettered' by genetic engineering? It may be that there is some, albeit limited, case that can be made for such research if it seeks to genuinely enhance the welfare of the individual animals concerned. But in the case of the oncomouse we are dealing not with any bettering of nature either individually or generally but rather with a process that involves the deliberate and artificial creation of disease, suffering and premature death. What is more, the purpose of patenting is so to secure the legal rights to this 'invention' that the patent holders concerned may uniquely secure any benefits that may flow from it, not least of all commercial gain. If successful, therefore, the granting of a patent would not only legitimize a morally questionable line of research, it would also financially reward those who carried it out.

While it cannot be claimed that all nature in every instance should be regarded as sacred and inviolable, it is a mistake to suppose that the pursuance of every conceivable human advantage no matter how indirect or trivial justifies each and every intervention in nature. While creation may be disordered, it does not follow that there is a total absence of integrity; maintaining and promoting the good that already exists is an essential task of stewardship. The artificial creation of disease in animals can hardly be claimed to be compatible with the designs of a holy, loving, Creator.

Moreover, while it may not strictly speaking be an implication of creation doctrine, opposition to cruelty has been a long-standing feature of traditional moral theology. Whatever else may be said in favour of the oncomouse, it is difficult to see how it can pass any test of moral necessity. To show that something is necessary we have to show that it is essential, unavoidable or, arguably at its very weakest, that some higher good requires it and could not in any way be obtained without it. Even within those sub-traditions of Christendom which have been pro-foundly unreflective about animal welfare, there is a strong conviction that the infliction of pain can only be justified, if at all, on the most stringent criteria. Animals pose special problems in this regard. They cannot give consent to experimental procedures performed upon them; they cannot merit any infliction of pain, and moreover they cannot intellectually comprehend the meaning of the procedures to which they are subjected. These considerations always tell against the infliction of pain upon innocents, whether they be children, or the mentally handicapped, or animals.

In short: the innocence and defencelessness of animals, far from being considerations which should push animals away from our field of moral concern, are precisely those which should make us exercise special care and enjoin extraordinary scrupulosity. Whatever views may be held generally about the use of animals in scientific research, patenting represents the attempt to perpetuate, to institutionalize, and to commercialize, suffering to animals. It seems predicated on the assumption that animal suffering is justifiable no matter how indirect the benefit to humans.

The objection may be raised that the oncomouse is, after all, only a mouse. According to many people, including Christians, a mouse has little value in comparison with a human being.

Proponents of patenting have certainly been clever in choosing a species which apparently commands limited public sympathy. Because mice interact with human environments in ways which are disadvantageous to us, they are frequently classed as a pest species and often killed inhumanely. The limited sympathy this species can invoke is, however, irrelevant to its moral status and therefore to the issue of principle. Mice are intelligent, sentient, warm-blooded creatures. There are no rational grounds on which we can include some sentient species while excluding others from moral consideration.

It is important to remember that the patent for the oncomouse constitutes a test case. The oncorabbit, the oncocow, the oncopig, the oncochimp will inevitably follow. There is no limit to the species or the numbers which may be patented. If the arguments in favour of patenting succeed in the case of the oncomouse, there can be no rational grounds why they should not succeed in others. We shall wake up and find that we have reduced innumerable species of animals to a class of human inventions, tailor-made to laboratory needs and arguably unprotected in law. If successful, the patenting of animals will represent the victory of short-term utilitarianism over the constraints of Christian theology (however unimplemented these may have been in the past). It may be no exaggeration to say that we stand on the brink of a wholly new relationship to other creatures: no longer custodians of our fellow creatures, but rather dealers in new commodities.

The Discredited Theology of Genetic Engineering

I was going to call this chapter 'the discredited theology of genetic engineering' but some individuals protested that it might be read as assuming that genetic engineering *had* a theology. In fact, as we have seen, it does and a strong and powerful one at that. The Christian tradition, fed by powerful Aristotelian notions, has been largely responsible for its propagation. For many centuries Christians have simply read their scriptures as legitimizing the Aristotelian dicta: 'existing for and belonging to'. The notion of 'dominion' in Genesis has been interpreted as licensed tyranny over the world, and animals in particular. God, it was supposed, cared only for humans within creation, and as for the rest, they simply existed for the human 'goodies'. According to this view, the whole world belongs to humans by divine right, and the only moral constraints as regards the use of animals was whether animal cruelty brutalizes humans or how we should treat them if they were other humans' property.[20] This god – not unfairly described as a 'macho-god' – essentially masculine and despotical, who rules the world with fire and expects his human subjects to do the same, has trampled through years of Christian history, but his influence is now waning. There are many reasons for this and two in particular: First, most Christians do not believe in him any more. You will have to search high and low for any reputable theologian who defends the view that God is despotic in power and wants human creatures to be as well. Second, as we have seen, having re-examined their scriptures most theologians conclude that we misunderstand dominion if we think of it simply in terms of domination. What dominion now means, according to these scholars, is that humans have a divine-like responsibility to look after the world and to care for its creatures.[21] Indeed, for those who still hold to the 'macho-god' version of divinity, I have some worrying news. Not only theologians (who tend in the nature of things to be either ahead of or behind the times) but also churchpeople, even church leaders, have disposed of this old deity:

> The temptation is that we will usurp God's place as Creator and exercise a *tyrannical* dominion over creation ... At the present time, when we are beginning to appreciate the wholeness and inter-relatedness of all that is in the cosmos, preoccupation with humanity will seem distinctly parochial ... too often our theology of creation, especially here in the so-called 'developed' world, has been distorted by being too man-centred. We need to maintain the value, the

preciousness of the human by affirming the preciousness of the non-human also – of all that is. For our concept of God forbids the idea of a *cheap* creation, of a throwaway universe in which everything is expendable save human existence. The whole universe is a work of love. And nothing which is made in love is cheap. The value, the worth of natural things is not found in Man's view of himself but in the goodness of God who made all things good and precious in his sight ... As Barbara Ward used to say, 'We have only one earth. Is it not worth our love?'[22]

These words come from a lecture given in 1988 by the then Archbishop of Canterbury, Robert Runcie. Notice how the earlier tradition is here confronted and corrected. God is a God of love. God's world is a manifestation of costly, self-sacrificial love. We humans are to love and reverence the world entrusted to us. And lest you should think that this is just 'Anglican' theology which may at times tend to be a little fashionable, it is worth mentioning that an encyclical from that rather unfashionable, undoubtedly conservative Pope, John Paul II, specifically speaks of the need to respect 'the nature of each being' within creation, and underlines the modern view that the 'dominion granted to man ... is not an absolute power, nor can one speak of a freedom to "use and misuse", or to dispose of things as one pleases'.[23]

We have not yet brought our argument to its sharpest point, however. It is this: *No human being can be justified in claiming absolute ownership of animals for the simple reason that God alone owns creation. Animals do not simply exist for us nor belong to us. They exist primarily for God and belong to God. The human patenting of animals is nothing less than idolatrous.* The practice of genetic engineering implicitly involves the claim that animals are ours, to do with as we wish and to change their nature as we wish. The reason why it is wrong to use human beings as slaves is also precisely the reason why we should now oppose the whole biotech endeavour with animals as theologically erroneous. We have no right to misappropriate God's own.

Four Objections

I anticipate four objections to this conclusion which I shall consider briefly in turn.

The first objection is as follows: We have always made animals our slaves. Our culture is based upon the use of animals. It is therefore absurd to suppose that we can change our ways.

I agree with the first part of this objection. It is true that human culture is based on the slavery of animals. I, for one, would like to see a root and branch cultural change. Christians may legitimately disagree about how far we can and should use animals. But one thing should be clear: we cannot own them, we should not treat them as property, and we should not pervert their nature for the sole purpose of human consumption. Genetic engineering – while part of this cultural abuse of animals – also represents its highest, or lowest, point. Because we have exploited animals in the past and now do so, is no good reason for intensifying that enslavement and bringing the armoury of modern technology to bear in order to create and perpetuate a permanently enslaved species.

The second objection is that the record of Christianity has been so terrible as regards the non-human that we must surely despair of any specifically theological attempt to defend animals.

I agree with the first part of this objection. Christianity has a terrible record on animals. But not only animals – also on slaves, gays, women, the mentally handicapped, and a sizeable number of other moral issues as well. I see no point in trying to disguise the poor record of Christianity, although I have to say that I do not quite share Voltaire's moral protest to the effect that 'every sensible man, every honourable man, must hold the Christian sect in horror'.[24] All traditions, religious or secular, have their good and bad points.

But to take one issue as an example: Recall my earlier point that if we go back in history two hundred years or so, we will find intelligent, conscientious, respectable Christians defending slavery as an institution. The quite staggering fact to grapple with is that this very same community which had in some ways provided the major ideological impetus for the defence of slavery came within a historically short period, one hundred, perhaps only fifty, years, to change its mind. The same tradition which helped keep slavery alive was the same community, one hundred or fifty years later, that helped end it.[25] So successful indeed has this change been that I suppose that among Christians today we shall have difficulty in finding *one* slave trader, even *one* individual Christian who regards the practice as anything other than inimical to the moral demands of the Christian faith. While it is true that Christian churches have been and are frequently awful on the subject of animals, it is just possible, even plausible, that given say fifty or one hundred years we shall witness among this same community shifts of consciousness as we have witnessed on other moral issues, no less complex or controversial. In sum: Christian churches have been agents of slavery – I do not doubt – but they have also been, and can be now, forces for liberation.

The third objection is that genetic engineers are really good, honest, loving, generous, well-meaning people only trying to do their best for the sake of humanity, or at the very least they are no more awful than the rest of us. Why criticize what they are doing, when in point of fact *everybody* is in the difficult situation of moral compromise to a greater or lesser extent?

Again, I agree with the first part of this objection. I have no reason for doubting the sincerity, the motivation, and the moral character of those who are actively engaged in biotech research. One of the really sad aspects of the campaign for the abolition of the slave trade was the way in which abolitionists tended, during the time of their ascendancy, to vilify their opponents by regarding them as the source of all evil. I have no desire to do the same. Indeed, what I want to suggest is that genetic engineers are really doing what they say they are doing, namely pursuing the cause of humanity according to their own lights. What I want to question, however, is whether a simple utilitarian humanist standard is sufficient to prevent great wrong. From the slave trader's perspective, it was only right and good to use slaves for the sake of the masters. From the genetic engineer's perspective it is only right and good to treat animals as utilities in order to benefit the human species. I doubt whether simple utilitarian calculation based on the interests of one's *own* class, or race, or species can lead otherwise than to the detriment of *another's* class, race, or species. Once we adopt this framework of thinking, there is no right, good or value that cannot be bargained away, at least in principle, in pursuit of a supposedly 'higher' interest.

The fourth objection is to the analogy so far drawn between human and animal slavery. Animals are only animals, it is argued. Animals are not human.

This argument, which emphasizes a clear demarcation between animals and humans, whatever its merits in other spheres, is exceedingly problematic when applied to genetic engineering. After all, are not genetic engineers involved in the injection of *human* genes into non-human animals? According to a recent report, Vernon G. Pursel, a research scientist at the US Department of Agriculture's research faculty in Beltsville, responded to a recent move by various humane agencies and churches against genetic engineering by saying, 'I don't know what they mean when they talk about species integrity.' He went on to make a most revealing statement: 'Much of all genetic material is the same, from worms to humans.'[26] This statement is revealing precisely because it supposes what transgenic procedures must implicitly accept, namely that there is not a watertight distinction between humans and animals. Some may think that this is an argument in favour of treating animals in a more humane fashion, and so in a way it should be, but the argument is used to the practical detriment of non-human creatures. Here we have curious confirmation of the anxiety that besets bystanders like myself. For the question that must be asked is this: if the genetic material is much the same – from worms to humans – what is there logically to prevent us experimenting upon humans if we accept its legitimacy in the case of animals? Indeed genetic experiments on humans are not new. And neither is the view that there should be an eugenic programme for human beings. This view has received strong support from Christians at various times. One Christian writer in 1918 made clear that

> The man who is thoroughly fit to have children, and who either through love of comfort, or some indulgence of sentiment, refrains from marriage, defrauds not only himself and his nation, but human society and the Ruler of it ... But the man or woman who knowing themselves unfit to have healthy children yet marry, are clearly guilty of an even more serious offence.

This writer does not just advocate these moral imperatives as personal guidelines, rather he seeks to have them enshrined in law:

> The only kinds of legislation *for which the times are ripe* seem to be two. In the first place, marriage might be forbidden in the case of those mentally deficient, or suffering from certain hereditary diseases. And in the second place, much more might be done at present in the way of providing cottages in the country, and well-arranged dwellings in the towns, and by encouraging in every way the production of healthy children.[27]

This work by Percy Gardner was entitled *Evolution in Christian Ethics*. Gardner's view was straightforward: only those who are fit have the right to propagate the race. The well-being of the race was, as he saw it, threatened by the First World War because only the 'weaker, and especially those whose vital organs are least sound, we retain at home to carry on the race'.[28]

Eugenics and Genetic Engineering

Gardner's views had to wait another fifteen years before his ideas reached their fullest and most persuasive expression in the work of another writer, a political philosopher, of immense influence:

> [The state] must see to it that only the healthy beget children; but there is only one disgrace: despite one's own sicknesses and deficiencies, to bring children into the world, and one highest honour to renounce doing so ... [The state] must put the most modern medical means in the service of this knowledge. It must declare unfit for propagation all who are in any way visibly sick or who have inherited a disease.

And according to this view:

> [The state's philosophy] of life must succeed in bringing about that nobler age in which men no longer are concerned with breeding dogs, horses, and cats, but in elevating man himself, an age in which the one knowingly and silently renounces, the other joyfully sacrifices and gives.[29]

These views are taken from the well-known work, *Mein Kampf,* and the author is, of course, Adolf Hitler.

Some may object that the analogy here breaks down. After all Hitler would hardly have approved of infecting Aryan blood with the genes of animals or, more accurately, allowing Aryan genes to be wasted on animals. He was hardly in favour of 'hybrid humans' – as he called the children of mixed marriages – so he might well have had a certain disdain for the very idea of transgenic animals. And yet we cannot dismiss the fact that Hitler popularized, indeed did apparently much to develop, a medical science which aimed at 'preserving the best humanity' as he saw it. And what is more his ideas of genetic control exercised through force, coercion, and legislation are by no means dead. Indeed the notion of creating a 'super animal' is faintly reminiscent of the Hitler doctrine of creating a 'superior' race.

Some may still feel that human eugenics and genetic engineering with animals are two quite separate things. Some may think that I am being simply alarmist. But *Mein Kampf* is, in my view, a much more important work of political philosophy than its detractors allow. But that is beside the point. What is the point is that I can find no good arguments for allowing genetic experiments on animals which do not also justify such experiments (or genetic programmes) in the case of human beings. I am alarmed by the way in which we have simply failed to recognize that animal experiments are often a precursor to experiments on human beings. Even in current established practice, animal experiments frequently precede the clinical trials on human subjects. We should not be oblivious to the fact that the century which has seen the most sustained and ruthless use of animals in scientific research is also the century that has seen experiments on human subjects as diverse as Jews, blacks, embryos, and prisoners of war. If 'much of all genetic material is the same, from worms to humans', as Dr Pursel maintains, what real difference does it make if the subjects are animals or humans?

If some of this still appears alarmist, it is perhaps worth emphasizing that one of the main planks of the case for anti-vivisection has always been that the experimental method, if morally valid, must logically extend to humans. C. S. Lewis based his critique on this very idea. His words deserve to be read in full:

> But the most sinister thing about modern vivisection is this. If a mere sentiment justifies cruelty, why stop at a sentiment for the whole human race? There is also a sentiment for the white man against the black, for a *Herrenvolk* against the Non-Aryan, for 'civilized' or 'progressive' peoples against 'savage' or 'backward' peoples. Finally, for our own country, party, or class against others. Once the old Christian idea of a total difference in kind between man and beast has bee n abandoned, then no argument for experiments on animals can be found which is not also an argument for experiments on inferior men. If we cut up beasts simply because they cannot prevent us and because we are backing our own side in the struggle for existence, it is only logical to cut up imbeciles, criminals, enemies, or capitalists for the same reasons. Indeed experiments on men have already begun. We all hear that Nazi scientists have done them. We all suspect that our own scientists may begin to do so, in secret, at any moment.[30]

Lewis was writing in 1947 and may be accused of hindsight. No such accusation, however, could be levelled at Lewis Carroll who seventy-two years earlier, when vivisection was just beginning at Oxford, argued on precisely the same basis but with even more vigour. Of the thirteen 'Popular Fallacies about Vivisection', it was the thirteenth 'that the practice of vivisection shall never be extended so as to include human subjects' that earned his greatest mockery:

That is, in other words, that while science arrogates to herself the right of torturing at her pleasure the whole sentient creation up to man himself, some inscrutable boundary line is there drawn, over which she will never venture to pass ... And when that day shall come, O my brother-man, you who claim for yourself and for me so proud an ancestry – tracing our pedigree through the anthropomorphoid ape up to the primeval zoophyte – what potent spell have *you* in store to win exception from the common doom? Will you represent to that grim spectre, as he gloats over you, scalpel in hand, the inalienable rights of man? He will tell you that it is merely a question of relative expediency, – that, with so feeble a physique as yours, you have only to be thankful that natural selection has spared you so long. Will you reproach him with the needless torture he proposes to inflict upon you? He will smilingly assure you that the *hyperaesthesia*, which he hopes to induce, is in itself a most interesting phenomenon, deserving much patient study. Will you then, gathering up all your strength for one last desperate appeal, plead with him as with a fellow-man, and with an agonized cry for 'Mercy!' seek to rouse some dormant spark of pity in that icy-breast? Ask it rather of the nether mill-stone.[31]

There is one important sense, however, in which Pursel was right. In addition to the nature appropriate to each individual species, there is a nature which is common to all human and non-human animals. But this realization alone should make us think twice about genetic engineering. Animals, it is sometimes supposed, are simply 'out there', external to ourselves like nature itself. Likewise, it is thought, what we do to animals does not really affect *us*. In fact, however, humans are not just tied to nature, they *are part of nature*, indeed inseparable from nature. Because of this there is a profound sense in which we cannot abuse nature without abusing ourselves.[32] The genetic manipulation of animal nature is not just some small welfare problem of how we should treat some kinds of animal species, it is part of a much more disturbing theological question about 'who do we think we are' in creation, and whether we can acknowledge moral limits to our awesome power, not only over animals, but also over our own species.

At the beginning of this chapter I invited you to imagine the Old Major addressing his fellow animal comrades and complaining that their state was none other than 'misery and slavery'. You may recall that a little provocatively the Old Major thought that the answer was the abolition of 'Man'. In one sense the Old Major was right. We need to abolish what St Paul calls the 'old man' which is humanity in moral bondage or slavery to sin.[33] Demythologized a little, what St Paul might have said is that we must stop looking on God's beautiful world as though it was given to us so that we can devour, consume, and manipulate it without limit. I look forward to the final death of the 'old man' – of which St Paul speaks – both in myself as well as in other human beings. Then, and only then, when we have surrendered our idolatrous power, which is nothing short of tyranny, over God's good creation, shall we be worthy to have that moral dominion over all which God has promised us.

Notes

Full bibliographical details of works cited here will be found in the *Guide to the Literature.*

1. Reverence, Responsibility and Rights

1. Andrew Linzey, *Animal Rights: A Christian Assessment*, pp. 20–29, and *Christianity and the Rights of Animals*, pp. 68–98.
2. A series of symposia sponsored by the British Veterinary Association among others has helped to bring the issue of animals to the front of contemporary debate. See, esp., R. D. Ryder and David Paterson (eds), *Animals' Rights – A Symposium*, based on the Conference held at Trinity College, Cambridge in 1977; David Paterson (ed), *Humane Education – A Symposium*, based on the Conference at the University of Sussex in 1980, and R. D. Ryder (ed), *Animal Welfare and the Environment*, based on the Conference at Christ Church, Oxford in 1990.
3. The key biblical texts are anthologized in Andrew Linzey and Tom Regan (eds), *Animals and Christianity: A Book of Readings*. Referred to below as *AAC*; see also discussion of key texts, pp. 33–35, 103–106, 125–132.
4. For an anthology of some of the best animal poetry (as I see it), see Andrew Linzey and Tom Regan (eds), *The Song of Creation*, and on saints and sages, see Andrew Linzey, *Brother and Sister Creatures: The Saints and Animals.*
5. Albert Schweitzer, *Civilization and Ethics*, preface, pp. 5–6. All the relevant sections from Schweitzer, Barth, Aquinas and Primatt are anthologized in *AAC*, and future references will be preponderantly to those edited sections.
6. Schweitzer, *Civilization and Ethics*, p. 212.
7. Schweitzer, in *AAC*, p. 188.
8. Schweitzer, in *AAC*, p. 119.
9. Schweitzer, in *AAC*, p. 118.
10. See Schweitzer's discussion of experimentation in *AAC*, p. 120.
11. Schweitzer, in *AAC*, p. 119; my emphasis.
12. Schweitzer, in *AAC*, p. 119.
13. Schweitzer, in *AAC*, p. 120; my emphasis.
14. See James Brabazon, *Albert Schweitzer: A Biography*, p. 255.
15. Schweitzer, *Civilization and Ethics*, p. 227.
16. Schweitzer, *Civilization and Ethics*, p. 209.
17. Schweitzer, *Civilization and Ethics*, p. 212.

18. Peter Singer, *Practical Ethics*, p. 91. I have previously defended Schweitzer against some of his religious critics who I think misunderstand him in my 'Moral Education and Reverence for Life' in David Paterson, *Humane Education: A Symposium*, pp. 117–125.
19. Paul Tillich, *Morality and Beyond*, p. 12.
20. Charles R. Joy (ed), *Albert Schweitzer: An Anthology*, p. 231.
21. Karl Barth, *Church Dogmatics*, Vol. 111, *The Doctrine of Creation*, Part 4, p. 349. Hereafter *CD*, 111/4.
22. Barth, *CD*, 111/4, p. 349.
23. Barth, *CD*, 111/4, p. 350.
24. Barth, *CD*, 111/4, p. 352.
25. Barth, *CD*, 111/4, p. 350.
26. Barth, *CD*, 111/4, p. 351.
27. Barth, *Church Dogmatics*, Vol. 111, *The Doctrine of Creation*, Part 1, p. 18.
28. See, for example, the discussion in Stephen R. L. Clark, *The Moral Status of Animals*, pp. 169–174.
29. Barth, *CD*, 111/4, p. 352.
30. See Andrew Linzey, *Christianity and the Rights of Animals*, pp. 77–86, and also later discussion below, pp. 33–35.
31. See Andrew Linzey, *The Neglected Creature: The Doctrine of the Non-Human Creation and its Relationship with the Human in the Thought of Karl Barth*, PhD thesis.
32. St Maximus, *Selected Writings*, p. 186.
33. E. L. Mascall, *The Christian Universe*, p. 163.
34. St Athanasius, *Ad Seraphionem*, 1. 31, cited and discussed in T. F. Torrance, *Theology in Reconstruction*; my emphasis.
35. St John of the Cross, *The Complete Works*, pp. 48–9; also in Linzey, *Christianity and the Rights of Animals*, p. 62.
36. Eph. 1.10 (RSV).
37. Rom. 8.28f. (RSV).
38. St Athanasius, *AAC*, p. 97.
39. St Irenaeus, *Against Heresies*, in *The Writings of Irenaeus*, Vol. 1, v 28, 3, pp. 105–6; also extract in *AAC*, p. 91.
40. St Chrysostom, cited in Donald Attwater, *St John Chrysostom*, pp. 59–60; my emphasis.
41. St Bonaventure, *The Life of St Francis*, pp. 254–5; my emphasis.
42. Thomas Traherne, 'Second Century' in *Selected Writings*, para. 66, p. 83.
43. See, for example, the encyclical *Sollicitudo Rei Socialis* which suggests (para. 34) that 'one cannot use with impunity the different natural elements' within the cosmos. For a pioneering Roman Catholic study, see Robert Murray, *The Cosmic Covenant*, esp. chapter 6 on 'Relationships Within the Kingdom of Peace', pp. 94–125.
44. See Linzey, *Christianity and the Rights of Animals*, pp. 68–98.

45. St Thomas Aquinas, *Summa Theologica*, Question 64, Article 1. Extract in *AAC*, pp. 124–6.
46. Aquinas, in *AAC*, p. 124.
47. Aquinas, in *AAC*, p. 124.
48. Aquinas, in *AAC*, p. 125.
49. Aquinas, in *AAC*, p. 125; see Aristotle, *The Politics*, pp. 78–9 (1, viii) for the similarity.
50. Aquinas, in *CAA*, p. 125.
51. Aquinas, *Summa Contra Gentiles*, Book 111, Ch. CX11, reprinted in Tom Regan and Peter Singer (eds), *Animal Rights and Human Obligations*, p. 56.
52. See Ambrose Agius, *God's Animals*, pp. 8, 17–18.
53. Aquinas, *Summa Theologica*, Question 65, Article 3; reprinted in *AAC*, pp. 125–127.
54. Aquinas, in *AAC*, p. 126.
55. Aquinas, in *AAC*, p. 126.
56. P. Palazzini (ed), *Dictionary of Moral Theology*, p. 73.
57. Keith Thomas, *Man and the Natural World: Changing Attitudes in England 1500–1800*.
58. Humphry Primatt, *Dissertation on the Duty of Mercy and the Sin of Cruelty to Brute Animals*, p. 10; extract in *AAC*, pp. 127–130.
59. Primatt, in *AAC*, p. 127.
60. Primatt, in *AAC*, p. 127.
61. Primatt, in *AAC*, p. 128.
62. Primatt, in *AAC*, p. 129; his emphases.
63. Primatt, in *AAC*, p. 129; his emphasis.
64. Primatt, in *AAC*, p. 129.
65. Primatt, *Dissertation*, p. 288f.
66. Primatt, *Dissertation*, p. 288.
67. Aquinas, in *AAC*, p. 126.
68. Aristotle, *The Politics*, p. 79 (1, viii).
69. Aquinas, in *AAC*, p. 124–6.
70. Aquinas, in *AAC*, pp. 124–6.
71. See, for example, Claus Westerman, *Creation*.
72. Robin Attfield, *The Ethics of Environmental Concern*, p. 26.
73. W. A. Whitehouse, 'New Heavens and a New Earth' in Ann Loades (ed), *The Authority of Grace*, p. 210.
74. See James Turner, *Reckoning with the Beast: Animals, Pain and Humanity in the Victorian Mind*, p. 43.
75. Cited and discussed in James Gaffney, 'The Relevance of Animal Experimentation to Roman Catholic Ethical Methodology' in Tom Regan (ed), *Animal Sacrifices: Religious Perspectives on the Use of Animals in Science*, p. 149.
76. Thomas Tryon, 'Complaints of the birds and fowls of heaven to their

Creator' in *The Countryman's Companion*, pp. 141–173, cited in Charles R. Magel (ed), *Keyguide to Information Sources in Animal Rights*. I acknowledge my indebtedness to Magel for this reference and for his comprehensive work.

77. Primatt, *Dissertation*, p. 136.
78. For a discussion of 'positive and negative rights' see Stephen R. L. Clark, *The Moral Status of Animals*, and extract in *AAC*, pp. 143–4.
79. Justus George Lawler, 'On the Rights of Animals', p. 6.
80. Andrew Linzey, *Animal Rights: A Christian Assessment*, p. 28.
81. Peter Singer, *Animal Liberation*.
82. See especially R. G. Frey, 'What has sentiency to do with the possession of rights?' in David Paterson and R. D. Ryder (eds), *Animals' Rights – A Symposium*, and, more positively, Tom Regan, 'An Examination and Defense of One Argument Concerning Animal Rights', *Inquiry* Vol. 22, 1979, pp. 189–219.
83. Richard Griffiths, *The Human Use of Animals*, p. 18.
84. Griffiths, p. 6.
85. Griffiths, p. 8.
86. Griffiths, p. 8.
87. Though Griffiths is clearly wrong in supposing that Genesis 9 (which concerns the permission given by God to eat flesh under certain conditions) is the 'basic' text (p. 6). This is simply loading the evidence. The prior text is Genesis 1.29 where humans are prescribed a vegetarian diet.
88. Andrew Linzey, *Christianity and the Rights of Animals*.
89. Barth, *Dogmatics in Outline*, p. 54.
90. Dietrich Bonhoeffer, *Ethics*, p. 127.
91. See Linzey, *Christianity and the Rights of Animals*, p. 8.
92. See, especially, chapter 2, pp. 33–35 and chapter 8, *passim*.
93. James Gustafson, *Theology and Ethics*, p. 96.
94. Barth, *CD*, 111/2, p. 388.
95. Oliver Wendell Holmes Sr., *Life and Letters of Oliver Wendell Holmes*, Vol. 1, p. 274. I am grateful to Peter J. Wexler for this reference.
96. Jürgen Moltmann, *The Crucified God*, p. 275. Moltmann does go some way to remedy this deficiency in his *God in Creation*. However, he almost entirely omits discussion of the status of animals.
97. A. D. Galloway's *The Cosmic Christ* is still a foundational text in this regard. However Galloway does not specifically consider the status of sentient creation.
98. Linzey, *Christianity and the Rights of Animals*, p. 97.
99. See, for example, the discussion paper issued by the General Synod of the Church of England, *Human Rights: Our Understanding and our Responsibilities*. For a recent review of the significance of rights language in Roman Catholic and Protestant theology, see Charles Villa-Vicencio, *A*

Theology of Reconstruction: Nation-Building and Human Rights. Although entirely concerned with human rights, he gives a convincing account of how rights theory is central to moral theology together with some account of how theology can make a distinctive contribution to the development of rights theory in general. See, esp., pp. 117–195.

100. Linzey, *Christianity and the Rights of Animals*, p. 97.
101. Ibid, p. 98.

2. The Moral Priority of the Weak

1. Peter Singer, 'All Animals are Equal', *Philosophic Exchange*, Vol. 1, No. 5, Summer 1974. Parts of the article appeared in a review of S. and R. Godlovitch and J. Harris (eds), *Animals, Men and Morals* in *The New York Review of Books*, 5 April 1973. Also reprinted in Tom Regan and Peter Singer (eds), *Animal Rights and Human Obligations*, pp. 148–162, and in P. A. B. Clarke and Andrew Linzey (eds), *Political Theory and Animal Rights*, pp. 162–167. All subsequent page references are to the 1976 reprint in *Animal Rights and Human Obligations*.
2. Singer, p. 149.
3. Singer, p. 150.
4. Singer, p. 154.
5. Mary Midgley, *Animals and Why They Matter*, pp. 65–73.
6. Singer, pp. 158–9. The references in Singer's text are to William Frankena, 'The Concept of Social Justice' in R. Brant (ed), *Social Justice*, p. 19; H. A. Bedau, 'Egalitarianism and the Idea of Equality' in J. R. Pennock and J. W. Chapman (eds), *Nomos IX: Equality*, and G. Vastos, 'Justice and Equality' in Brant, *Social Justice*, p. 48.
7. Singer, p. 159.
8. Karl Barth, 'The Yes of God the Creator', 'Creation as Justification' in *Church Dogmatics*, III/1, pp. 383–4.
9. Karl Barth, *The Humanity of God*, p. 45.
10. Karl Barth, *Humanity of God*, pp. 69–70; my emphasis.
11. Karl Barth, *Church Dogmatics*, III/1, p. 181 n.
12. See John Austin Baker, 'Biblical Attitudes to Nature' in Hugh Montefiore (ed), *Man and Nature*, p. 95.
13. Karl Barth, *Church Dogmatics*, III/1, p. 178.
14. John Austin Baker, in *Man and Nature*, p. 105.
15. *Man and Nature*, ibid.
16. For a collection of readings from these and other saints, see Andrew Linzey and Tom Regan (eds), *Compassion for Animals: Readings and Prayers*. The prayer of St Basil is reproduced on p. 34.
17. Arthur Broome, 'Prospectus of the SPCA', 25 June 1824, from *RSPCA*

Records, Vol. II (1823–26) pp. 203–4. I am grateful to Olive Martyn, the librarian of the RSPCA, for a copy of this document.

18. Lord Shaftesbury, letter 30 April 1881, cited by Roberta Kalechofsky in *Between the Species: A Journal of Ethics*, Vol. 6, No. 3, Summer 1990, p. 160.

19. See E. G. Fairholme and W. Pain, *A Century of Work for Animals: The History of the RSPCA, 1824–1924*, pp. 165f, and Gerald Carson, *Men, Beasts and Gods: A History of Cruelty and Kindness to Animals*, pp. 103f.

20. Bishop of Exeter (Robert Mortimer) cited in Andrew Linzey, *Animal Rights*, p. 5.

21. Peter Singer, *Practical Ethics*, p. 133.

22. This is the argument I also deploy *against* the institutionalization of experiments on embryos; see P. A. B. Clarke and Andrew Linzey, *Research on Embryos: Politics, Theology and Law*, pp. 37–61.

23. The view that animals may suffer more than humans is implicitly supported in Bernard E. Rollin, *The Unheeded Cry: Animal Consciousness, Animal Pain and Science*, p. 145.

24. Peter Singer, *Practical Ethics*, p. 46.

25. Peter Singer, 'All Animals are Equal', p. 156.

26. Peter Singer, *Practical Ethics*, p. 58; my emphasis.

27. Lord Shaftesbury, letter to Frances Power Cobbe, 3 September 1878, extract in Jon Wynne-Tyson (ed), *The Extended Circle: A Dictionary of Humane Thought*, p. 321. Though it may be noted that Shaftesbury did previously support revision rather than abolition because he feared that 'abolition would be a dead letter', Speech on the Cruelty to Animals Bill, *Hansard*, 22 May 1876, pp. 1016f. I am grateful to Vanessa Clarke for this reference.

28. It is worth remembering how comparatively recent is the declaration of the rights of children, see *The UN Declaration of the Rights of the Child*; also John Bradford, *The Spiritual Rights of the Child*, A Discussion Paper. In 1989 the United Nations unanimously adopted a new Convention on the Rights of the Child. The Convention passed into international law in September 1990. To date over 70 countries have ratified the Convention *not* including the United Kingdom; see *The Needs and Rights of Children*, 'Principles', p. 1.

29. *Focus on Bats: Their Conservation and the Law*, p. 9. For precise details of the legislation see *Wildlife and Countryside Act 1981*, section 12; schedule 7.

30. See *Focus on Bats*.

3. Humans as the Servant Species

1. See, e.g., Oliver Barclay, 'Animal Rights: A Critique' and Andrew Linzey, 'Animal Rights: A Reply to Barclay'.

2. James Barr, 'The Image of God in the Book of Genesis – a Study in Terminology', *Bulletin of the John Rylands Library*, Vol. 51, No. 1, Autumn

1968, pp. 12–13. Barr appears to reject absolutely any 'referential meaning' of the phrase 'image of God'. He writes that there is 'no reason to believe that this writer (P) has in his mind any definite idea about the content or the location of the image of God'. Such a view should not obscure, however, the possibility of developing an understanding of the 'image' in a way that links it with the further notion of 'dominion', and which may enhance the view of the priestly role of humanity which I have advocated here.

3. Robert Runcie, 'Theology, the University and the Modern World' in Paul A. B. Clarke and Andrew Linzey (eds), *Theology, the University and the Modern World*, pp. 19–20.

4. Desmond Morris, *The Naked Ape*, p. 210.

5. Aristotle, *The Politics*, I, viii.

6. Aquinas, *Summa Contra Gentiles*, Book III, Part II, Ch. CXII. Extract in Tom Regan and Peter Singer (eds), *Animal Rights and Human Obligations*, pp. 56–9.

7. See Andrew Linzey, *Christianity and the Rights of Animals*, p. 18.

8. John Austin Baker, *Travels in Oudamovia*, pp. 53–4.

9. Baker, p. 54.

10. Helen Waddell, *Peter Abelard*, Granada edn, pp. 194–6. Used by permission of Constable & Co.

11. Thomas Torrance, *The Trinitarian Faith*, pp. 285f.

12. Charles Raven, *The Creator Spirit*, p. 120; cited and discussed in A. Richard Kingston, 'Theodicy and Animal Welfare' in Andrew Linzey and Tom Regan (eds), *Animals and Christianity*, p. 77.

13. Julian of Norwich, *Showings*, pp. 130–1.

14. Margery Kempe cited in Ambrose Agius, *God's Animals*, p. 46.

15. Joseph Plunkett (1887–1916), 'I See His Blood Upon the Rose'.

16. Edith Sitwell, 'Still Falls the Rain', *Collected Poems*, Sinclair Stevenson 1993. Used by permission.

17. The Byzantine Rite, verse from the Mattins of Holy Saturday in *The Lenten Triodion*, cited and discussed in A. M. Allchin, *The Dynamic of Tradition*, and anthologized in Andrew Linzey and Tom Regan (eds), *Compassion for Animals: Prayers and Readings*, p. 86.

18. Alexander Pope, 'Essay on Man', extract in Linzey and Regan, *Song of Creation*, p. 33. The Plunkett and Sitwell poems are included here, too.

19. Archbishop Leighton, cited and discussed in Michael Paternoster, *Man: The World's High Priest*, pp. 7f. I am grateful to Paternoster for the inspiration for this chapter.

20. Cf. 'It was during this expedition, in the stillness of the vast solitude of the Ordos desert, that one Easter Sunday he finished the mystical and philosophical poem, *Mass Upon the Altar of the World*. Alone before God, he prays with lyrical fervour: "Christ of glory, hidden power stirring in the heart of matter, glowing centre in which the unnumbered strands of the manifold

are knit together; strength inexorable as the world and warm as life; you whose brow is of snow, whose eyes are of fire, whose feet are more dazzling than gold poured from the furnace; you whose hands hold captive the stars; you, the first and the last, the living, the dead, the reborn; you, who gather up in your superabundant oneness every delight, every taste, every energy, every phase of existence, to you my being cries out with a longing as vast as the universe: for you indeed are my Lord and my God."' Pierre Leroy, 'Teilhard de Chardin; The Man' in P. Teilhard de Chardin, *Le Milieu Divin*, p. 26. See also P. Teilhard de Chardin, *Hymn of the Universe*.

21. S. T. Coleridge, 'To Nature', included in Linzey and Regan, *Song of Creation*, p. 68.
22. George Herbert, 'Providence', cited and discussed in Paternoster, *Man*, pp. 8f.
23. Thomas Torrance, *Divine and Contingent Order*, pp. 129–130; my emphasis.
24. John Zizioulas, 'Preserving God's Creation. Three Lectures on Theology and Ecology, 1', p. 3.
25. Barth, *Church Dogmatics*, III/4, p. 355.
26. See my discussion in chapter 6, pp. 103–106.
27. Rom. 8.19–22 (RSV).
28. Nietzsche, *Thoughts Out of Season*, p. 149. I am grateful to Ildi Clarke for this reference.
29. Nietzsche, p. 154.
30. St Isaac the Syrian cited in Vladimir Lossky, *The Mystical Theology of the Eastern Church*, p. 111; also cited and discussed in A. M. Allchin, *The World is a Wedding*, p. 85.
31. Stephen R. L. Clark, *The Moral Status of Animals*, preface.
32. Humphry Primatt, *Dissertation on the Duty of Mercy*, pp. 288–9; also extract in *AAC*, pp. 127–130.
33. Torrance drawing upon scientific models offers a most satisfying interpretation of natural evil, see *Divine and Contingent Order*, pp. 113–128.
34. Zizioulas, 'Preserving God's Creation', p. 1.
35. I was helped in my change of view by reading H. Maurice Relton's excellent essay on 'Patripassianism' in his *Studies in Christian Doctrine*, pp. 61–91. Relton concludes his study by asking this question: 'Why was it that when God did at last reveal Himself – when He could be seen, touched, handled, when He actually walked this Earth and wandered in the streets of Jerusalem – why was it that He appeared *as a man of Sorrows*? Christian theology would answer this question by pointing to the Sin of the World which broke the heart of the Crucified', (p. 91; his emphasis).
36. Schweitzer, *My Life and Thought: An Autobiography*, pp. 279–80.

4. Liberation Theology for Animals

1. John Clare (1793–1864), 'Written in Northampton Country Asylum'. See also William Kean Seymour and John Smith (eds), *The Pattern of Poetry*, p. 136.
2. Gustavo Gutierrez, *A Theology of Liberation*, pp. 24f.; my emphasis.
3. Gutierrez, p. 90; my emphasis.
4. See Gutierrez, pp. 83–105, and Leonardo and Clodovis Boff, *Introducing Liberation Theology*, pp. 43–65.
5. Gutierrez, p. 90; my emphasis.
6. See Mary Midgley, *Animals and Why They Matter: A Journey Around the Species Barrier*, pp. 12–18.
7. Anyone who doubts the difficulty of mainstream Western Christian tradition accommodating ecological perspectives need look no further than the unwavering humanocentricity of the Second Vatican Council. All amply documented in Austin Flannery (ed), *Vatican Council II: The Conciliar and Post Conciliar Documents*.
8. Leonardo Boff, *Saint Francis: A Model for Human Liberation*, p. 4.
9. Boff, *Saint Francis*, p. 15.
10. Boff, *Saint Francis*, p. 18.
11. St Bonaventure, cited by Boff, *Saint Francis*, p. 37; my emphasis.
12. Boff, *Saint Francis*, p. 46; my emphasis.
13. See Boff, *Saint Francis*, chs 2 and 4.
14. Roger D. Sorrell, *St Francis of Assisi and Nature*.
15. Andrew Linzey, *Brother and Sister Creatures: The Saints and Animals*, unpublished manuscript, p. 34.
16. Gutierrez, p. 165.
17. See Edward Carpenter et al, *Animals and Ethics*, p. 21.
18. Gutierrez, citing Karl Barth, p. 6.
19. For my detailed discussion, see Andrew Linzey, *The Neglected Creature: The Doctrine of the Non-Human Creation and its Relationship with the Human in the Thought of Karl Barth*, unpublished PhD thesis.
20. St Athanasius, *Contra Gentes and De Incarnatione*, pp. 113–5.
21. John 1.3 (RSV).
22. For a critique of Küng, see Andrew Linzey, 'Is Anthropocentricity Christian?'
23. St Athanasius, p. 115; my emphasis.
24. See Henry Davis, *Moral and Pastoral Theology*, Vol. II, pp. 258–9; extract in Andrew Linzey and Tom Regan (eds), *AAC*, pp. 130–1.
25. Bernard Häring, *The Law of Christ*, Vol. II, Mercier Press 1963 pp. 361–2.
26. Dostoyevsky, *The Brothers Karamazov*, Vol. I, p. 375.
27. St Athanasius, p. 5.
28. Karl Barth, *The Knowledge of God and the Service of God According to the Teaching of the Reformation* p. 44; my emphasis.

29. Boff, *Jesus Christ Liberator* p. 211; my emphasis.
30. Jon Sobrino, *The True Church and the Poor*, p. 49.
31. Boff, *Jesus Christ Liberator*, 69.
32. Gutierrez, p. 81.
33. Keith Ward, *The Promise*, p. 2.
34. Rom. 8.18–24 (RSV).
35. Konrad Lorenz, *On Aggression* p. 195; cited and discussed in Miriam Rothschild, *Animals and Man*, p. 52; my emphasis.
36. Tom Regan, *The Case for Animal Rights*, pp. 232–265.
37. For example, John Wesley in his sermon on 'The General Deliverance', *Sermons on Several Occasions*, Vol. ii, pp. 324–343. He specifically envisages an other worldly redemption for all creatures; also extract in *Animals and Christianity*, pp. 101–3.

5. Animal Rights and Parasitical Nature

1. Anne Rice, *Interview with the Vampire*, pp. 10–20.
2. Rice, p. 73.
3. The other titles are *The Vampire Lestat* and *The Queen of the Damned* both published by Ballantine Books. I am grateful to Marly Cornell for introducing me to this literature.
4. Rice, p. 83.
5. Rice, p. 88; my emphasis.
6. Rice, p. 169.
7. Plato, 'The Statesman' in Harold N. Fowler and W. R. M. Lamb (tr), *Plato*, 271d–4c; extract in P. A. B. Clarke and Andrew Linzey (eds), *Political Theory and Animal Rights*, pp. 53–55.
8. See Gen. 1.29.
9. Samuel Pufendorf (1632–92), *The Law of Nature and Nations*, Vol. II, pp. 530–1; extract in *Political Theory and Animal Rights*, pp. 116–119.
10. John Macquarrie, 'Rethinking Natural Law' in *Three Issues in Ethics*, p. 92.
11. Macquarrie, p. 97; my emphasis.
12. Macquarrie, p. 110; my emphasis.
13. John Armstrong, *The Idea of Holiness and the Humane Response*, p. 44.
14. W. R. Inge, 'The Rights of Animals' in *Lay Thoughts of a Dean*, p. 199; cited and discussed also in Andrew Linzey, *Christianity and the Rights of Animals*, pp. 145f.
15. Stephen R. L. Clark, *The Moral Status of Animals*, p. 83.
16. Gerard Manley Hopkins (1844–89), 'God's Grandeur'.
17. Charles Davis, *God's Grace in History*, pp. 21f; the reference to Davis is lifted from my *Animal Rights*, p. 16.
18. Karl Barth, 'Creation as Justification' in *Church Dogmatics*, III/1, pp. 348f.
19. Clark, p. 196.

20. Macquarrie, p. 109.
21. Eph. 1.9–10 (REB).
22. Col. 1.20 (REB).
23. Barth, *Church Dogmatics*, III/4, 'The Command of God the Creator', p. 256.
24. William Godwin (1756–1836), *Enquiry Concerning Political Justice and Its Influence on Modern Morals and Happiness*, pp. 216–18; extract in *Political Theory and Animal Rights*, pp. 132–4.
25. Godwin, ibid.
26. Werner Jaeger, *The Theology of the Early Greek Philosophers*, pp. 36, 115–6. The translation from Heraclitus is from Jaeger; cited and discussed in Macquarrie, pp. 93f.

6. Animal Experiments as Un-Godly Sacrifices

1. Hugh Montefiore (ed), *Man and Nature*, p. 67. Hereafter referred to as Montefiore, *Man*. Unfortunately, however, the Report does not feel it right to 'lay down general principles derived from theological insights' (pp. 80f.) and thus does not consider the question of animal treatment directly. One can only point out, however, that this procedure has been followed for many years in moral theology, and many publications of the Board for Social Responsibility attempt to offer analysis and critique based on theological insight.
2. H. P. Owen, *Concepts of Deity*, p. 1. For a discussion of these terms, see pp. 4–34. Chapter 3 will have shown, however, that I reject the notion of divine impassibility in fidelity to the Gospel narratives.
3. E. L. Mascall, *The Importance of Being Human*, p. 83. Hereafter referred to as Mascall, *Importance*.
4. '… in all things like unto us, sin only excepted; begotten of the Father before ages as to his Godhead, and in the last days, the Same, for us and for our salvation, of Mary the Virgin *Theotokos* as to his manhood' (from the Council definition). See Aloys Grillmeier, *Christ in Christian Tradition*, p. 481. This book gives a useful discussion of the development of Christian doctrine up to the time of Chalcedon.
5. E. L. Mascall, *The Openness of Being*, p. 146. Mascall also argues that it is the rationality of humans that especially enables them to be open to God in a rational and personal way, a capacity he judges impossible for other creatures (p. 148).
6. E.g., 'Salvation by means of a flight out of the world, an escape of the spirit from the world, will appear as a limitation or spiritualistic deformation. In reality we are dealing with a way of salvation which does not tear us out of the world but is rather opened *for* this created world, in the Word become flesh'; Vladimir Lossky, *The Vision of God*, p. 58; his emphasis.
7. Brian Horne, *A World to Gain: Incarnation and the Hope of Renewal*, p. 55.

Hereafter referred to as Horne, *World*. Horne also writes: 'My concern is to argue that if there is to be a halt to the destruction of our environment and a restoration of the world of nature, then a change must begin in the Church at a fundamental level. Quite simply, the Church should be less concerned about the salvation of souls and more concerned about the sanctification of life, or, to be more precisely theological, less concerned about 'justification by faith' and more concerned about 're-creation by grace'; and the re-creation will extend to the whole of the natural order. We are not souls to be plucked from matter on the day of our salvation, we are part of a universe which along with us waits for the consummation that has been promised by God in Christ. At the level of doctrine this means the reintegration of the doctrines of creation, incarnation, and atonement. Wholly interdependent, each must be read in terms of others' (p. 53).

8. For example, Mascall suggests: 'Insofar as the evolutionary process may have been distorted before the advent of man, it is reasonable to explain this distortion by the common Christian doctrine that one of the functions which God has committed to the angels is the supervision of the lower creation, so that the defection of certain of the angels has had as one of its consequences a disorganization of the material world and the dislocation of its functions' (Mascall, *Importance*, p. 80).

9. Paul Tillich, *Systematic Theology*, Vol. 2, Part III, p. 96. Tillich also writes: 'If there are non-human "worlds" in which existential estrangement is not only real – as it is in the whole universe – but in which there is also a type of awareness of this estrangement, such worlds cannot be without the operation of saving power within them ... The manifestation of saving power in one place implies that saving power is operating in all places' (p. 96). It is interesting to note that the kind of awareness Tillich postulates is firmly held by many biologists, e.g., W. H. Thorpe, *Animal Nature and Human Nature*, p. 320, and Marian Stamp Dawkins, *Animal Suffering: The Science of Animal Welfare*, pp. 10 ff.

10. *Man in His Living Environment*, p. 65.

11. Mascall, *The Christian Universe*, p. 107.

12. Montefiore, *Man*, p. 63.

13. Keith Ward, *Rational Theology and the Creativity of God*, pp. 201–202. Also: 'If there is any sentient being which suffers pain, that being – whatever it is and however it is manifested – must find that pain transfigured by greater joy. I am quite agnostic as to how this is to happen; but that it must be asserted to be true follows from the doctrine that God is love, and would not therefore create any being whose sole destiny was to suffer pain' (Ward, *The Concept of God*, p. 223).

14. For example, C. F. D. Moule argues: 'To what, then, is man's true sonship going to lead nature? To some spurious immortality? By no means! The emancipation of nature from its servitude to decay consists, exactly as in the

emancipation of an individual from lust, in its material still being used – indeed being used up – but in an overall purpose that is part of God's design' (*Man and Nature in the New Testament*, p. 14). Hereafter referred to as Moule, *Man and Nature*. But the point that Moule overlooks is that animals (unlike lust) have intrinsic value.

15. See Bishop Butler and John Wesley (James Turner, *Reckoning with the Beast*, p. 8). Also C. S. Lewis' theory about tame animals, *The Problem of Pain*, pp. 127–8. For a discussion of Lewis' views, see C. E. M. Joad and C. S. Lewis, 'The Pains of Animals', *The Month*, February 1950, pp. 95–104.

16. Montefiore, *Man*, p. 67.

17. Karl Barth, *Church Dogmatics*, Vol. III, Part 2, p. 78.

18. Edward Carpenter et al., *Animals and Ethics*, p. 6. This report was the result of 'A group of biologists, theologians, veterinarians and others concerned with the welfare of animals [who] met during 1977–1979 to prepare an agreed statement on man's relationship with animals which would reflect an ethical approach within a factual context' (p. 5).

19. Mascall, *Corpus Christi*, pp. 86–87. Hereafter referred to as Mascall, *Corpus*.

20. Masure cited by Mascall, *Corpus*, p. 92; my emphasis. For a supporting view, see Frances Young, *The Use of Sacrificial Ideas in Greek Christian Writers from the New Testament to John Chrysostom*, Patristic Monograph Series, No. 5, pp. 54 ff.

21. Mascall, *Corpus*, p. 93.

22. See, e.g., Robert Dobbie, 'Sacrifice and Morality in the Old Testament', pp. 297–300, and H. H. Rowley, 'Sacrifice and Morality: A Rejoinder', pp. 341–342.

23. See, for example, the argument of Heb. 2.14ff.; also Mascall, *Corpus*, pp. 94ff. Jesus' rejection of animal sacrifice may be deduced, e.g., in Mark, by the cleansing of the temple (11.51) and the wise reply to the scribe (12.32–35).

24. H. H. Rowley goes as far as to suggest that 'all the animal sacrifices of the Temple were abolished for the Church' and that in doing so it 'repudiated a part of the inheritance of Judaism', *The Biblical Doctrine of Election*, p. 163.

25. Moule comes to a similar conclusion: 'His [humankind's] distinctive contribution to the ecological set-up is meant to be rational and conscious manipulation in accordance with the will of God. It seems to me that such a view is integral with the confession of real incarnation and of new creation in Christ' (*Man and Nature*, p. 16). But he appears to overlook that this 'manipulation' in accordance with God's will might have a moral dimension in the light of the incarnation. Once again the implication that animals are simply things to be 'manipulated' ignores their intrinsic value.

26. Patrick Corbett, 'Postscript' in Stanley and Roslind Godlovitch and John Harris (eds), *Animals, Men and Morals*, p. 236.

27. *The Proposed International Guidelines for Biochemical Research Involving Human Subjects*, p. 22, paras 1f.

28. *Trials of War Criminals Before the Nuremberg Military Tribunals Under Control Council Law No. 10*, vol. 2, pp. 181f. I am grateful to J. M. Finnis for this reference and note 27 above.

29. Tom Regan, *The Case for Animal Rights*, p. 377.

30. See chapter 2, pp. 42–44

31. Hans Ruesch, *Slaughter of the Innocent*, p. 35. Also my review in *Resurgence*, September–October 1979, p. 35.

32. See, e.g., the discussion in chapter 3, pp. 45–47. It is a matter of continuing debate to what extent the Western Christian tradition is responsible for the current misuse of nature. Horne offers a favourable interpretation of Aquinas: 'The idea of the divine *order*, almost a hierarchy of things in the universe, is central to Thomas Aquinas' understanding of creation. Each thing in the universe occupies its proper place and exists to serve those things that are ranged above it ... The proper function of every particle of the created order is ordained by God. On grounds of Thomist theology alone one could argue that the use to which man has put the world in which he lives and has responsibilities is a disruption of God's beneficent ordering of nature' (*World*, p. 45; his emphasis). I think it is right that we should seek the most charitable interpretation of theologians, even those whose views we may regard as erroneous. Too much critical engagement (including my own) has been infected with a prosecuting zeal at the expense of understanding. I regret to add that much in Peter Singer's *Animal Liberation*, pp. 203–220, exhibits this deficiency. The problem with Aquinas it seems to me is not his notion of an overarching divine order but his oversimplification (we can now judge with hindsight and with the benefit of knowledge simply not at his disposal at the time of writing) of what constitutes this divine order and its moral significance. It is not so obvious to us that the created order as we now know it 'serves' the human species in the way postulated.

33. W. H. Vanstone, 'On the Being of Nature', p. 283.

34. See chapter 2, especially pp. 30–33, 36–41.

7. Hunting as the Anti-Gospel of Predation

1. St Francs de Sales, *Introduction to the Devout Life*, p. 175.

2. William H. Ammon, *The Christian Hunter's Survival Guide*, pp. 18, 25, 35, 39–40, 62, 69. I am grateful to Bernard Unti for bringing this book to my attention.

3. Ammon, p. 17. See Cleveland Amory, *Man-Kind? Our Incredible War on Wildlife*.

4. Ammon, p. 58.

5. Peter Singer, *Animal Liberation*, p. 9: cited in Ammon, p. 50.

6. Ammon, p. 44.

7. Ammon, p. 44.

8. Ammon, p. 10.
9. Ammon, p. 42.
10. Ammon, p. 42.
11. Ammon, pp. 64–65.
12. See chapter 8 on vegetarianism, esp. pp. 127–129.
13. Ammon, p. 41.
14. Richard Cartwright Austin, *Beauty of the Lord*, pp. 196–197.
15. Matthew Fox and Jonathon Porritt, 'Green Spirituality', pp. 14–15. Eco-theologians in providing a rationale for predation take up one of the hunter's favourite defences; see, e.g., Jim Ritchoff, 'Epilogue to a Hunting Moment of Truth' in *Mixed Bag: Reminiscences of a Master Raconteur*, pp. 244 f. I am grateful to Stephen Bales for this reference.
16. Peter Kropotkin, *Mutual Aid: A Factor in Evolution*, esp. pp. 60–62, 72–73; extract in Paul Clarke and Andrew Linzey (eds), *Political Theory and Animal Rights*, pp. 88–90.
17. 'The Easter Anthems', *The Alternative Service Book*, Clowes, SPCK, CUP, 1980, pp. 63–64.
18. See Louis Bouyer, *Eucharist*, esp. pp. 130–131f.
19. Edward Carpenter, 'Christian Faith and the Moral Aspects of Hunting' in Patrick Moore (ed), *Against Hunting: A Symposium*, p. 137.
20. See T. F. Torrance, *Divine and Contingent Order*, esp. pp. 113–142 to which reference has already been made in chapter 3 above, p. 54.
21. Ammon, p. 48.

8. Vegetarianism as a Biblical Ideal

1. John Calvin, *Commentaries on the First Book of Moses*, Vol. 1, pp. 291–292. Extract in Andrew Linzey and Tom Regan (eds), *Animals and Christianity*, pp. 199–200.
2. This argument is developed at length in Andrew Linzey, *Christianity and the Rights of Animals*, pp. 141–149.
3. *Where We Stand on Animal Welfare*, p. 1.
4. John Austin Baker, 'Biblical Attitudes to Nature' in Hugh Montefiore (ed), *Man and Nature*, p. 96; see also pp. 93–4.
5. Anthony Phillips, 'Respect for Life in the Old Testament', p. 32. I am indebted to this article, though I am perplexed by the subsequent line: 'While animals, like all God's creation, *were made for man*, he must still order that creation in accordance with God's will' (my emphasis, p. 32). I think a fundamental distinction must be drawn between our dominion over creation and the notion that it was made for our use.
6. Karl Barth, CD 111/4, p. 352; extract in *Animals and Christianity*, pp. 191–193.
7. Barth, p. 353 n.

8. Barth, p. 354.

9. Abraham Isaac Kook, *The Lights of Penitence* etc., pp. 317–323. I am grateful to Jonathan Sacks for this reference.

10. See, *inter alia, Christianity and the Rights of Animals*, p. 148.

11. See, e.g., the discussion in J. Jeremias, *The Eucharistic Words of Jesus*.

12. See, e.g., Geoffrey L. Rudd, *Why Kill for Food?*, pp. 78–90, and Steven Rosen, *Food for the Spirit: Vegetarianism and the World Religions*, pp. 33–39.

13. See, e.g., V. A. Holmes-Gore, *These We Have Not Loved*, pp. 86–9.

14. E.g., J. Todd Ferrier, *On Behalf of the Creatures*, pp. 111f.

15. See, e.g., *The Gospel of the Holy Twelve* and *The Essene Humane Gospel of Jesus*, cited and discussed in Rosen, op. cit.

16. 'The Gospel of the Ebionites' in Montague R. James (ed), *The Apocryphal New Testament*, pp. 8–10.

17. See, e.g., 'The Gospel of Thomas', pp. 49–56; 'The Acts of Thomas', pp. 396–402 and 'The Acts of Philip, pp. 446–448, all in James, op. cit. See also 'The Acts of Peter' in E. Hennecke (ed), *New Testament Apocrypha*, Vol. II, *Apostolic and Early Church Writings*, pp. 294–297.

18. J. A. T. Robinson, 'Need Jesus have been Perfect?' in S. W. Sykes and J. P. Clayton (eds), *Christ, Faith and History*, pp. 39–52.

19. 'Introduction' to Linzey and Regan (eds), *Compassion for Animals*, p. xv.

20. I am grateful to Richard Bauckham for a lecture at Essex University on this theme and for bringing to my attention the significance of this verse. I understand that his work will be published as *Jesus and the Greening of Christianity*.

21. St Richard of Chichester, cited in Butler's *Lives of the Saints*, p. 157; also extract in *Compassion for Animals*, p. 66.

22. *Rule of St Benedict*, ch. 39, p. 46.

23. See Richard D. Ryder, *Animal Revolution*, p. 96. For a history of the Church in America see *The History of the Philadelphia Bible-Christian Church, 1817–1917*. I am grateful to Bernard Unti for this last reference.

9. Genetic Engineering as Animal Slavery

1. George Orwell, *Animal Farm*, Penguin edn, pp. 5–10. Used by permission of Secker and Warburg.

2. For an illustration of some of the dramatic parallels between the two systems, see Marjorie Spiegel, *The Dreaded Comparison: Human and Animal Slavery*, esp. pp. 37–57.

3. Aristotle, *The Politics*, I, viii, p. 79.

4. Aristotle, I, v, pp. 68–9.

5. Aristotle, I, iv, p. 65.

6. See Aristotle, I, v, esp. pp. 67–8.

7. See the discussion in chapter 1, pp. 17–19.

8. Aquinas, *Summa Theologica*, Part 1, Question 93, Article 4, p. 289.
9. The Anti-Slavery Society (180 Brixton Road, London SW9 6AT) campaigns against chattel slavery, debt bondage, serfdom, child exploitation and servile forms of marriage.
10. William Henry Holcombe cited in David Brion Davis, *Slavery and Human Progress*, p. 23.
11. Aristotle, I, v, p. 68.
12. Davis, p. 25.
13. Theodore Weld in Davis, p. 146; his emphasis.
14. See Trevor Dennis, 'Man Beyond Price: Gregory of Nyssa and Slavery' in Andrew Linzey and Peter J. Wexler (eds), *Heaven and Earth*, p. 138. Dennis' essay is a much expanded version of a paper entitled 'The relationship between Gregory of Nyssa's attack on slavery in his fourth homily on *Ecclesiastes* and his treatise *De hominis opiticio*', in *Studia Patristica*, Vol. XVIII, ed. E. A. Livingstone, 1982, pp. 1065–72. I acknowledge my indebtedness to Dennis' essay, not least of all for providing the inspiration for this chapter.
15. See Dennis, p. 137.
16. Davis, p. 13. His emphasis.
17. Robert Schank, cited in *Omni*, January 1988 and in *Agscene*, May 1988, p. 3.
18. Cited in 'Gene Splicing Aims for "Super Animals"', *St Louis Post-Dispatch*, Monday 8 December 1986, p. 4.
19. Aristotle, I, iv, p. 65.
20. For the Roman Catholic view that animals have a moral status identical to that of human property, see Henry Davis, *Moral and Pastoral Theology*, Vol. II, p. 258.
21. See, e.g., John Rogerson, *Genesis 1–11*, See also the discussion in chapter 2 above, esp. pp. 34f.
22. Robert Runcie, 'Address at the Global Forum of Spiritual and Parliamentary Leaders on Human Survival', pp. 13–4; his emphasis. I am grateful to Marion Wells for this reference.
23. Pope John Paul II, *Sollicitudo Rei Socialis*, para. 34, pp. 64–5. I am grateful to have read 'Pope John Paul II on the environment and the place of animals' (1988) by Dr Petroc Willey, formerly of Plater College, Oxford, who explains the significance of the encyclical for Roman Catholic theology.
24. Voltaire cited in Davis, p. 130.
25. See Davis, esp. pp. 129–153. I have utilized this illustration in my 'Moral Dreams and Practical Realities'.
26. Vernon G. Pursel, cited in *St Louis Post-Dispatch*, art. cit., p. 5.
27. Percy Gardner, *Evolution in Christian Ethics*, pp. 188–9; my emphasis.
28. Gardner, p. 190.
29. Adolf Hitler, *Mein Kampf*, pp. 367–369.
30. C. S. Lewis, *Vivisection*, pp. 9–10. Lewis wrote this essay while a Fellow of Magdalen College, Oxford, at the request of George R. Farnum who was

then President of the New England Anti-Vivisection Society. Apparently Farnum was a friend of Richard W. Livingstone, then President of Corpus Christi College, Oxford and Vice-Chancellor of the University, who first called Farnum's attention to Lewis' work on this subject as shown in his book *The Problem of Pain*. See Farnum's Foreword, p. 4.

31. Lewis Carroll, *Some Popular Fallacies about Vivisection*, pp. 14–16; his emphasis. I am grateful to Richard Bell of the Bodleian Library for this document.

32. For a theological discussion of nature which underlines this point see Paulos Mar Gregorios, *The Human Presence: Ecological Spirituality and the Age of the Spirit*, esp. pp. 85–93.

33. See, e.g., Rom.6.6. Paul understands Christian discipleship as 'dying and rising with Christ' in baptism whereby our old selfish natures are transformed.

Guide to the Literature

including works cited in text

Adams, Carol J., *The Sexual Politics of Meat: A Feminist-Vegetarian Critical Theory*, Crossroad, New York 1990. A pioneering and original book exploring the connection between the exploitation of women and the exploitation of animals.

Agius, Ambrose, *God's Animals*, foreword by John Heenan, Catholic Study Circle for Animal Welfare 1970. Largely a compendium of statements by Roman Catholic authorities on the right use of animals.

Allchin, A. M., *The World is a Wedding: Explorations in Christian Spirituality*, Darton, Longman and Todd 1978.

—— *The Dynamic of Tradition*, Darton, Longman and Todd 1981.

Two of the many Allchin books appropriating Orthodox insights about, *inter alia*, this worldly spirituality and the renewal of the earth. The first contains his piece on 'Wholeness and Transfiguration in the lives of St Francis and St Seraphim' (pp. 80–94).

Ammon, William, H., *The Christian Hunter's Survival Guide*, Fleming H. Revell Company, New Jersey 1989. A biblical and practical defence of sport hunting from a conservative evangelical.

Amory, Cleveland, *Man-Kind? Our Incredible War on Wildlife*, Harper and Row, New York 1974. Pioneering moral and practical critique of sport hunting in the US.

Aquinas, St Thomas, *Summa Theologica*, ET by the English Dominican Fathers, Benziger Brothers, New York 1918, Question 64, Article 1; Question 65, Article 3.

—— *Summa Theologica*, ET by the English Dominican Fathers, Burns and Oates and Wasborne, 2nd revd edn 1922, Part 1, Question 93, Article 4.

—— *Summa Contra Gentiles*, ET by the English Dominican Fathers, Benziger Brothers, New York 1928, Book III, Ch. XII.

Key texts concerning the theological status of animals.

Aristotle, *The Politics*, 1, viii, ET by T.A. Sinclair, Penguin Books 1985. Key section on the 'natural' use of animals.

Armstrong, John, *The Idea of Holiness and the Humane Response: A Study in the Concept of Holiness and its Social Consequences*, Allen and Unwin 1981. Discusses the humanitarian laws concerning animals in the Hebrew Bible.

Athanasius, St, *Contra Gentes and De Incarnatione*, ed and ET by Robert W. Thomson, Clarendon Press 1971. *De Incarnatione* offers an impressively inclusive doctrine of the *Logos* which could provide a basis for both eco- and animal theology.

Attfield, Robin, *The Ethics of Environmental Concern*, Blackwell 1983. Another philosophical discussion significant only for the fact that he defends the Christian tradition (more or less successfully) against Singer and others (see chapter 2, 'Man's Dominion and the Judaeo-Christian Heritage', pp. 20–34).

Attwater, Donald, *St John Chrysostom*, Catholic Book Club 1960. Highlights Chrysostom's theological concern for animals.

Augustine, St, *Concerning the City of God against the Pagans*, ET by Henry Bettenson, intro. by David Knowles, Penguin Books, 4th edn 1980. The rational endowment of humans makes them uniquely capable of 'enjoying eternal peace' in the 'Heavenly City'. Salvation consists in liberation from the 'animal body' which weighs down the soul (see pp. 872–78).

Austin, Richard Cartwright, *Baptized into Wilderness: A Christian Perspective on John Muir*, John Knox Press, Atlanta 1987.

—— *Beauty of the Lord: Awakening the Senses*, John Knox Press, Atlanta 1988.

—— *Hope for the Land: Nature in the Bible*, John Knox Press, Atlanta 1988.

—— *Reclaiming America: Restoring Nature to Culture*, Creekside Press, Abingdon, VA 1990.

Austin is the Presbyterian Church's leading practical eco-theologian in the US. Austin rarely deals with questions of justice to individual animals. He extols the beauty of predation (*Beauty of the Lord*, p. 197). While he endorses a charter of civil rights for the earth (*Reclaiming America*, pp. 156–172) individual animal rights as such do not get a look in.

Baker, John Austin, *Travels in Oudamovia*, Faith Press 1976. Short work of theological fantasy containing many imaginative insights not least of all into the world of the non-human.

—— 'Biblical Attitudes to Nature' in Montefiore, *Man and Nature* (see below). Exemplary essay harmonizing biblical insights towards nature and animals in particular.

Barclay, Oliver, 'Animal Rights: A Critique', *Science and Christian Belief*, Vol. 4, No. 10, 1992, pp. 49–61. A critique of my *Christianity and the Rights of Animals* (1987) from a conservative evangelical standpoint. See my reply (below).

Barr, James, 'The Image of God in the Book of Genesis – A Study in Terminology', *Bulletin of the John Rylands Library*, Vol. 51, No. 1, Autumn 1968. Takes issue with the common view that the *imago dei* has a 'referential meaning'.

Barth, Karl, *Church Dogmatics, The Doctrine of Creation*, Vol. III/1–4, ed and ET by G. W. Bromiley and T. F. Torrance, T. & T. Clark, Edinburgh and Scribners, New York, 1958–61. In my view, Barth's work on creation, although sadly humanocentric, can be restructured to provide a pleasing trinitarian basis for animal theology. See my *The Neglected Creature* (below).

—— *The Knowledge of God and the Service of God According to the Teaching of the Reformation*, Hodder and Stoughton 1949.

—— *Dogmatics in Outline*, SCM Press, London and Harper, New York, 1949.

—— *Evangelical Theology: An Introduction*, Collins, 3rd edn 1971.

—— *The Humanity of God*, Collins Fontana 1961.

—— *Ethics*, ed by Dietrich Braun, ET by G. W. Bromiley, T. & T. Clark 1981.

Bedau, H. A., 'Egalitarianism and the Idea of Equality' in J. R. Pennock and J. W. Chapman (eds), *Nomos IX: Equality*, New York 1967. Defends a humanocentric view of moral equality. Criticized by Peter Singer in 'All Animals are Equal' (below).

Benton, Ted, *Natural Relations: Ecology, Animal Rights and Social Justice*, Verso 1993. A rather unsystematic critique of animal rights from a socialist perspective. Its general thesis against ascribing individual rights to animals ignores the function of rights discourse in the historical struggle for emancipation.

Birch, Charles, Eakin, William, McDaniel, Jay B. (eds), *Liberating Life: Contemporary Approaches to Ecological Theology*, Orbis Books, Maryknoll 1990. Despite its many limitations (see my review in *Studies in Christian Ethics* (1992) Vol. 5, No. 1, pp. 64–7), it is the only currently comprehensive anthology available. The Appendix reproduces the sadly discarded Annecy Report on Liberating Life written for the World Council of Churches.

Black, John, *The Dominion of Man: The Search for Ecological Responsibility*, University of Edinburgh Press 1970. Argues that there are two traditions in Genesis, one of domination and the other of stewardship.

Boff, Leonardo, *Jesus Christ Liberator: A Critical Christology for Our Time* (1972), Orbis Books, Maryknoll 1978 and SPCK, London 1980.

—— *Saint Francis: A Model for Human Liberation*, Crossroad, New York 1982 and SCM Press, London 1985. An attempt to spell out the meaning of Francis for human liberation and care for creation by a major figure in liberation theology. Disappointingly humanocentric. No specific consideration of animals.

—— and Boff, Clodovis, *Introducing Liberation Theology*, Burns and Oates 1990.

Bonaventure, St, *The Life of St Francis*, SPCK 1978. Contains Bonaventure's theological defence of St Francis on the grounds of a similar ontology between humans and non-human creatures.

Bonhoeffer, Dietrich, *Ethics*, SCM Press, London and Macmillan, New York, 2nd edn 1971. In a much neglected section, Bonhoeffer argues for the rights of the natural world and in particular that duties flow from rights and not vice versa (pp. 176 f.).

Bostock, Stephen St C., *Zoos and Animals Rights: The Ethics of Keeping Animals*, Routledge 1993. A practical defence of zoos weak on theoretical and ethical aspects.

Bouyer, Louis, *Eucharist: Theology and Spirituality of the Eucharistic Prayer*, University of Notre Dame Press 1968. Includes extracts from early eucharistic prayers indicating a keen awareness of the goodness of creation.

Brabazon, James, *Albert Schweitzer: A Biography*, Gollancz 1976. A critical and sympathetic biography of the man who has yet to be rehabilitated from premature scorn.

Bracken, Joseph A., *Society and Spirit: A Trinitarian Cosmology*, foreword by John B. Cobb, Jr., Susquehanna University Press/Associated University Presses 1991. A ground-breaking attempt to formulate a new trinitarian cosmology arguing that creation is ordered to life within the divine community itself.

Bradford, John, *The Spiritual Rights of the Child: A Discussion Paper*, Church of England Children's Society 1979. It is striking how church bodies frequently accept the need for rights language in relation to weaker and vulnerable human beings – for example children – but not to other sentients such as animals.

Bridger, Francis, 'Ecology and Eschatology: A Neglected Dimension', *Tyndale Bulletin*, Vol. 41, No. 2, 1990. An impressive discussion of the significance of eschatological language for ecology and the Pauline vision of a consummated creation.

Broome, Arthur, 'Prospectus of the SPCA', 25 June 1824, *RSPCA Records*, Vol. II (1823–26). One of the earliest statements of the aims of the animal protection movement.

Brown, Les, *Cruelty to Animals: The Moral Debt*, The Macmillan Press 1988. The central theme of the book is 'the limited human capacity for impartiality in giving consideration to the interests of animals' (p. x). A useful philosophical discussion with consideration of practical issues. Lacks engagement with animal rights theory, however.

Butler, Alban, *Lives of the Saints*, revised by Herbert Thurston and Donald Attwater, P. J. Kennedy & Sons, New York 1946. Indispensable source of folk-lore about the saints and animals.

Butler, Joseph (Bishop), *The Analogy of Religion, Natural and Revealed to the Constitution and Course of Nature*, intro. by Henry Morley, George Routledge and Sons, 3rd edn 1887. Butler argues that we are mistaken in our common belief that our sensible change of form at death is equivalent to destruction and that such a view is 'equally applicable to brutes'. A strong defence of animal rationality and immortality (see, esp., pp. 12–21).

Button, John, *A Dictionary of Green Ideas*, Routledge 1988. Disappointing as a Dictionary but does elaborate some key concepts.

Callicott, J. Baird (ed), *A Companion to A Sand County Almanac*, University of Wisconsin Press 1987. Callicott's philosophical defence and restatement of Leopold's famous 'land ethic'.

Calvin, John, *Commentaries on the First Book of Moses*, Vol. 1, Calvin Translation Society, Edinburgh 1847. Comprises his interpretation of the first creation saga and his rejection of vegetarianism.

—— *Commentaries: The Epistle of Paul the Apostle to the Romans and to the Thessalonians*, ed by D. W. Torrance and T. F. Torrance, Oliver and Boyd 1961. On Romans 8: Animals have been cursed because of human sin but they will be delivered. 'Let us, therefore, be content with this simple doctrine – their [the animals'] constitution will be such, and their order so complete, that no appearance of deformity or of impermanence will be seen' (p. 173).

Caring for the Earth: A Strategy for Sustainable Living, IUCN/UNEP/WWF, Geneva 1991. This is the conservation strategy for sustainable living devised by the World Conservation Union. Heavy on practical prescription, weak on ethical theory. One one hand it wants to oppose cruelty and wanton destruction; on the other it defends fur trapping, whaling and the 'harvesting' of wild creatures such as elephants as renewable resources (see pp. 9, 14–5). In my view the circle cannot be squared; it is unethical to regard sentients as resources.

Carpenter, Edward, 'Christian Faith and the Moral Aspects of Hunting' in Patrick Moore (ed), *Against Hunting: A Symposium*, Gollancz 1965. Pioneering essay critical of the predatory defence of sport hunting.

—— et al., *Animals and Ethics*, Watkins Publishing 1980. The former Dean of Westminster's Working Group Report on animal welfare. It broke new ground in recommending minimum standards for the care of all managed animals.

Carroll, Lewis (Charles L. Dodgson), *Some Popular Fallacies about Vivisection*, printed for private circulation, Oxford, June 1875. Carroll's satire on animal experimentation.

Carson, Gerald, *Men, Beasts and Gods: A History of Cruelty and Kindness to Animals*, Charles Scribner's Sons, New York 1972. A history of animal protection work in the US.

Cavalieri, Paola, and Singer, Peter (eds), *The Great Ape Project: Equality beyond Humanity*, Fourth Estate 1993. A collection of essays defending the moral status of apes. Some essays (e.g. by Stephen Clark and James Rachels) are good but all lack theological discussion.

Choosing a Sustainable Future, The Report of the National Commission on the Environment, Island Press, Washington DC 1993. A detailed report on sustainable strategies for the US. Justice for animals is not a topic considered here.

Clark, Stephen R. L., *The Moral Status of Animals*, Clarendon Press 1977. A ground-breaking philosophical discussion – and one that is sensitive to the theological dimension of the subject. Now reissued as an Oxford paperback.

—— *The Nature of the Beast: Are Animals Moral?*, OUP 1982. A philosophical dialogue with biology about the moral status of animals leaving open the possibility of altruism in animals.

—— *How to Think about the Earth: Philosophical and Theological Models for Ecology*, Mowbray 1994. Clark's latest book providing a new critique of ecological pantheism.

Clarke, Paul and Linzey, Andrew, *Research on Embryos: Politics, Theology and Law*, Lester Crook Academic Press 1988. An argument against experimentation on embryos drawn, *inter alia*, from considerations of their innocence and vulnerability.

—— (eds), *Political Theory and Animal Rights*, Pluto Press, London and Winchester, Mass. 1990. A collection of more than 60 readings from Plato to Singer. Three sections: Differences between Humans and Animals; Dominion and the Limits to Power; and Justice, Rights and Obligations.

Cobb Jr., John, *Is It Too Late? A Theology of Ecology*, Bruce Publishing, California, 1972. A pioneering work relating theology to environmental issues by the famous process theologian.

—— and Birch, Charles, *From Cell to Community: The Liberation of Life?*, CUP 1970. The famous process theology of creation.

Cochrane, Charles Norris, *Christianity and Classical Culture: A Study of Thought and Action from Augustus to Augustine*, OUP, London and New York 1944. Important work on the development of the *Logos* doctrine. 'In Christ, therefore, they [early Christians] claimed to possess a principle of understanding superior to anything existing in the classical world. By this claim they were prepared to stand or fall' (p. vi). One wonders what Christianity and the world would have been like if this conviction had been maintained.

Come Holy Spirit: Renew the Whole Creation: Six Bible Studies, WCC Publications, Geneva 1990. Resource book for the Seventh Assembly of the WCC at Canberra on the theme of Justice, Peace and the Integrity of Creation. Disappointingly slight and insubstantial.

Cooper, Tim, *Green Christianity: Caring for the Whole Creation*, Hodder and Stoughton 1990. A popular statement of the case for eco-theology.

Corbett, Patrick, 'Postscript' in Stanley and Roslind Godlovitch and John Harris (eds), *Animals, Men and Morals* (below). His line on vivisection inspired my own, e.g.: 'The only possible justification of such vivisection would have to take the form that the interest of every other living creature must yield to the growth of human scientific knowledge and technological power as the supreme interest of the most complex creature ... But not only is that interest not supreme, since moral and emotional growth are at least as important, but also that animals are in many respects superior to ourselves, the argument collapses' (p. 237). Since these lines were written in 1971, we have witnessed the increasing use of animals worldwide in new forms of biotech research.

Cronin, Kieran, *Rights and Christian Ethics*, New Studies in Christian Ethics, CUP 1992. Neglectful and dismissive of the theological and philosophical literature on animal rights. It is difficult to avoid the conclusion that here is humanocentric prejudice wrapped up in philosophy.

Davis, Charles, *God's Grace in History*, Collins Fontana 1966. His Maurice lectures at King's College, London in which he castigates emerging eco-sensitivity.

Davis, David Brion, *Slavery and Human Progress*, OUP, Oxford and New York
    1986. Documents Christian support for – and opposition to – slavery (esp.
    pp. 129–153) and also animal analogies to human slavery (pp. 25f.).
    Exemplary scholarly study.

Davis, Henry, *Moral and Pastoral Theology, Vol. II, Commandments of God;
    Precepts of the Church*, Sheed and Ward 1946. Articulates the standard
    Roman Catholic line that animals are classable as human property.

Dawkins, Marian Stamp, *Animal Suffering: The Science of Animal Welfare*,
    Chapman and Hall, London and New York 1980. An attempt to base
    concern for animal welfare on experimental work on the actual preferences
    of, for example, battery hens.

Dennis, Trevor, 'The relationship between Gregory of Nyssa's attack on slavery
    in his fourth homily on *Ecclesiastes* and his treatise *De hominis opticio*', *Studia
    Patristica*, Vol. XVIII, ed by E. A. Livingstone, 1982.

—— 'Man Beyond Price: Gregory of Nyssa and Slavery' in Andrew Linzey and
    Peter J. Wexler (eds), *Heaven and Earth: Essex Essays in Theology and Ethics*,
    Churchman Publishing 1986. Fascinating analysis of a lone Christian voice
    against human slavery.

Descartes, Rene, 'Discourse on Method' in *Philosophical Works of Descartes*, Vol.
    1, ET by E. S. Haldane and G. R. T. Ross, CUP 1965.

—— letter to the Marquess of Newcastle (23 November 1646) and letter to
    Henry More (5 February 1649), *Descartes: Philosophical Letters*, ET and ed
    by Anthony Kenny, Clarendon Press 1970. Key works for understanding his
    view that animals possess no rational consciousness and operate like
    machines.

Devall, Bill and Sessions, George, *Deep Ecology: Living as if Nature Mattered*,
    Peregrine Smith Books, Salt Lake City 1985. Essential introduction to the
    concept of 'deep ecology'. The interview with Arne Naess reveals the
    unmistakably mystical character of deep eco-principles: 'There is a basic
    intuition in deep ecology that we have no right to destroy other living beings
    without sufficient reason. Another norm is that, with maturity, human beings
    will experience joy when other life forms experience joy, and sorrow when
    other life forms experience sorrow. Not only will we feel sad when our
    brother or a dog or a cat feels sad, but we will grieve when living beings,
    including landscapes, are destroyed. In our civilization, we have vast means
    of destruction at our disposal but extremely little maturity in our feelings' (p.
    75). There is a hinterland here between deep ecology and animal theology
    worth exploring.

Dobbie, Robert, 'Sacrifice and Morality in the Old Testament', *The Expository
    Times*, Vol. 17, October 1958. A rare discussion of animal sacrifice from an
    ethical perspective; see Rowley's rejoinder (below).

Dombrowski, Daniel A., *Vegetarianism: The Philosophy behind the Ethical Diet*,
    University of Massachusetts Press and Thorsons 1985. Traces vegetarian

philosophy back to its Hellenistic origins. Scant consideration of theology.

—— *Hartshorne and the Metaphysics of Animal Rights*, State University of New York Press 1988. A largely philosophical discussion based on process thinkers such as Hartshorne and Whitehead.

Dorr, Donal, *Integral Spirituality: Resources for Community, Peace, Justice and the Earth*, Orbis Books, Maryknoll 1990. Imaginative attempt to achieve a practical integrative spirituality. Beyond eco-sensitivity, he fails to grasp the challenges posed for theology by taking animal suffering seriously.

Dostoyevsky, Fyodor, *The Brothers Karamazov*, Vol. 1, ET by David Magarshack, Penguin edn 1958. Contains Father Zossima's advice on the treatment of animals and children.

Ehrenfeld, David, *The Arrogance of Humanism*, OUP, New York 1978. A powerful critique by an environmental biologist of humanist attempts to protect the environment. 'Thus the conservation dilemma is exposed: humanists will not normally be interested in saving any non-resource, any fragment of Nature that is not manifestly useful to humankind, and the various reasons advanced to demonstrate that these non-resources really are useful or potentially valuable are not likely to be convincing even when they are truthful and correct' (p. 192).

Evans, E. P., *The Criminal Prosecution and Capital Punishment of Animals* (1906), foreword by Nicholas Humphrey, Faber 1987. Details the shocking history of mutilation, torture and death inflicted on animals by ecclesiastical courts from the 9th to the 19th century.

Fairholme, E. G., and Pain, W., *A Century of Work for Animals: The History of the RSPCA, 1824–1924*, John Murray 1924. A useful, if insufficiently referenced, centenary history of the world's first national animal protection society.

Farrer, Austin, *Love Almighty and Ills Unlimited* (1962), Fontana Library of Theology and Philosophy, Collins Fontana 1966. Sensitive discussion of the issues raised for theodicy by animal pain. Contains his famous line: 'It must never be forgotten that God is the God of hawks no less than of sparrows, of microbes no less than of men' (pp. 104–5).

Ferrier, J. Todd, *On Behalf of the Creatures* (1926), The Order of the Cross edn, 1983. One of the many works of Ferrier – a mystic – who founded the Order of the Cross. He held that Jesus was really a vegetarian who advocated Essene-like ascetic principles.

Flannery, Austin (ed), *Vatican Council II: The Conciliar and Post Conciliar Documents*, Dominican Publications, Dublin 1975. Astonishingly not one word of eco concern from Vatican II.

Focus on Bats: Their Conservation and the Law, Nature Conservancy Council 1982. Guide to the UK Wildlife and Countryside Act 1981 in relation to the protection of bats.

Fox, Matthew, *Original Blessing: A Primer in Creation Spirituality*, Bear and

Company, Santa Fe 1983. Fox's best selling book espousing his vision of creation spirituality. In rejecting the fall of creation, Fox inevitably accepts eat and be eaten as the God-given law of the universe. His use of sources has been questioned.

—— and Porritt, Jonathon, 'Green Spirituality', *Creation Spirituality*, Vol. VII, No. 3, May–June 1991. Discussion on creation spirituality including predation and vegetarianism.

Fox, Michael W., *Superpigs and Wondercorn*, St Martin's Press, New York 1992. A critique of the genetic engineering of animals and a sober analysis of its implications for humans as well as animals.

Francis de Sales, St, *Introduction to the Devout Life*, ET by Michael Day, Burns and Oates, 1956 edn. Contains his defence of hunting as a morally innocent recreation.

Frankena, William, 'The Concept of Social Justice' in R. Brant (ed), *Social Justice*, Prentice-Hall, New Jersey 1962. Defends a humanocentric conception of justice criticized by Singer in 'All Animals are Equal' (below).

Frey, R. G., 'What has sentiency to do with the possession of rights?' in Ryder and Paterson, *Animals' Rights: A Symposium* (1979), below.

—— *Interests and Rights: The Case Against Animals*, Clarendon Press 1980.

—— *Rights, Killing and Suffering: Moral Vegetarianism and Applied Ethics*, Blackwell, 1983.
Frey's work in applied philosophy has been almost entirely devoted to finding a theoretical basis for opposing animal rights. Frey's candour – at least in one area – provides grounds for giving my anti-vivisectionist line more than a second thought. He holds that benefits from experimentation justify the use of humans as well as animals. '... if securing the benefit licenses (painful) experiments on animals, it equally licenses (painful) experiments on humans, since the benefit may be secured by either means' (*Rights, Killing and Suffering*, p. 113).

Galloway, A. D., *The Cosmic Christ*, Nisbet and Sons 1951. A theme which desperately needs updating to include eco-concerns and animal theology.

Gardner, Percy, *Evolution in Christian Ethics*, Crown Theological Library, Williams and Northgate, London 1918. An early Christian argument for eugenics.

Garner, Robert, *Animals, Politics and Morality*, Issues in Environmental Politics, Manchester University Press 1993. A useful exploration and critique of the various strategies for reform advanced by animal advocates.

Geach, Peter, *Providence and Evil*, CUP 1977. Argues that God is indifferent to the suffering of animals caused by the teleological structures of life. 'God cannot share with his creatures' the 'virtue of sympathy with physical suffering' (see pp. 76–80). It is difficult to conceive of a more anti-Christian doctrine of God.

Godlovitch, Stanley and Roslind, and Harris, John (eds), *Animals, Men and Morals: An Inquiry into the Maltreatment of the Non-Human*, Gollancz 1971.

The first modern collection of philosophical papers – edited by three graduate students at Oxford – which challenged the traditional moral view of animals.

Godwin, William, *Enquiry Concerning Political Justice and Its Influence on Modern Morals and Happiness* (1798), J. Watson, London 1842. Argues for a strongly pessimistic view of nature as a theatre of suffering. Perhaps he was the first to coin the phrase 'all nature suffers'.

Granberg-Michaelson, Wesley (ed), *Tending the Garden: Essays on the Gospel and the Earth*, Wm. B. Eerdmans, Grand Rapids 1987. A better than usual collection with some provocative, idiosyncratic and lively essays. Paulos Mar Gregorios' essay on 'New Testament Foundations for Understanding the Creation' (pp. 83–93) offers an eco-reading of Colossians.

Gregorios, Paulos Mar, *The Human Presence: Ecological Spirituality and the Age of the Spirit*, Amity House, New York 1987. An account of Orthodoxy's understanding of nature in relation to contemporary problems. Some maintain that Orthodoxy's emphasis upon 'man as a microcosm' of creation offers a potentially creative holism.

Gregory of Nyssa, St, *The Great Catechism*, ET and ed by H. Wace and P. Schaff, A Select Library of Nicene and Post-Nicene Fathers of the Christian Church, 2nd Series, Vol. 4, Parker and Co., Oxford and The Christian Literature Co., New York 1893. Impressive eco-reading of the second creation saga: 'Now, by a provision of the supreme Mind there is an intermixture of the intellectual with the sensible world, in order that nothing in creation may be thrown aside as worthless ... or left without its portion of the Divine fellowship ... It [Genesis] tells us that God, taking dust of the ground, formed the man, and by an inspiration from Himself He planted life in the work of His hand, and that thus the earthly might be raised up to the Divine, and so one certain grace of equal value might pervade the whole creation' (ch. VI, p. 480).

Griffiths, Richard, *The Human Use of Animals*, Grove Books 1982. A critique of my book *Animal Rights* (1976) from a conservative evangelical standpoint.

Grillmeier, Aloys, *Christ in Christian Tradition*, Mowbray 1965. An authoritative history of the development of early christological doctrine.

Gunn, Alastair S., 'Traditional Ethics and the Moral Status of Animals', *Environmental Ethics*, Vol. 5, No. 2, Summer 1983. Argues that nature is a Hobbesian state 'where the terms *right* and *wrong*, *just* and *unjust*, have no proper application' (his emphases; p. 152). If this is true, it would also be difficult to hold that these terms have any application to the human natural world as well.

Gunton, C. E., *Christ and Creation: The Didsbury Lectures*, Paternoster Press 1993. An impressive scholarly, if overcompressed, survey (127 pages) of the relevance of christological doctrine to contemporary eco-discussion. Vegetarianism is considered in the last 3 pages.

Gustafson, James, *Theology and Ethics*, Blackwell 1981. Admirable defence of a truly theocentric Christian ethic. His critique of humanistic ethics – religious or secular – provides a strong basis for animal theology (see pp. 96 f.).

Gutierrez, Gustavo, *A Theology of Liberation* (1971) ET by Caridad Inda and John Eagleson, revd edn Orbis Books, Maryknoll and SCM Press, London 1988. Pioneering work which opened a new chapter in theological consciousness about the poor.

Halkes, Catharina J.M., *New Creation: Christian Feminism and the Renewal of the Earth*, SPCK 1989. An exploration of the link between feminist theology and eco-theology.

Hargrove, E.C. (ed), *The Animal Rights/Environmental Ethics Debate*, State University of New York Press 1993. Impressive new collection of readings on the animal/eco-divide.

Hart, John, *The Spirit of the Land: A Theology of the Land*, Paulist Press, New York 1984. An enterprising theological exploration of the idea of 'the land' as found in the Judeao-Christian tradition and in native American society. His discussion of native culture is arguably a eulogy, however.

Hendry, George S., *Theology of Nature*, Westminster Press, Philadelphia 1980. A useful, if rather unfocussed, study linking natural theology to a theology of nature.

Hennecke, E. (ed), *New Testament Apocrypha, Vol. II, Apostolic and Early Church Writings*, Lutterworth Press 1965; reissued SCM Press 1974. Source for apocryphal material on Jesus and animals.

Herbert, George, *The Works of George Herbert*, ed with comm. by F. E. Hutchinson, Clarendon Press 1967. Herbert's sympathy for animals is enshrined in his great poem 'Providence'.

Hick, John, *Evil and the God of Love*, Fontana Library of Theology and Philosophy, Collins, 4th edn 1975. Defends an Augustinian theodicy in which the suffering of non-human creatures is necessary for human 'soul-making' and essential to the fullness of the created world (see pp. 345–53).

History of the Philadelphia Bible-Christian Church, 1817–1917, J. B. Lippincott Company, Philadelphia 1922. The American history of the church which made vegetarianism compulsory among its members.

Hitler, Adolf, *Mein Kampf*, ET by Ralph Manheim, intro. by D. C. Watt, Hutchinson, 1974 edn. His views on eugenics make disturbingly contemporary reading.

Holmes Snr., Oliver Wendell, *Life and Letters of Oliver Wendell Holmes*, Vol. I. Defends the concept of rights legally and theologically.

Holmes-Gore, V. A., *These We Have Not Loved* (1942), C. W. Daniel, 1946 edn. Follows the view of Ferrier that Jesus was a vegetarian.

Hormann, Karl, *An Introduction to Moral Theology*, Burns and Oates 1961. Modified Thomist line somewhat more favourable to animals. For example: 'If there is no good reason for it, then it must be considered a sin to kill an animal' (p. 275).

Horne, Brian, *A World to Gain: Incarnation and the Hope of Renewal*, Darton, Longman and Todd 1983. A modern apologetic defending incarnation as a means of understanding the world especially sympathetic to environmental issues.

Houston, Walter, *Purity and Monotheism: Clean and Unclean Animals in Biblical Law*, JSOT Press/Sheffield Academic Press 1993. Exemplary and comprehensive interpretation of dietary laws. Concludes that the law of animal kinds 'stands for the order and peace of civil society over against the disorder and violence of the wild ... for the possibility, not confined to Israel alone, of living in peace with God's creatures and in the experience of his presence' (p. 258).

Human Rights: Our Understanding and Our Responsibilities, Discussion paper issued by the Board for Social Responsibility of the General Synod of the Church of England, Church Information Office 1976. A slight but constructive discussion of rights.

Hume, C. W., *The Status of Animals in the Christian Religion*, Universities Federation for Animal Welfare, 2nd edn 1957. A rather unsophisticated theological study.

Inge, W. R., *Lay Thoughts of a Dean*, The Knickerbocker Press, London and New York 1926. Contains his strong anti-cruelty essay entitled 'The Rights of Animals'.

Irenaeus of Lyons, St, *Against Heresies, The Writings of Irenaeus*, 2 Vols, ET by A. Roberts and W. H. Rambaut, T. & T. Clark, no date. Contains Irenaeus' well-known doctrine of the summation of all things in the *Logos*.

Jaeger, Werner, *The Theology of the Early Greek Philosophers*, OUP 1967. Interprets Heraclitus on natural law and the *Logos*.

James, Montague R. (ed), *The Apocryphal New Testament* (1924), OUP 1955 edn. Provides edited extracts from a wide range of apocryphal material a significant amount of which includes references to animals.

Jeremias, Joachim, *The Eucharistic Words of Jesus*, SCM Press 1966. Contains the discussion about whether Jesus ate the Passover meal.

John of the Cross, St, *The Complete Works*, ed and ET by A. E. Peers, 3 vols in one edition, Vol. 2, Part v, Anthony Clarke 1974. Develops an interpretation of the incarnation which involves all created beings through a process of 'beautification'.

John Paul II, Pope, *Sollicitudo Rei Socialis*, Encyclical Letter, Catholic Truth Society 1987. Paragraph 34 almost suggests a non-instrumentalist view of the non-human world – quite a radical departure from standard Thomism.

Johnson, Andrew, *Factory Farming*, Blackwell 1991. The most up to date discussion of intensive farming in the UK with eco- and ethical discussion.

Johnson, Lawrence E., *A Morally Deep World: An Essay on Moral Significance and Environmental Ethics*, CUP 1991. A morally deep book full of insight by a philosopher: 'My overall conclusion I have come to is that we live in a morally deep world. We are morally significant ourselves, and we live in a world of beings, on many different levels, that are morally significant ... We live in a world of life, and all life processes, of whatever sort, define interests that count morally. It is respect for interests that is, at least, the core if not the whole of morality' (conclusion, p. 287). A useful prologemena to animal theology.

Jones, David Albert, 'Do Whales have Souls?' *New Blackfriars*, Vol. 73, No. 866, December 1992. A small sign of change in Roman Catholic thinking about the status of animals.

Jones, John D., 'Humans and Animals: Compassion and Dominion', *Anglican Theological Review*, Vol. LXII, No. 3, July 1981. Questions the view that animals are simply here for our use and argues that 'might is right' dominion is tantamount to tyranny.

Jonsson, Gunnlaugur, A., *The Image of God: Genesis 1:26–8 in a Century of Old Testament Research*, Almqvist & Wiksell International/Coniectanea, Old Testament Series 26, 1988. A fascinating survey showing how scholarly opinion has changed this century from viewing the *imago dei* as the rational endowment of humans to the current consensus that the image means sharing God's moral rule over creation. Also discusses liberation theology and feminist viewpoints. Admirable.

Joranson, Philip N. and Butigan, Ken (eds), *Cry of the Environment: Rebuilding the Christian Creation Tradition*, Bear and Company, Santa Fe 1984. A comprehensive collection from scholars covering a whole range of eco-theological themes – 470 pages. Although animals are a glaring omission, the book is an indispensable reader. A project of the Centre for Ethics and Social Policy, Berkeley, California.

Joy, Charles R., (ed), *Albert Schweitzer: An Anthology*, Adam and Charles Black 1952. A good anthology of his key writings.

Julian of Norwich, *Showings (Revelations of Divine Love)*. Classics of Western Spirituality, Paulist Press, New York and SPCK, London 1978, and many other editions. Suggests an inclusive understanding of Christ's suffering.

Kay, William J., Cohen, Susan P., Fudin, Carole E., Kutscher, Austin H., Nieburg, Herbert A., Grey, Ross E., and Osman, Mohamed M. (eds), *Euthanasia of the Companion Animal: The Impact on Pet Owners, Veterinarians, and Society*, The Charles Press, Philadelphia 1988. A comprehensive guide to the euthanasia debate with 31 essays ranging from the ethical aspects to practical means of disposal.

Kempe, Margery, cited in Agius, *God's Animals* (above). Fifteenth-century, illiterate English mystic. *The Book of Margery Kempe* is a narrative of her spiritual history. This extract includes her identification of animal suffering with the suffering of Christ crucified.

Kew, Barry, *A Pocketbook of Animal Facts and Figures*, Green Print 1991. A useful collection of factual information about animal exploitation in the UK.

Kingston, A. Richard, 'Theodicy and Animal Welfare', *Theology*, Vol. LXX, No. 569, November 1967. A ground-breaking analysis of available theodicies arguing that 'with a few noble exceptions theologians have done far more to discourage than to stimulate a concern for the lower creatures' (p. 482).

Kook, Abraham Isaac, *The Lights of Penitence, The Moral Principles, Lights of Holiness, Essays, Letters, and Poems*, Classics of Western Spirituality, Paulist Press, New York and SPCK, London 1979. Includes Kook's talmudic defence of vegetarianism as a biblical ideal.

Kropotkin, Peter, *Mutual Aid: A Factor in Evolution*, Penguin Books, 1939 edn. Much overlooked work which defends the view that the natural world is characterized as much by cooperation as competition.

Landsbury Coral, *The Old Brown Dog: Women, Workers and Vivisection in Edwardian England*, University of Wisconsin Press 1985. A brilliant historical analysis of the Brown Dog Riots of 1907 when an unlikely fusion of suffragettes, anti-vivisectionists and trade unionists battled with medical students over a statue of a brown dog in London's Battersea district. Provides a unique insight into the common threads which united three disparate movements.

Langley, Gill (ed), *Animal Experimentation: The Consensus Changes*, Chapman and Hall, New York 1989. Collection of essays focussing on the apparent change of moral consciousness – not least of all among scientists.

Lawler, Justus George, 'On the Rights of Animals', *Anglican Theological Review*, April 1965. Possibly the first theologian to articulate the sentiency criterion as a basis for moral rights. An important and much neglected essay.

Leahy, Michael P. T., *Against Liberation: Putting Animals in Perspective*, Routledge 1991. Spirited critique of animal rights. Not always accurate, e.g. on p. 227 where he incorrectly attributes to me the 'abolitionist' view about killing except for self-defence. I have always accepted – for example – the case for euthanasia of animals in times of extreme suffering.

Lenten Triodion, ET by Mother Mary and Bishop Kallistos, Faber 1978. Contains the significant verse on the creation suffering with Christ from the Mattins of Holy Saturday according to the Byzantine Rite.

Leopold, Aldo, *A Sand County Almanac*, OUP, New York 1949. Arguably *the* pioneering work on ecology (still in print) comprising Leopold's famous dictum: 'A thing is right when it tends to preserve the integrity, stability, and beauty of the biotic community. It is wrong when it tends otherwise' (p. 217). It is astonishing that contemporary eco-theologians should be so eager to incorporate this naturalistic principle into their systems.

Lewis, C. S., *The Abolition of Man* (1943), Collins Fount edn 1978. Lewis' prophetic work on 'Man's power over nature' so appropriate to the present genetic manipulation of animals, plants – and humans. 'For the power of Man to make himself what he pleases means ... the power of some men to make other men what *they* please' (p. 37; his emphasis).

—— *Vivisection*, foreword by George R. Farnum, New England Anti-Vivisection Society, Boston 1947. His argument for the complete abolition of experiments on animals.

—— *The Problem of Pain*, Fontana edn 1967. Chapter 9 on 'Animal Pain' gives Lewis' sympathetic discussion of animal suffering and his theory of 'animal resurrection' (see, esp., pp. 127–8).

—— and Joad, C. E. M., 'The Pains of Animals', *The Month*, Vol. 3, No.2, February 1950. A fascinating discussion on the origins of evil as it relates to the suffering of animals.

Lewis, Martin W., *Green Delusions: An Environmental Critique of Radical Environmentalism*, Duke University Press, Durham 1992. A trenchant, if not always convincing, critique of eco-theory and practice. Useful for – among other things – its critique of the view that indigenous cultures represent (in their treatment of the environment and animals in particular) some pristine ecotopia. His lack of balance, however, can be detected in his brief dismissal of religion as an inspiration for eco-concerns (pp. 248 f.).

Linzey, Andrew, *Animal Rights: A Christian Assessment*, SCM Press 1976. My first work which heralded the beginning of the modern animal rights movement.

—— 'Is Anthropocentricity Christian?', *Theology*, Vol. LXXXIV, No. 697, January 1981.

—— 'Moral Education and Reverence for Life' in David Paterson (ed), *Humane Education: A Symposium*, Humane Education Council 1981.

—— 'Animals' in John Macquarrie and James Childress (eds), *A New Dictionary of Christian Ethics*, SCM Press, London and Westminster Press, Philadelphia 1985.

—— *The Neglected Creature: The Doctrine of the Non-Human Creation and its Relationship with the Human Creation in the Thought of Karl Barth*, Doctoral Dissertation, University of London 1986.

—— *Christianity and the Rights of Animals*, SPCK, London and Crossroad, New York 1987 My second attempt at a systematic theological analysis.

—— 'Moral Dreams and Practical Realities', *Between the Species: A Journal of Ethics*, Vol. 7, No. 2, Spring 1991.

—— 'The Christian Case Against Cruelty' in Andrew Linzey (ed), *Cruelty and Christian Conscience*, Lynx Educational Trust 1992.

—— 'Animal Rights: A Reply to Barclay', *Science and Christian Belief*, Vol. 5, No. 1, 1993.

—— *Brother and Sister Creatures: The Saints and Animals*, unpublished manuscript.

—— (ed), *Animal Rights and Modern Literature*, University of Illinois Press 1994. An anthology of fiction drawn from modern writers such as Orwell, Saroyan, Steinbeck, Bashevis Singer, Turgenev, and Van de Post on the morality of our exploitation of animals.

—— and Regan, Tom (eds), *Animals and Christianity: A Book of Readings*,

SPCK, London and Crossroad, New York 1989. A collection of readings from partisans of both sides of the debate including extracts from Augustine, Aquinas, Bonaventure, Calvin, Wesley, Tillich, Barth, Austin Farrer and John Hick. Text book for university courses in the US and the UK.

—— and Regan, Tom (eds), *The Song of Creation*, Marshall Pickering 1988. Collection of some of the finest poetry celebrating the non-human creation including pieces from Blake, Clare, Cowper, Donne, Emerson, Hardy, Longfellow, Pope, Shelley and Vaughan.

—— and Regan, Tom (eds), *Compassion for Animals: Readings and Prayers*, SPCK, London and Crossroad, New York 1989. Collection of pieces for liturgical and pastoral use.

List, Peter C. (ed), *Radical Environmentalism: Philosophy and Tactics*, Wadsworth Publishing Company, California 1993. An important book offering a serious discussion of eco-activism, eco-tactics and eco-tage.

Lorenz, Konrad, *On Aggression*, Methuen 1966. Contains his view about the justifiability of anthropomorphism.

Lossky, Vladimir, *The Vision of God*, ET by A. Moorhouse, preface by J. Meyendorff, The Library of Orthodox Theology and Spirituality, Faith Press and American Orthodox Press 1963. Defends an inclusive vision of salvation.

—— *The Mystical Theology of the Eastern Church*, ET by the Fellowship of St Alban and St Sergius, James Clarke 1973. Discusses St Maximus and St Isaac the Syrian on creation, compassion and union with God.

—— *In the Image and Likeness of God*, ed by John H. Erickson and Thomas E. Bird, intro. by John Meyendorff, St Vladimir's Seminary Press 1974. His last essay on 'Dominion and Kingship: An Eschatological Study' argues that God's dominion will be ultimately triumphant resulting in the sanctification of the whole creation.

Luther, Martin, *Lectures on Romans*, The Library of Christian Classics, Vol. XV, SCM Press, London and Westminster Press, Philadelphia 1961. An apparently non-humanocentric reading of Romans 8. His line of exegesis strikes me as prophetic: 'We conclude, therefore, that anyone who searches into the essences and functionings of the creatures rather than into their sighings and earnest expectations is certainly foolish and blind. He does not know that also the creatures are created for an end' (p. 237).

Lynne, Finn, *Arctic Wars: Animal Rights and Endangered Peoples*, University Press of New England 1992. Passionate defence of sealing, whaling and fur trapping. The abysmal level of the discussion can be gleaned from the following: 'It will probably be no easy matter, however, to convince the churches – the Evangelical-Lutheran and the Roman Catholic – to join the antifur crusade. After all, it has never been a matter of doctrine that Jesus died on the cross so that animals could go to heaven. More important, the churches have always been for everyone, and they tend to be strongly conservative' (pp. 69–70).

Macquarrie, John, *Three Issues in Ethics* SCM Press, London and Harper, New York 1970. Comprises his thoughtful discussion of natural law.

McDaniel, Jay B., *Of God and Pelicans: A Theology of Reverence for Life*, Westminster/John Knox Press, Louisville 1989. A pioneering exposition of a 'Life-Centred Ethic' by a process theologian.

—— *Earth, Sky, Gods and Mortals: Developing an Ecological Spirituality*, Twenty-Third Publications, Mystic 1990. A survey of ecological themes (including animals) from a process theological perspective. A useful 'map' especially appropriate for university students.

McDonagh, Sean, *To Care for the Earth*, Geoffrey Chapman 1988. A pioneering, if somewhat unsystematic, defence of eco concerns from a Roman Catholic perspective.

—— *The Greening of the Church*, Orbis Books, Maryknoll 1990. A largely pastoral sequel to the above. Chapter 9 on 'The Environment in the Modern Catholic Church' is illuminating.

McFague, Sallie, *The Body of God: An Ecological Theology*, SCM Press, London and Fortress Press, Minneapolis 1993. A sequel to her *Models of God* in which she systematically elaborates on her doctrine of the world as God's own embodied reality. Many problems here from an animal theology perspective including the belittling of human moral transcendence, parasitism as God's will, the eclipsing of transcendence and the seeming impossibility of redemption for suffering non-human creatures. McFague will resist this but I judge that she has fundamentally deified nature.

McKenna, Virginia, Travers, Bill, and Wray, Jonathan (eds), *Beyond the Bars: The Zoo Dilemma*, Thorsons 1987. Thoughtful collection of essays critical of zoos. Richard Adams' essay on animals in religious imagery repays reflection.

Magel, Charles R., *Keyguide to Information Sources in Animal Rights*, Mansell Press, London and New York 1989. Indispensable resource for scholars working in this area.

Man in His Living Environment: An Ethical Assessment, Church Information Office 1970. An early eco- report of the Church of England Board for Social Responsibility Working Party. One of the very few church reports to stand the test of time. Unlike its successors (too numerous to mention) it contains exemplary ethical and theological discussion about the status of animals. I hope it will not be too long before the Church of England addresses itself seriously to this issue again.

Marshall, Paul, 'Does Creation have Rights?', *Studies in Christian Ethics*, Vol. 6, No. 2, Autumn 1993. One of the few Christian responses to the debate about animal rights. He completely fails, however, to engage any *theology*. He dismisses my own view that God is the source of rights as an 'indirect duty' view (note p. 33). But from a theological perspective, God has to be the ultimate source and ground of all value and rights. It is precisely *because* God values sentient life that it is possible to speak meaningfully of its 'inherent worth'.

Mascall, E. L., *The Importance of Being Human*, OUP 1959. Defends a meta-physical fall of creation.

—— *Corpus Christi*, Longmans 1965. Contains his analysis of animal sacrifice and its relationship to theories of the atonement.

—— *The Christian Universe*, Darton, Longman and Todd 1966. Insists on the significance of Christ for the entire universe and offers a theory of the (progressive) 'Christification' of the natural order.

—— *The Openness of Being*, Darton, Longman and Todd 1971. Vigorous defence of Thomist categories of creation especially in relation to the non-human.

Mason, Jim, *An Unnatural Order: Uncovering the Roots of Our Domination of Nature and Each Other*, Simon and Schuster, New York 1993. Fresh analysis of the philosophy of domination.

—— and Singer, Peter (eds), *Animal Factories*, Crown Publishing, New York 1980. Well-documented critique of factory farming, especially in the US.

Maximus the Confessor, St, *Selected Writings*, Classics of Western Spirituality, SPCK, London and Paulist Press, New York 1985. Maximus is one of the rediscovered treasures of those seeking an eco- theology. For commentary and interpretation, see Gregorios, *The Human Presence* (above).

Midgley, Mary, *Animals and Why they Matter: A Journey Around the Species Barrier*, Penguin Books 1983. Another philosophical discussion favourable to animals but one which stops short at moral equality and rights for animals.

Moltmann, Jürgen, *The Crucified God: The Cross of Christ as the Foundation and Criticism of Christian Theology*, SCM Press, London and Harper, New York 1974. If only Moltmann had seen the connection between the suffering non-human creation and the crucified Christ, he would have written a different book.

—— *God in Creation: An Ecological Doctrine of Creation*, SCM Press, London and Harper, New York 1985. One of the very few full systematic works on eco-theology. More a survey than an argument, however. Animals get a brief mention.

Montefiore, Hugh (ed), *Man and Nature*, Collins 1975. A report of a Working Party set up by Michael Ramsey in 1970. Its joint report (pp. 3–84) is an example of constructive theological work although almost entirely neglectful of animals. Some of the individual essays, e.g. by John Austin Baker (see above) broke new ground at the time.

Morris, Desmond, *The Naked Ape*, Corgi Books 1969. The best-selling book which helped popularize the evolutionary view of human ancestry. Specifically critical of claims to human uniqueness.

Moses, John, *The Sacrifice of God: A Holistic Theory of Atonement*, foreword by Stephen W. Sykes, The Canterbury Press 1992. One of the very few works on atonement doctrine that seeks to interpret Christ's saving work in the light of the interdependence of creation.

Moule, C. F. D., *Man and Nature in the New Testament*, The Athlone Press 1964. A slight but provocative survey of some New Testament themes comprising a strong rejection of animal immortality.

Murray, Robert, *The Cosmic Covenant: Biblical Themes of Justice, Peace and the Integrity of Creation*, Sheed and Ward 1992. Impressive examination of the biblical material about animals and creation with detailed consideration of key texts. Chapter 6 develops a very strong argument drawn from the kingship tradition with respect to animals; the ethical implications are not explored but they are far reaching in practice.

Nagel, Thomas, *Mortal Questions*, CUP, 1990 edn. Contains his famous essay on 'What is it like to be a bat?' His conclusion that 'there are facts which do not consist in the truth of propositions expressible in a human language' (p. 171) may sound elementary to theologians but if taken seriously might shake some of the usual humanocentric prejudice about animals.

Nash, Roderick Frazier, *The Rights of Nature: A History of Environmental Ethics*, University of Wisconsin Press 1989. More a survey than a complete history. No engagement with theological perspectives.

Nietzsche, Frederick, *Thoughts Out of Season*, T. N. Foulis, Edinburgh 1909. Contains his view about how nature needs to be redeemed.

Needs and Rights of Children, A Child Protection Agenda, National Society for the Prevention of Cruelty to Children 1991. Isolates far-reaching principles which should govern our conduct towards the weaker members of the human community.

Orwell, George, *Animal Farm*, Secker and Warburg 1945; Penguin 1961. Political satire on inequality and oppression especially appropriate to the human use of animals. The opening narrative is used to illustrate my argument on genetic engineering in chapter 9.

Owen, H. P., *Concepts of Deity*, Macmillan 1971. Steely defence of the classical view of God against various forms of pantheism and panentheism. Admirably succinct.

Palazzini, P. (ed), *Dictionary of Moral Theology*, Burns and Oates 1962. Reproduces the standard Thomist line that animals have no rights and that animals were made for human use.

Passmore, John, *Man's Responsibility for Nature: Ecological Problems and Western Traditions*, Duckworth 1974. A critique of the humanocentricity of the Christian tradition. Now published in a revised and expanded edition.

Paternoster, Michael, *Man: The World's High Priest*, SLG Press 1976. A short paper making connections between priesthood and ecology.

Paterson, David (ed), *Humane Education – A Symposium*, Humane Education Council 1981. Proceedings of the first conference on humane education in the UK at the University of Sussex in 1980.

—— and Palmer, Mary (eds), *The Status of Animals: Ethics, Education and Welfare*, CAB International 1989. One of the significant symposia of the

1980s – based on the British Veterinary Association conference at Nottingham University in 1988.

Paton, William, *Man and Mouse: Animals in Medical Research*, OUP 1984. Defence of animal experiments by the former Professor of Pharmacology at Oxford. Astonishingly, he incorrectly attributes to me an indirect-duties view of our obligation to animals (p. 36). See my *Animal Rights* (1976) (above) pp. 22 f. for actual text.

Phillips, Anthony, 'Respect for Life in the Old Testament', *King's Theological Review*, Autumn 1983. Perceptive analysis of Hebrew attitudes to issues of life and death, including killing animals.

—— *Lower than the Angels: Questions raised by Genesis 1–11*, Bible Reading Fellowship 1983. Concise survey of the major issues. Admirably succint.

Pinches, Charles and McDaniel, Jay B. (eds), *Good News for Animals? Christian Approaches to Animal Well-Being*, Orbis Books, Maryknoll 1993. A groundbreaking collection of theological pieces drawn from the Duke University Conference in 1990.

Plato, 'The Statesman', *Plato*, ET by Harold W. Fowler and W. R. M. Lamb, Heinemann 1925. Source for Plato's conception of 'the Golden Age'.

Pratt, Dallas, *Painful Experiments on Animals*, Argus Archives, New York 1976. An objective analysis of the extent of suffering in US laboratories.

Preece, Rod and Chamberlain, Lorna, *Animal Welfare and Human Values*, Wilfrid Laurier University Press, Ontario 1993. An attempt to construct a moderate humanocentric ethic for our use of animals, but its theoretical basis is much weaker than that of animal rights which it attacks. Animal experimentation, hunting, culling and meat-eating are all justified.

Primatt, Humphry, *Dissertation on the Duty of Mercy and the Sin of Cruelty to Brute Animals*, T. Constable 1776. The first full systematic theological defence of animals.

Primavesi, Anne, *From Apocalypse to Genesis: Ecology, Feminism and Christianity*, Fortress Press, Minneapolis 1991. Another theo-eco- feminist analysis which seems to deify the natural world. See my review in the *Scottish Journal of Theology*, 1992, Vol. 45, No. 2, pp. 265–270.

Proposed International Guidelines for Biochemical Research Involving Human Subjects, A Joint Project of the World Health Organization and the Council for Organizations of Medical Sciences, Geneva 1982. Proscribes experimental procedures on human subjects without full consent.

Pufendorf, Samuel, *The Law of Nature and Nations* (1688), ET by C. H. and W. A. Oldfather, Oceana, New York 1931. One of the early discussions of natural law and its implications for the right treatment of animals.

Quinn, Edward, 'Animals in Heaven?' *New Blackfriars*, Vol. 65, No. 767, May 1984. Suggests that there might be room for animals in a new world transfigured by God's grace.

Rachels, James, *Created from Animals: The Moral Implications of Darwinism*, OUP 1991. A refreshing philosophical defence of Darwin as the harbinger of a moral revolution concerning the status of animals. Chapter 5 on 'Morality without the Idea that Humans are Special' (pp. 173–224) is a provocation not to be missed.

Raven, Charles, *The Creator Spirit*, Macmillan 1927. Work of the celebrated natural theologian. Dismissive of animals to the extent of doubting that they can experience suffering.

Regan, Tom, 'An Examination and Defense of One Argument Concerning Animal Rights', *Inquiry*, Vol. 22, Nos. 1–2, Summer 1979. Takes up the argument from marginal cases in my *Animal Rights* (1976).

—— *The Case for Animal Rights*, University of California Press 1983. A major philosophical defence of the rights of animals based on notions of 'inherent value' and animals as 'subjects of a life'. No theology.

—— (ed), *Animal Sacrifices: Religious Perspectives on the Use of Animals in Science*, Temple University Press, Philadelphia 1985. Eight perspectives on the morality of animal experimentation from scholars representing different world religions.

—— and Singer, Peter (eds), *Animal Rights and Human Obligations* (1976), Prentice-Hall, New Jersey, 2nd edn 1989. Revised edition of the influential text book with partisans for and against specific views on animals. Little theological depth, however.

Regenstein, Lewis G., *Replenish the Earth: A History of Organized Religion's Treatment of Animals and Nature – including the Bible's Message of Conservation and Kindness to Animals*, foreword by John A. Hoyt, SCM Press, London and Crossroad, New York 1991. Essentially a collection of sources rather than an historical analysis or systematic survey.

Relton, H. Maurice, *Studies in Christian Doctrine*, Macmillan 1960. Contains his interesting defence of divine passibility.

Rice, Anne, *Interview with the Vampire*, Ballantine Books, New York 1976. Among other things, a disturbing and theologically sensitive narrative about the rights and wrongs of killing to live. The basic plot is used to illustrate the dilemma of meat eating today in chapter 5.

Ridley, Jane, *Fox Hunting*, Collins 1990. A strongly pro-social history of hunting. Shows how from early times hunters have preserved foxes for hunting (pp. 14 f.).

Ritchoff, Jim, *Mixed Bag: Reminiscences of a Master Raconteur*, National Rifle Association, Washington 1975. Reproduces the familiar pro-hunting argument that hunters are only bigger and better predators serving the interests of the ecological whole.

Robinson, John A. T., 'Need Jesus have been Perfect?' in S. W. Sykes and J. P. Clayton (eds), *Christ, Faith and History*, Cambridge Studies in Christology, CUP 1972. Robinson's essay queries the view that orthodox christology requires a morally perfect Jesus.

Rockefeller, Steven C. and Elder, John C. (eds), *Spirit and Nature: Why the Environment is a Religious Issue – An Interfaith Dialogue*, Beacon Press, Boston

1992. Pan religious anthology with essays of varying quality. Robert Prescott-Allen's chapter endorses the IUCN's view of animals as renewable resources.

Rodd, Rosemary, *Biology, Ethics and Animals*, OUP 1990. A much-overlooked biological/philosophical discussion arguing for a reappraisal of the status of animals together with a defence of rights language.

Rogerson, John, *Genesis 1–11*, Old Testament Guides, JSOT/Sheffield Academic Press 1991. Brief survey of the exegetical possibilities and problems in reading the foundational chapters of Genesis.

Rollin, Bernard E., *Animal Rights and Human Morality*, Prometheus Books, New York 1992. Revised edition of the 1982 book defending an animal rights position. Rollin is one of the very few animal rights theorists equally versed in physiology, philosophy and bioethics. Scant theological discussion.

—— *The Unheeded Cry: Animal Consciousness, Animal Pain and Science*, OUP 1989. A consummately impressive book challenging the scientific and philosophical view that animals have no mental life and cannot suffer. Rollin developed the world's first course in veterinary ethics and animal rights at Colorado State University.

Rosen, Steven, *Food for the Spirit: Vegetarianism and the World Religions*, Bala Books, New York 1987. Contains extracts from apocryphal works such as 'The Gospel of the Holy Twelve'.

Rothschild, Miriam, *Animals and Man: The Romanes Lecture, 1984–5*, Clarendon Press 1986. Practical ethical discussion weak on philosophy and theology.

Rowley, H. H., *The Biblical Doctrine of Election*, Lutterworth Press 1950. Argues for a discontinuity between the church and temple in the matter of animal sacrifices.

—— 'Sacrifice and Morality: A Rejoinder', *The Expository Times*, Vol. 17, March 1959.

Royston III, Holmes, *Environmental Ethics: Duties to and Values in the Natural World*, Temple University Press, Philadelphia 1988. Probably the most thorough philosophical defence of environmental ethics so far. Duties to individual animals are considered but they clearly play second fiddle to wider eco-considerations. Theology only implicit.

—— 'Does Nature Need to be Redeemed?', *Horizons in Biblical Theology*, Vol. 14, No. 2, 1993. A rather tentative ecological Yes to this question.

Rudd, Geoffrey L., *Why Kill for Food?*, The Vegetarian Society 1970. Very selective use of the Bible maintaining an unambiguous biblical ethic of non-violence to animals and also that Jesus was a vegetarian.

Ruesch, Hans, *Slaughter of the Innocent*, Futura Publications 1979. Polemic against animal experiments.

Ruether, Rosemary Radford, *Gaia & God: An Ecofeminist Theology of Earth Healing*, SCM Press, London and Harper, New York 1993. A wide-ranging eco-feminist theological critique of the Judeao-Christian creation tradition from the foremost feminist theologian.

Rule of St Benedict, ET by Justin McCann, Spiritual Masters Series, Sheed and Ward 1976. Benedict's rule required abstinence from animal flesh.

Runcie, Robert, 'Theology, the University and the Modern World' in Paul Clarke and Andrew Linzey (eds), *Theology, the University and the Modern World*, Lester Crook Academic Publishing 1988.

—— 'Address at the Global Forum of Spiritual and Parliamentary Leaders on Human Survival', unpublished paper (11 April 1988). Both contain his memorable lines about how exclusive concern for human beings is parochial.

Ryder, Richard D., *Victims of Science: The Use of Animals in Research*, National Anti-Vivisection Society 1983. Originally published by Davis-Poynter in 1975, this book began a national debate in the UK about the use of animals in research – especially non-medical uses.

——*Animal Revolution: Changing Attitudes towards Speciesism*, Blackwell 1989. A personal history of the animal movement by the psychologist who coined the word 'speciesism', now canonized in *The Oxford Dictionary*.

—— (ed), *Animal Welfare and the Environment*, Duckworth 1992. A collection of essays spanning the animal/eco-divide based on the conference at Christ Church, Oxford in 1991.

—— and Paterson, David (eds), *Animals' Rights – A Symposium*, Centaur Press 1979. Papers from the first modern conference on the rights of animals at Trinity College, Cambridge in 1977.

Salt, Henry, *Animals' Rights considered in Relation to Social Progress*, preface by Peter Singer, Centaur Press 1980. Reprint of the 1892 book which provides a systematic argument for the legal rights of animals.

Sandys-Winsch, Godfrey, *Animal Law*, Shaw and Sons, 2nd edn 1984. A concise guide to the law relating to animals.

Santmire, Paul H., *The Travail of Nature: The Ambiguous Ecological Promise of Christian Theology*, Fortress Press, Philadelphia 1985. Still, in my view, the most outstanding work of eco-theology; one that recognizes the ambiguity of Christian teaching even in its eco-friendly modes. His detailed consideration of classical teachers and their teaching is incisive and illuminating. I await with eagerness the day when Santmire will address himself to animal theology specifically.

Sapontzis, S. F., *Morals, Reason and Animals*, Temple University Press, Philadelphia 1987. An important and thorough philosophical discussion with strong moral conclusions.

Scarce, Rik, *Eco-Warriors: Understanding the Radical Environmental Movement*, The Noble Press, Chicago 1990. An introduction to the theory and practice of radical environmentalism including direct action for animals.

Schwartz, Richard H., *Judaism and Vegetarianism*, Micah Publications, Marblehead, MA 1988. Links contemporary vegetarianism with the Jewish tradition of compassion for animals.

Schweitzer, Albert, *Civilization and Ethics* (1923), ET by C. T. Campion, Unwin

Books, 1967 edn. His wide-ranging critique of Western philosophy and his expanded doctrine of reverence for life.

—— *My Life and Thought: An Autobiography*, ET by C. T. Campion, Allen and Unwin 1933. Moving story of his dissatisfaction with religious orthodoxy and the founding of his hospital at Lambarene.

—— *Reverence for Life*, ET by R. H. Fuller, foreword by D. E. Trueblood, SPCK 1970. An edited collection of his powerful sermons on this theme.

Seymour, William Kean, and Smith, John (eds), *The Pattern of Poetry*, Burke Publishing 1967. Source for Clare's poetry and many others on the theme of communion with nature.

Shaftesbury, Seventh Earl of (Anthony Ashley Cooper), letter on service to the weak, 30 April 1881, cited and discussed by Roberta Kalechofsky in *Between the Species: A Journal of Ethics*, Vol. 6, No. 3, Summer 1990.

—— letter to Frances Power Cobbe, 3 September 1878, extract in John Wynne-Tyson (ed), *The Extended Circle* (see below).

—— Speech on the Cruelty to Animals Bill, *Hansard*, 22 May 1876, HMSO 1876.

Shaftesbury's leadership role in the anti-vivisection movement has received scant attention from historians and biographers.

Sharpe, Robert, *The Cruel Deception: The Use of Animals in Medical Research*, Thorsons 1988. A practical critique of the claim that animal experimentation is essential to medical progress. Argues that the 'obsession with animal experiments … has delayed the development and introduction of humane and more reliable approaches' (p. 115).

Singer, Peter, 'All Animals are Equal', *Philosophic Exchange*, Vol. 1, No. 5, Summer 1974. Singer's famous defence of the moral equality of all sentients. Parts of the article first appeared in a review of *Animals, Men and Morals* in *The New York Review of Books*, 5 April 1973.

—— *Animal Liberation: A New Ethics for Our Treatment of Animals*, Jonathan Cape 1976. Landmark book for philosophical debate. Now in its second revised edition. Its treatment of the Judaeo-Christian tradition is dismissive betokening a deeper failure to understand theological perspectives.

—— *Practical Ethics*, CUP 1979. Contains Singer's wide-ranging utilitarian views on practical issues from abortion to vegetarianism. He defends abortion, euthanasia and even infanticide (pp. 133f.) while opposing (most) animal experimentation and killing for food.

—— (ed), *In Defence of Animals*, Blackwell 1985. Another collection of essays of varying quality spanning the range of our current use of animals. Dale Jamieson's critique of zoos (pp. 108–117) is compelling.

Sobrino, Jon, *The True Church and The Poor* (1981) Orbis Books, Maryknoll 1984 and SCM Press, London 1985. More humanocentric liberation theology.

Sorrell, Roger, D., *St Francis of Assisi and Nature: Tradition and Innovation in Western Christian Attitudes toward the Environment*, OUP, New York 1988. An important book offering a fresh perspective on the Franciscan legend and placing it in some historical context.

Spiegel, Marjorie, *The Dreaded Comparison: Human and Animal Slavery*, preface by Alice Walker, Mirror Books, New York 1988. Shows how slaves were frequently regarded and treated as animals are today.

Stewart Jr., Claude Y., *Nature in Grace: A Study in the Theology of Nature*, Mercer University Press 1983. An exemplary scholarly study of the relationship between grace and nature.

Sweeney, Noel, *Animals and Cruelty and Law*, foreword by Peter Singer, Alibi Books 1990. A survey of how cruelty is permitted and sanctioned by many forms of law – written by a practising barrister.

Taylor, C. C. W. (ed), *Ethics and the Environment*, Corpus Christi College, Oxford 1992. Papers from a conference held at Oxford in 1991. Contains Bernard Williams' essay entitled: 'Must a concern for the environment be centred on human beings?' to which the answer given appears entirely in the affirmative (pp. 60–8).

Taylor, Paul W., *Respect for Nature: A Theory of Environmental Ethics*, Princeton University Press 1986. A scholarly and systematic defence of the biocentric (as distinct from the humanocentric) view of creation. Really no theology, however – and it shows.

Teilhard de Chardin, Pierre, *Le Milieu Divin*, ed and ET by Bernard Wall, Collins Fontana edn 1964.

—— *Hymn of the Universe*, ET by N.M. Wildiers, Collins Fontana edn 1970. Two of the great works on the cosmic Christ. Teilhard's vision is heavily humanocentric, however. He never seems to appreciate the Christ-like nature of the suffering of animals.

Tertullian, *Treatise on the Resurrection*, ed, ET and comm. by Ernest Evans, SPCK 1960. A seemingly inclusive vision of redemption: Different kinds of flesh and therefore different kinds of glory but the same substance will be redeemed (para. 52, pp. 156–7).

Tester, Keith, *Animals and Society: The Humanity of Animal Rights*, Routledge 1991. Socio-anthropological polemic against the animal movement arguing that the notion of 'rights' has become a fetish (pp. 194f.) and that animal people want 'no relationships with animals' (p. 193). Some of his critique could have been compelling if overall it was not so exaggerated.

Thomas, Keith, *Man and the Natural World: Changing Attitudes in England 1500–1800*, Allen Lane 1983. Not to be missed history of changing theological attitudes to nature and animals in particular (see especially chs 1–4 inclusive). Indispensable as background to contemporary animal theology. An exciting read now out as a Penguin paperback.

Thorpe, W. H., *Animal Nature and Human Nature*, Methuen 1974. Contains his defence of animal self-consciousness.

Tillich, Paul, 'Nature, also, Mourns for a Lost Good' in *The Shaking of the Foundations*, SCM Press 1949; reissued Pelican Books 1962. Tillich's important – but neglected – sermon on how nature itself will be redeemed. Preached in the chapel of Union Theological Seminary, New York, 1947.

—— *Morality and Beyond*, Collins Fontana 1969. A slim but searching account of the religious dimension to the moral imperative. Tillichian moral theology is well placed to accommodate Schweitzer's mysticism and also insights from deep ecology. The theological world awaits the scholars who can make the connection.

—— *Systematic Theology*, Vol. 2, Part III, University of Chicago Press and James Nisbet 1957; reissued SCM Press 1978. On 'Existence and the Christ' which comprises his discussion of the redemption of non-human worlds and the possibility of other incarnations within them.

Tolstoy, Leo, *Recollections and Essays*, ET with an intro. by Aylmer Maude, OUP, 4th edn 1961. His essay entitled 'The First Step' defends vegetarianism as a sign of spiritual awakening.

Torrance, Thomas F., *Theology in Reconstruction*, SCM Press 1969. A robust defence of theological objectivity and the significance of Christ as *Logos* for all created being.

—— *Space, Time and Incarnation*, OUP 1978. Few have expressed the relationship between Creator and created better than Torrance in this one line: 'When considered theologically, from a centre in God, the world is to be understood as subsisting in His creative Word, for God continues to maintain it in being, through His freedom to be present in it and to realise its relation as created reality towards Himself the Creator' (p. 59).

—— *Divine and Contingent Order*, OUP 1981. In my view, one of the profoundest works of modern theology. Leaving aside his masterful work on 'theology and scientific world-views', it is his discussion on 'Contingence and Disorder' (ch. 4) concerning the reality of evil in the world and the need for the exercise of sacrificial human priesthood which is breathtakingly impressive. Much overlooked contribution.

—— *The Trinitarian Faith*, T. & T. Clark 1988. Contains his sympathetic discussion of divine passibility.

Tracy, David, and Lash, Nicholas (eds), *Cosmology and Theology*, *Concilium*, Vol. 166, June 1983. Some thoughtful essays though astonishingly neglectful of the non-human realm as an issue for theology and ethics.

Traherne, Thomas, 'Second Century', *Selected Writings*, ed by D. A. Davis, Fyfield Books 1980. Traherne's poetry displays a keen theological interest in animals and a perception of their God-given worth.

Trials of War Criminals before the Nuremberg Military Tribunals under Control Council Law No 10, Vol. 2, US Government Printing Office, Washington, DC 1949. Gives details of experimental procedures on human subjects.

Tryon, Thomas, 'Complaints of the birds and fowls of heaven to their Creator', *The Countryman's Companion*, Andrew Sowle 1688. Tryon was possibly the first to utilize the notion of animal rights in a theological context.

Turner, James, *Reckoning with the Beast: Animals, Pain and Humanity in the*

Victorian Mind, The Johns Hopkins University Press 1980. An impressive historical study but marred by the author's desire to see concern for animals as mawkish Victorian sentiment.

United Nations Declaration of the Rights of the Child, United Nations Association/ International Year of the Child 1979. In my view, we need a similar declaration of the rights of animals. See also the United Nations World Charter for Nature (1983) obtainable from the United Nations Environment Programme (New York Office, Room DC2 -0803, NY 10017) reproduced as an Appendix to Rockefeller and Elder (eds), *Spirit and Nature* (above).

van de Veer, Donald and Pierce, Christine (eds), *People, Penguins and Plastic Trees: Basic Issues in Environmental Ethics*, Wadsworth Publishing Company, Belmont, California 1986. A useful reader for undergraduates but wholly lacking in theology.

—— *The Environmental Ethics and Policy Book: Philosophy, Ecology, Economics*, Wadsworth Publishing Company, Belmont, California 1994. The successor volume to the above. Useful as an introductory reader but only two slight theological pieces.

Vanstone, W. H., 'On the Being of Nature', *Theology*, Vol. LXXXI, No. 675, July 1977. Sharp critique of theological anthropocentricity.

—— *Love's Endeavour, Love's Expense: The Response of Being to the Love of God*, foreword by H. A. Williams, Darton, Longman and Todd 1977. Defends the view that nature and animals respond actively to the love of God.

Vastos, G., 'Justice and Equality' in Brant, *Social Justice* (above). Another humanocentric defence of moral equality challenged by Singer. See his 'All Animals are Equal' (above).

Villa-Vicencio, Charles, *A Theology of Reconstruction: Nation-Building and Human Rights*, CUP 1992. Contains many constructive insights into the relationship between theology and rights.

Waddell, Helen, *Peter Abelard*, Granada Publishing 1972; Constable 1987. Moving historical romance full of theological insight. Some of the narrative provides a basis for my discussion of divine passibility in chapter 3.

Ward, Keith, *The Concept of God*, Blackwell 1974. Contains his defence of the divine transfiguration of pain endured by sentients (p. 223).

—— *The Promise*, 1980. His translation and interpretation of the Old Testament.

—— *Rational Theology and the Creativity of God*, Blackwell 1982. Contains his argument that immortality for animals is a necessary condition of any acceptable theodicy (pp. 201–202).

—— *The Battle for the Soul: The End of Morality in a Secular Society*, Hodder and Stoughton 1985. Now argues that animals 'do not have rational consciousness . . . but it is *possible* that animal souls *could* survive death' (p. 152; my emphases).

Welty, Eberhard, *A Handbook of Christian Social Ethics, Vol. 1, Man in Society*, Nelson 1960. Traditional Thomist view on animals taking up St Thomas' line that the human person is 'the most perfect thing in the whole of nature' (p. 43).

Wesley, John, *Sermons on Several Occasions*, 4 Vols with biog. note by J. Beecham, Weslyan Conference Office 1874. Vol. ii contains his defence of animal immortality in his sermon 'The General Deliverance'.

Westacott, E., *A Century of Vivisection and Anti-Vivisection*, C. W. Daniel Co. 1949. Majesterial full-length (675 page) history.

Westerman, Claus, *Creation*, SPCK 1974. One of the first more eco-friendly readings of Genesis departing from a purely instrumentalist view of creation.

Where We Stand on Animal Welfare, Rabbinic Conference of the Union of Liberal and Progressive Synagogues, London, May 1990.

White, T. H., *The Book of Beasts*, Alan Sutton Publishing 1992. New edition of translations from a latin bestiary of the twelfth century first published in 1954. Many insights into mediaeval knowledge of animals and the natural world.

Whitehouse, W. A., 'New Heavens and a New Earth' in Ann Loades (ed), *The Authority of Grace: Essays in Response to Karl Barth*, T. & T. Clark 1981. Critiques the 'aristocrats of the mind' tradition and defends the view that materiality participates in redemption.

Wildlife and Countryside Act 1981, HMSO, reprint 1985. Important UK legislation concerning the conservation and protection of wild animal and plant species. Its principal weakness lies in its failure to extend this protection to hunted species (fox, deer, mink, hare and rabbit) who are classed as 'ground game'.

Willey, Petroc, *Pope John Paul II on the environment and the place of animals*, unpublished paper, 1988. Explains the significance of the encyclical *Sollicitudo Rei Socialis* (see above) for Roman Catholic theology.

Wrighton, Basil, *Reason, Religion and the Animals*, Catholic Study Circle for Animal Welfare 1987. A collection of his short but incisive papers given during a life-time of work for animal welfare in the Roman Catholic church. His early essays on animal rights (1952) and vegetarianism (1965) herald later secular concern.

Wynne-Tyson, Jon (ed), *The Extended Circle: A Dictionary of Humane Thought*, Centaur Press 1985. A useful collection of sources though not always adequately referenced.

Young, Frances, *The Use of Sacrificial Ideas in Greek Christian Writers from the New Testament to St John Chrysostom*, Patristic Monograph Series, no. 5, The Philadelphia Patristic Foundation 1979. Argues that the primary meaning of animal sacrifice consisted in the liberation of life rather than in the infliction of death.

Zizioulas, John, 'Preserving God's Creation: Three Lectures on Theology and Ecology, 1', *King's Theological Review*, Vol. Xll, No. 1, Spring 1989. A fresh treatment from an Orthodox perspective. Negectful of the precise issues raised by the contemporary debate about animals, however.

Acknowledgments

Chapters of this book appeared in earlier drafts as detailed below. All of them have been thoroughly revised for inclusion here. The author is deeply grateful to the many people, too numerous to mention, who have encouraged his work and made helpful comments on it, and he and the publisher acknowledge the kind permission of various editors to include here revised versions of earlier published work.

1. *Reverence, Responsibility and Rights*
First presented to an international conference on 'The Status of Animals' at the University of Nottingham in 1988, and then published in the conference proceedings entitled *The Status of Animals: Ethics, Education and Welfare*, ed by David Paterson and Mary Palmer, CAB International 1989.

2. *The Moral Priority of the Weak*
First presented to a conference on 'The Animal Kingdom and the Kingdom of God' jointly sponsored by the Church and Nation Committee of the Church of Scotland and the University of Edinburgh's Centre for Theology and Public Issues in 1991, and subsequently published as an occasional paper by the Centre for Theology and Public Issues.

3. *Humans as the Servant Species*
Originally prepared for a Working Group on Animals and Theology held under the auspices of the Centre for the Study of Theology in the University of Essex, and published in revised form as 'The Servant Species: Humanity as Priesthood' in *Between the Species: A Journal of Ethics*, Vol. 6, No.3, Summer 1991.

4. *Liberation Theology for Animals*
Originally delivered as one of a series of talks on Animals, Theology and Ethics arranged by the Centre for Social Ethics and Policy at the

University of Manchester in 1989, and revised for publication as 'Liberation Theology and the Oppression of Animals' in the *Scottish Journal of Theology*, Vol. 46, Part IV, December 1993.

5. Animal Rights and Parasitical Nature
Originally given at an international conference held at Duke Divinity School in 1990 entitled 'Good News for Animals?', and then published in *Good News for Animals? Christian Approaches to Animal Well-Being*, ed by Jay McDaniel and Charles Pinches, Orbis Books, Maryknoll 1993.

6. Animal Experiments as Un-Godly Sacrifices
Originally given at an international conference entitled 'Religious Perspectives on the Use of Animals in Science' held in London in 1985, and subsequently published as 'The Place of Animals in Creation: A Christian View' in *Animal Sacrifices: Religious Perspectives on the Use of Animals in Science*, ed by Tom Regan, Temple University Press, PA 1986.

7. Hunting as the Anti-Gospel of Predation
Originally given at an international conference on 'Wildlife and Animal Rights' arranged by the Philosophy Department of Pennsylvania State University in 1991 and published in a revised form as 'The Case Against the Christian Hunter' in the *Epworth Review*, Vol. 20, No. 2, May 1993.

8. Vegetarianism as a Biblical Ideal
In an earlier version, included as 'The Bible and Killing for Food' in *Using the Bible Today*, ed by Dan Cohn-Sherbok, Bellew Publishing 1991.

9. Genetic Engineering as Animal Slavery
Originally delivered at an international conference on the ethics of genetic engineering arranged by the Athene Trust in London in 1988, and published in an earlier form as 'Human and Animal Slavery: A Theological Critique of Genetic Engineering' in *The Bio-Revolution: Cornucopia or Pandora's Box?*, ed by Peter Wheale and Ruth McNally, Pluto Press 1990. Includes some material from an article originally published as 'Created Not Invented: A Theological Critique of Patenting Animals' in *Crucible*, the quarterly journal of the Board for Social Responsibility of the Church of England, April 1993.

Index